Re:ZeRo

-Starting Life in Another World-

The Frozen Bond

2

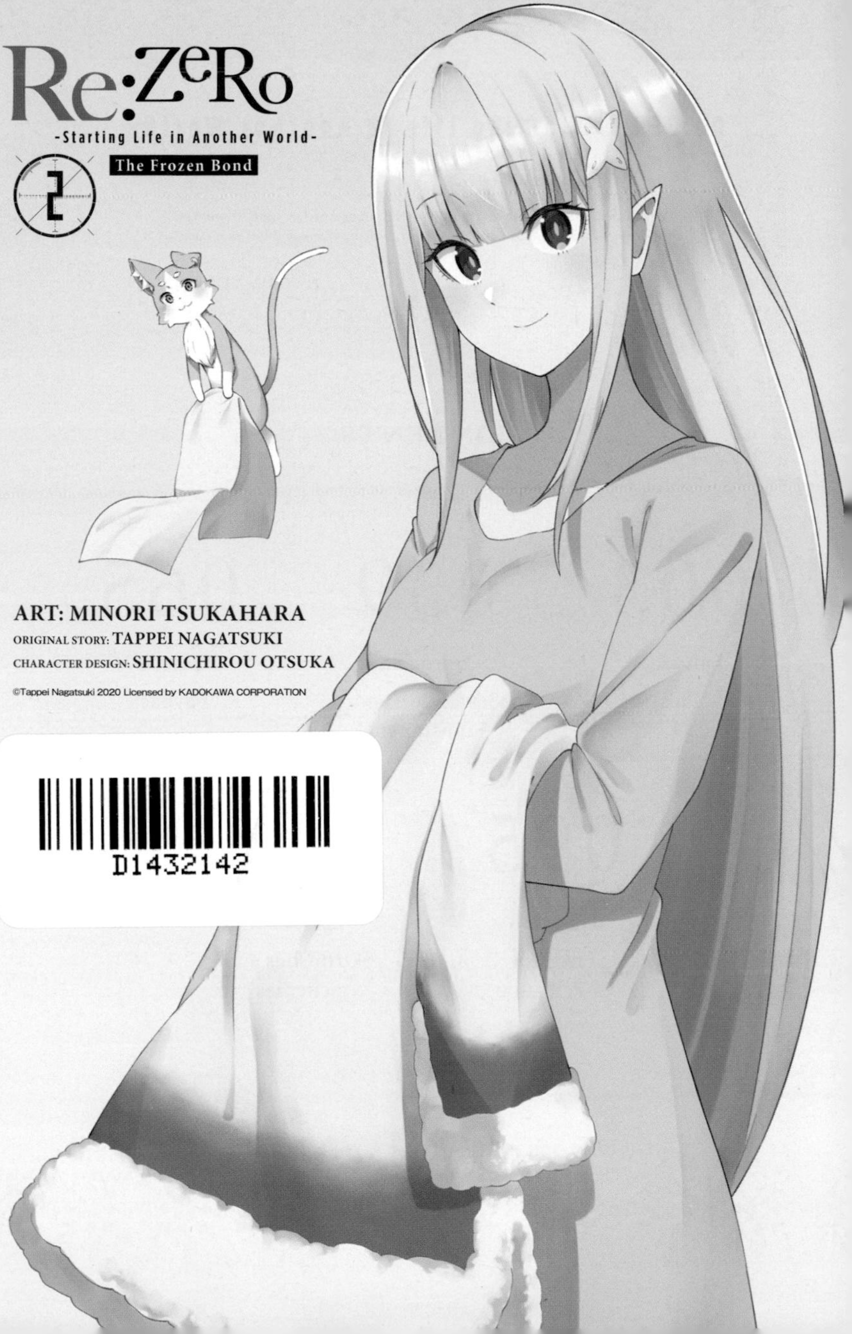

ART: MINORI TSUKAHARA

ORIGINAL STORY: **TAPPEI NAGATSUKI**

CHARACTER DESIGN: **SHINICHIROU OTSUKA**

Re:ZERO –Starting Life in Another World–

The Frozen Bond

The only ability Subaru Natsuki gets when he's summoned to another world is time travel via his own death. But to save her, he'll die as many times as it takes.

CONTENTS

003

Episode 5

Plea

039

Episode 6

Separation and Punishment

065

Episode 7

Payback

095

Episode 8

Envoy of Conciliation

127

Episode 9

Skirmishes and Schemes

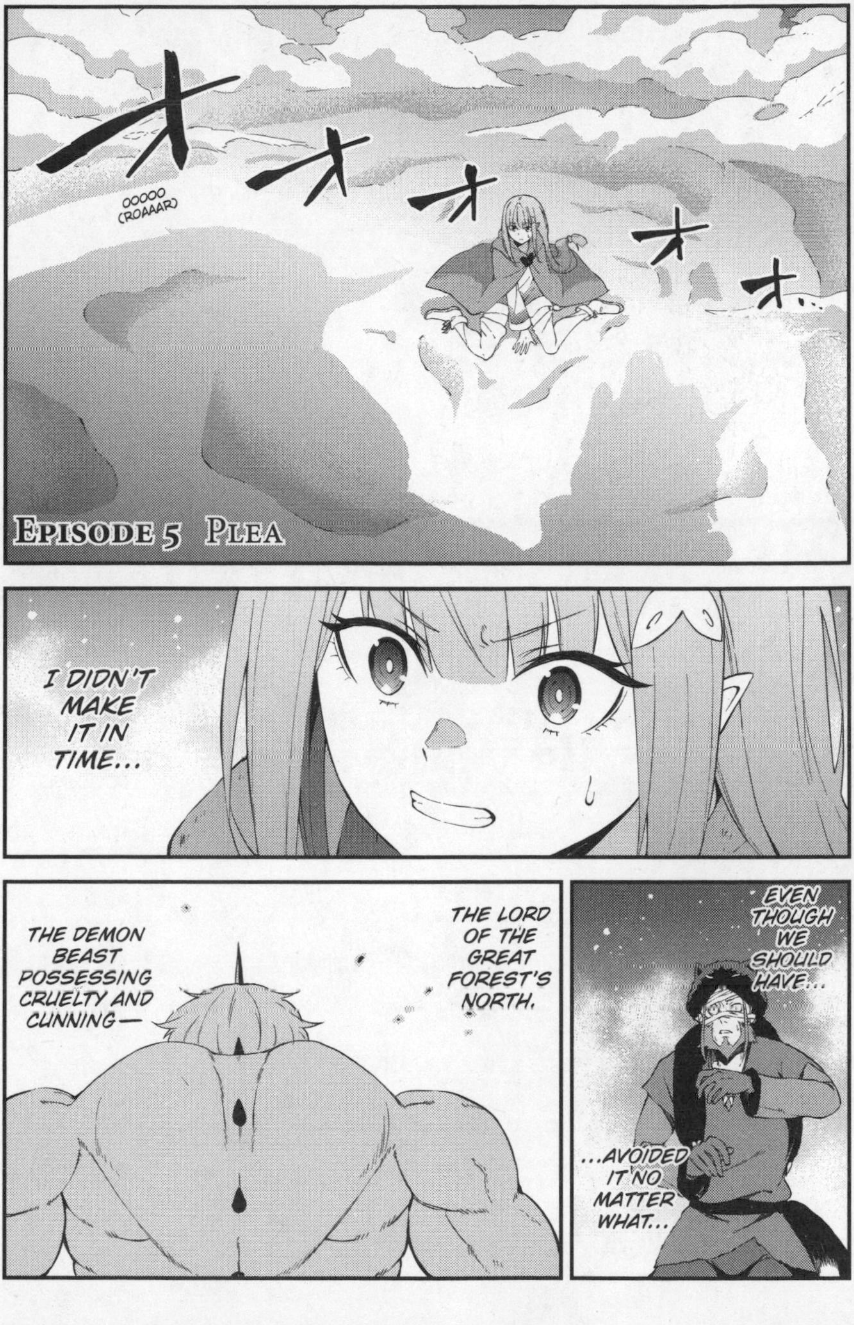
OOOOO (ROAAAR)
EPISODE 5 PLEA
I DIDN'T MAKE IT IN TIME...
EVEN THOUGH WE SHOULD HAVE...
...AVOIDED IT NO MATTER WHAT...
THE LORD OF THE GREAT FOREST'S NORTH.
THE DEMON BEAST POSSESSING CRUELTY AND CUNNING—

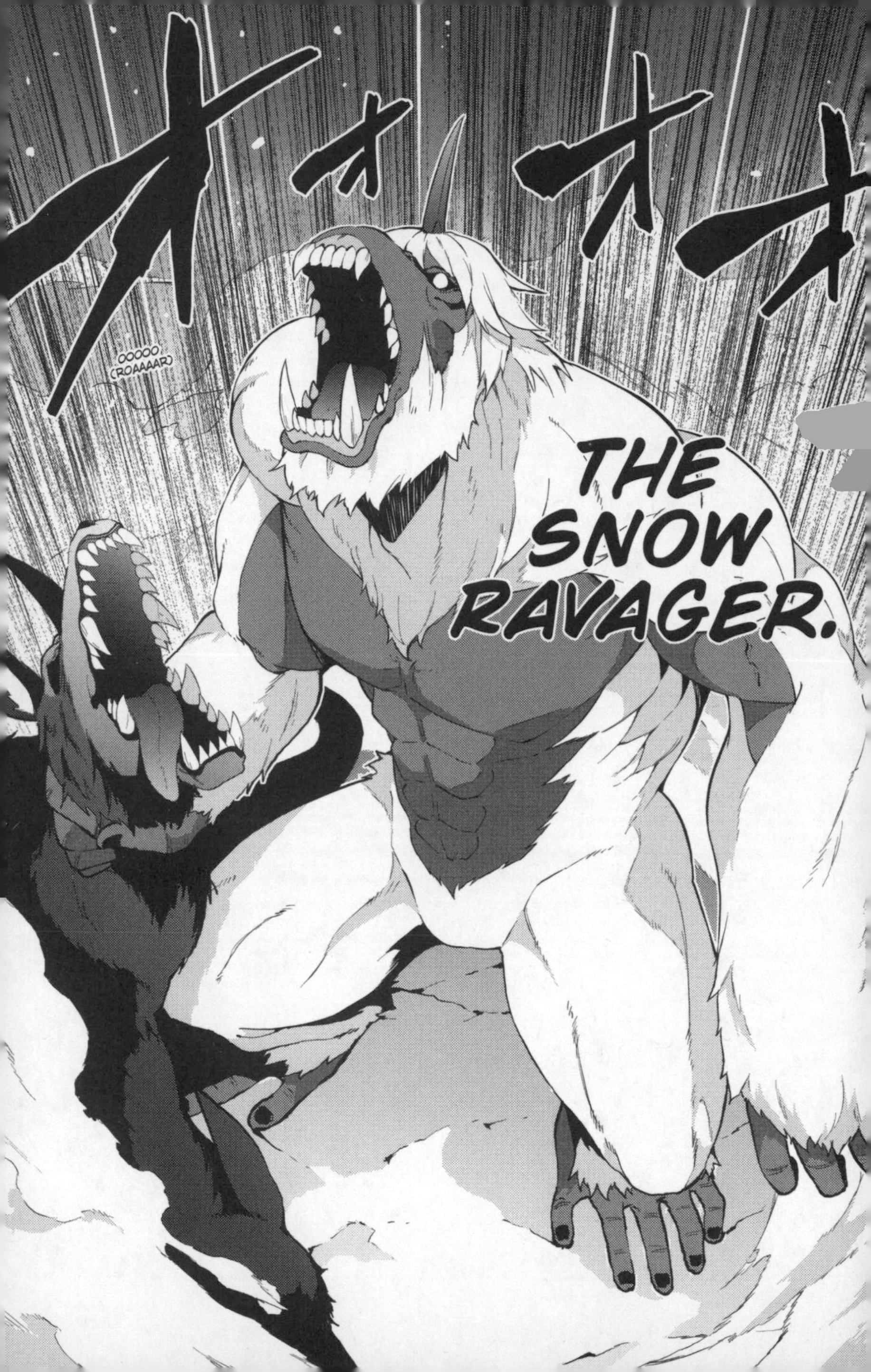
オォオオ
OOOOO
(ROAAAAR)
THE SNOW RAVAGER.

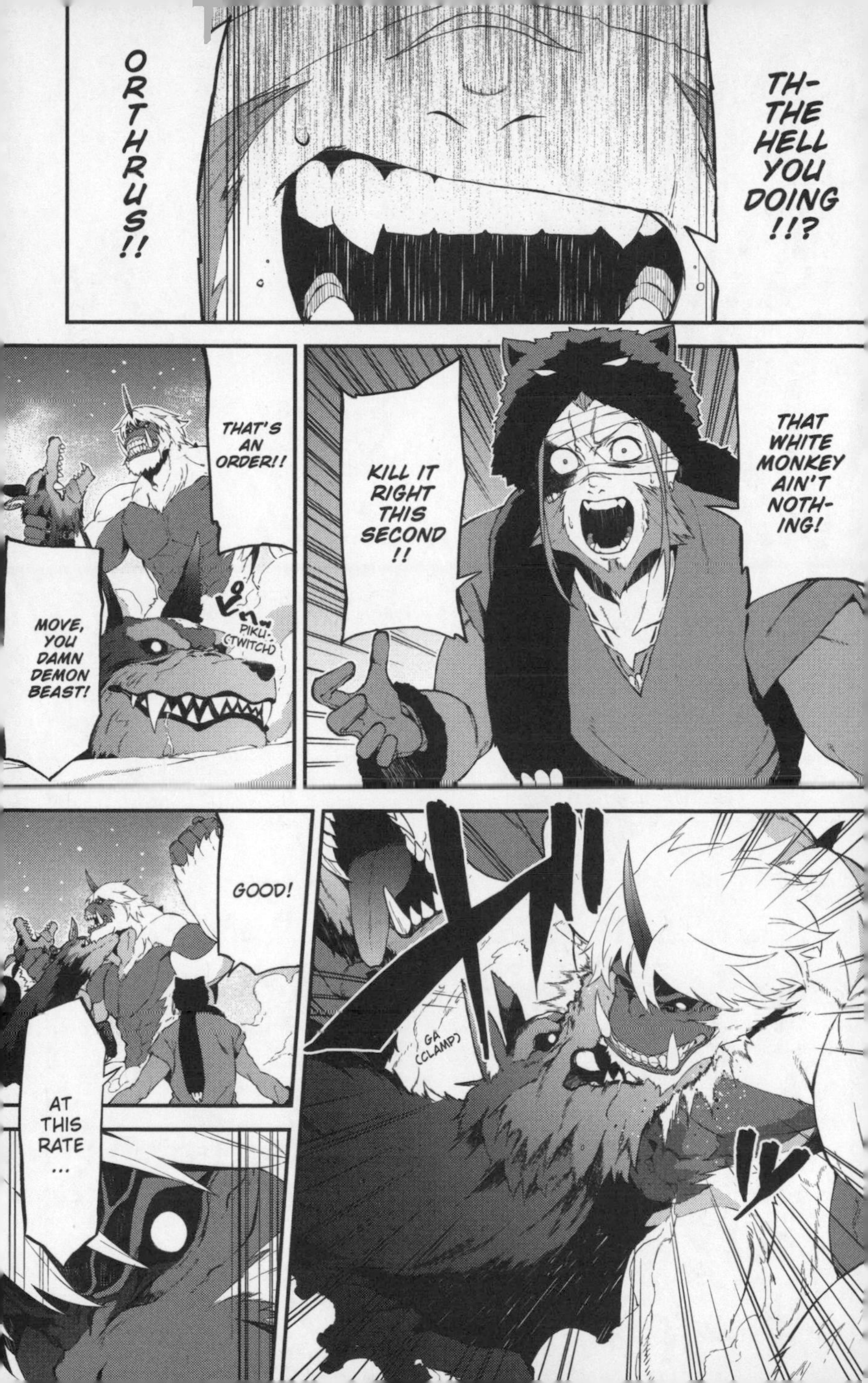
TH-THE HELL YOU DOING!!?
ORTHRUS!!
THAT WHITE MONKEY AIN'T NOTHING!
KILL IT RIGHT THIS SECOND!!
THAT'S AN ORDER!!
PIKU.. (TWITCH)
MOVE, YOU DAMN DEMON BEAST!
GA (CLAMP)
GOOD!
AT THIS RATE...

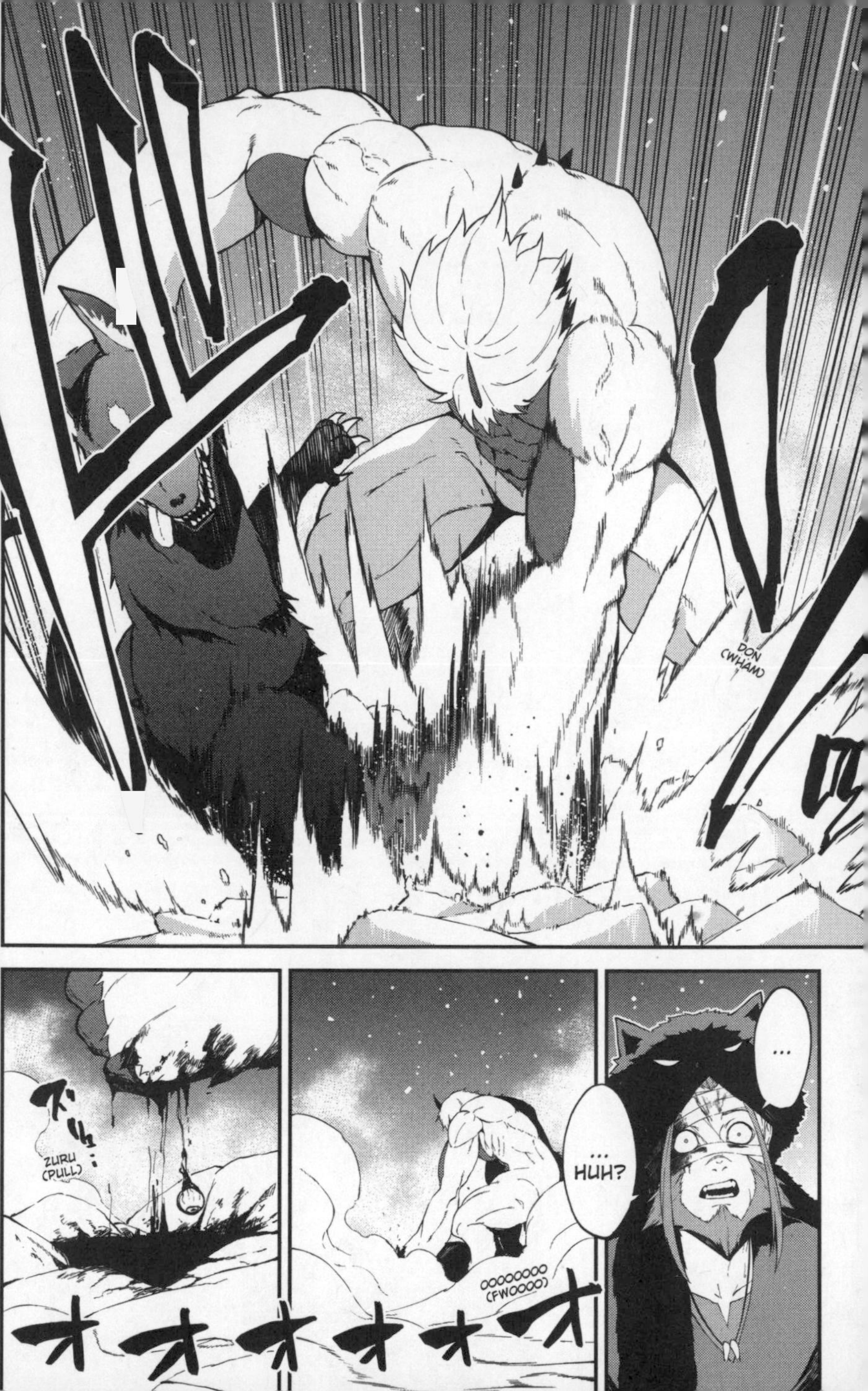
DON (WHAM)
...
... HUH?
OOOOOOOO (FWOOOO)
オオオオオオ
ズル…
ZURU (PULL)

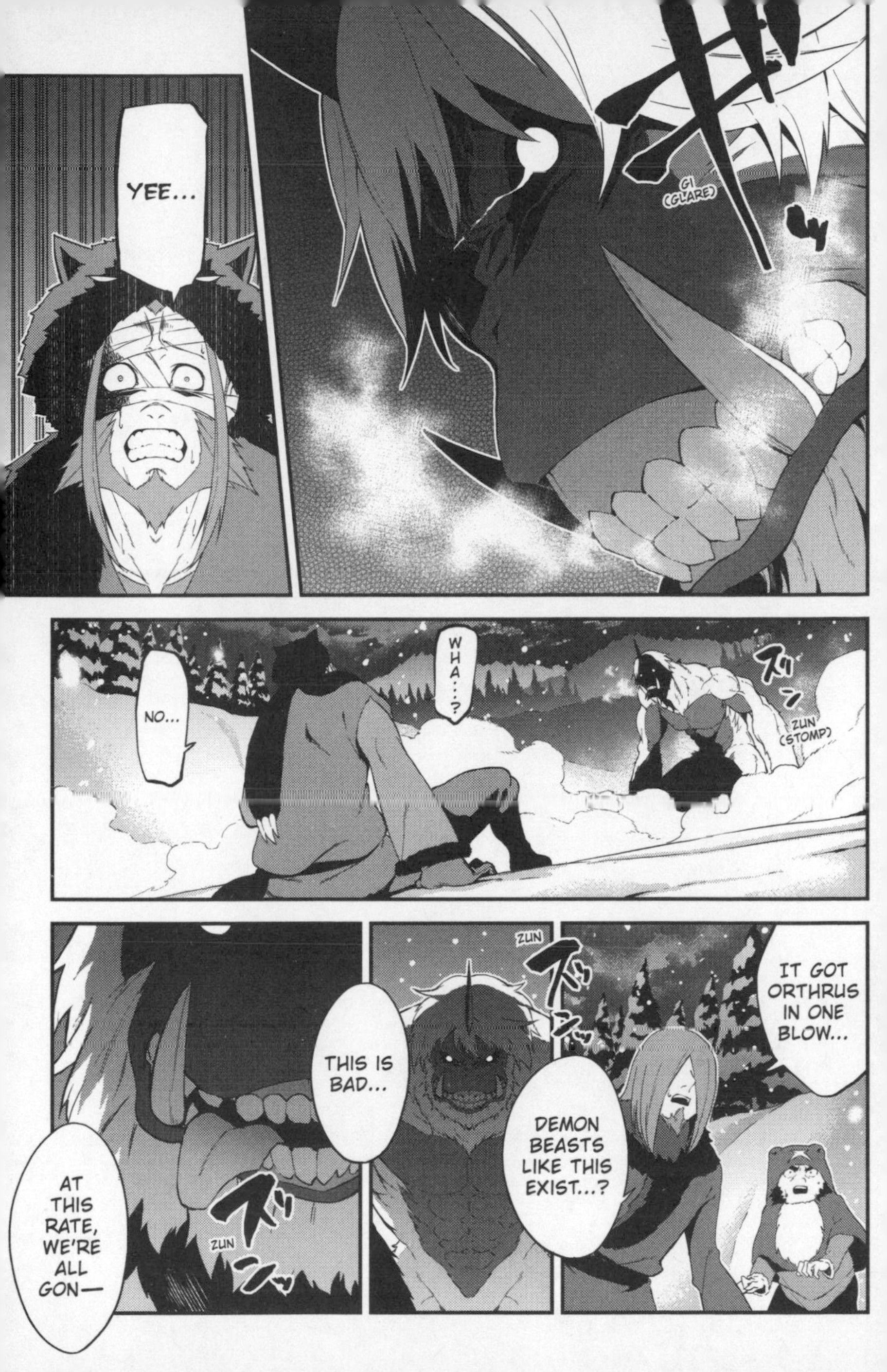
GI (GLARE)
YEE...
ZUN (STOMP)
WHA...?
NO...
IT GOT ORTHRUS IN ONE BLOW...
ZUN
THIS IS BAD...
DEMON BEASTS LIKE THIS EXIST...?
ZUN
AT THIS RATE, WE'RE ALL GON—

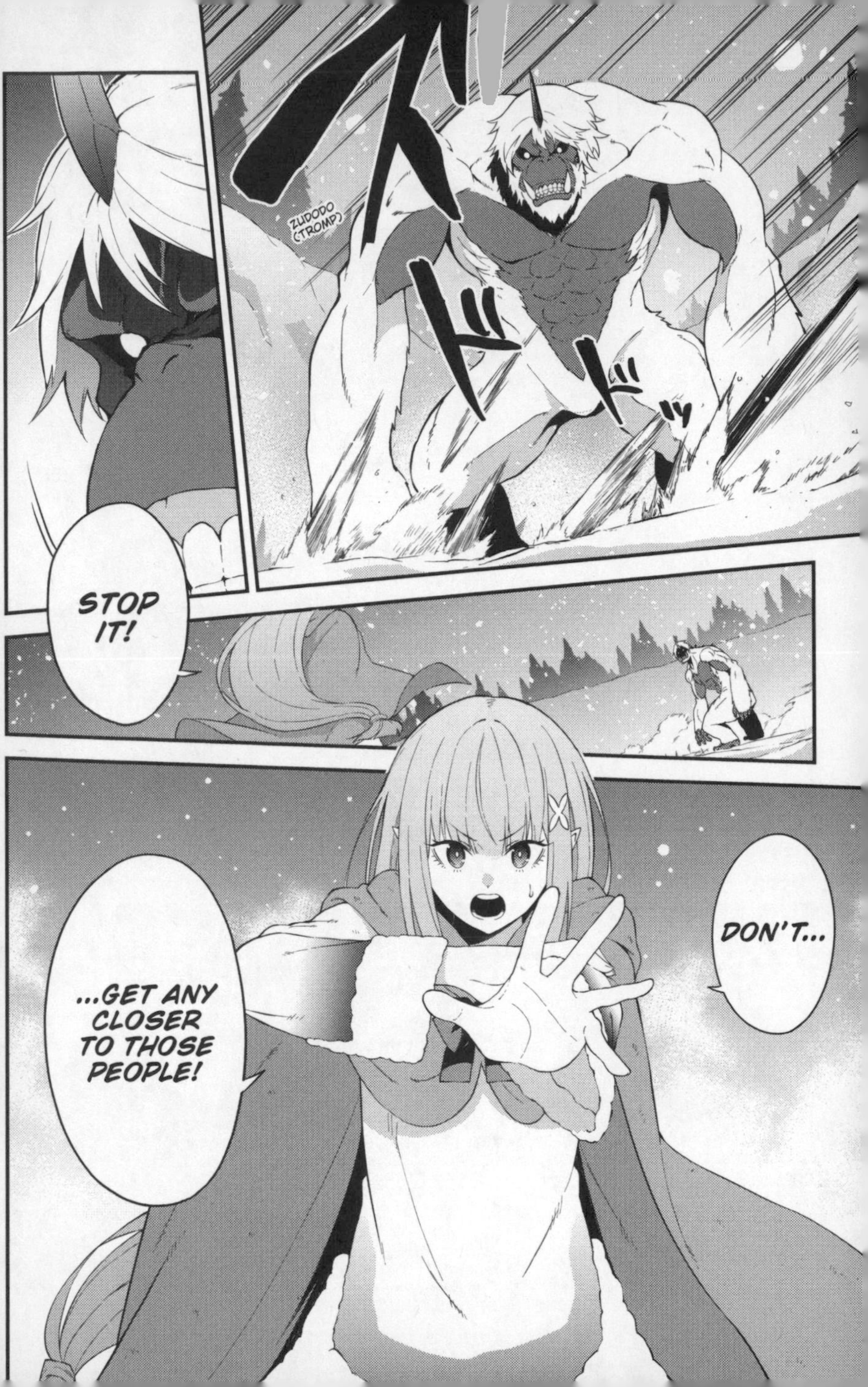
ZUDODO (TROMP)
STOP IT!
DON'T...
...GET ANY CLOSER TO THOSE PEOPLE!

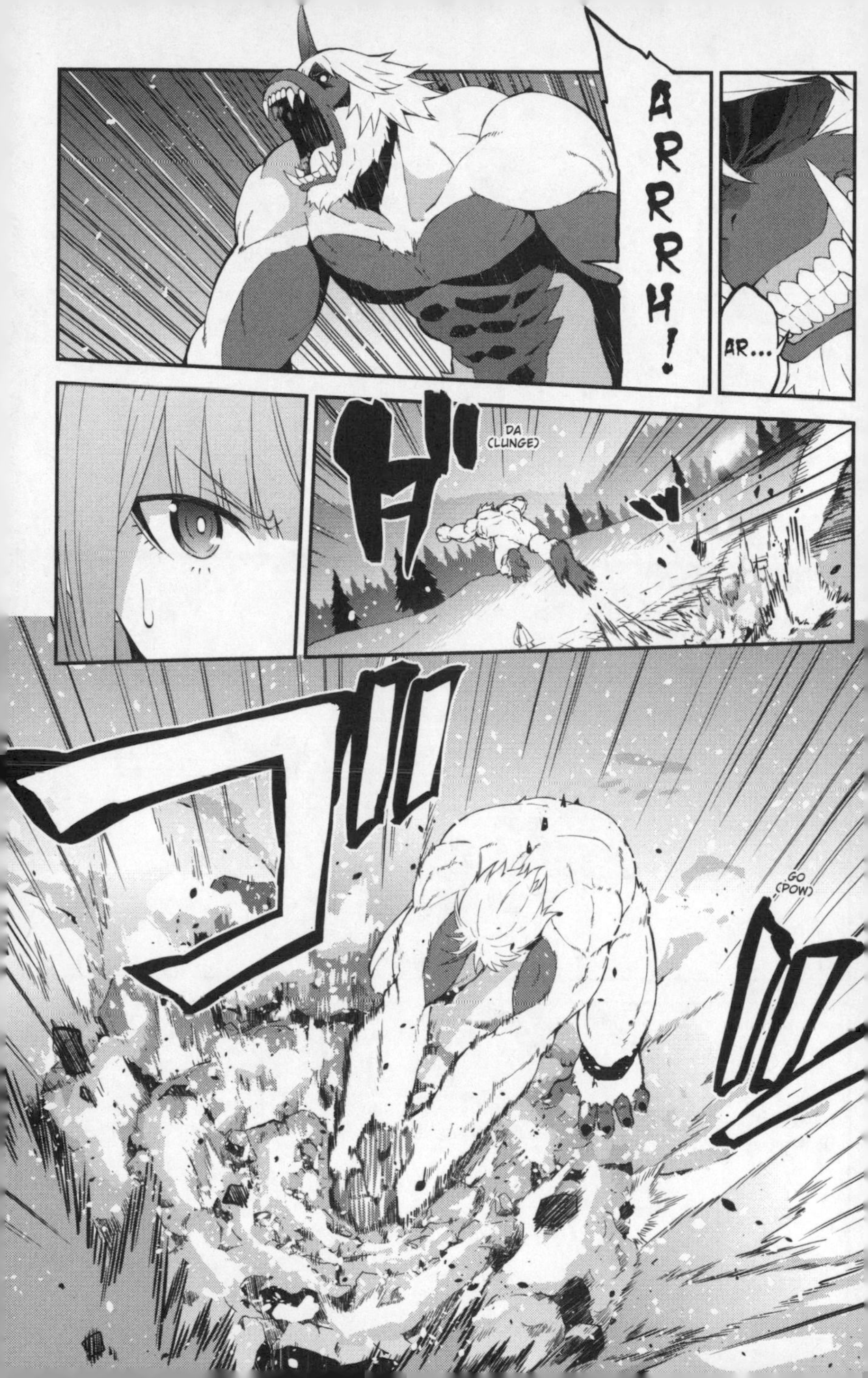
AR...
ARRRH!
DA (LUNGE)
GO (POW)

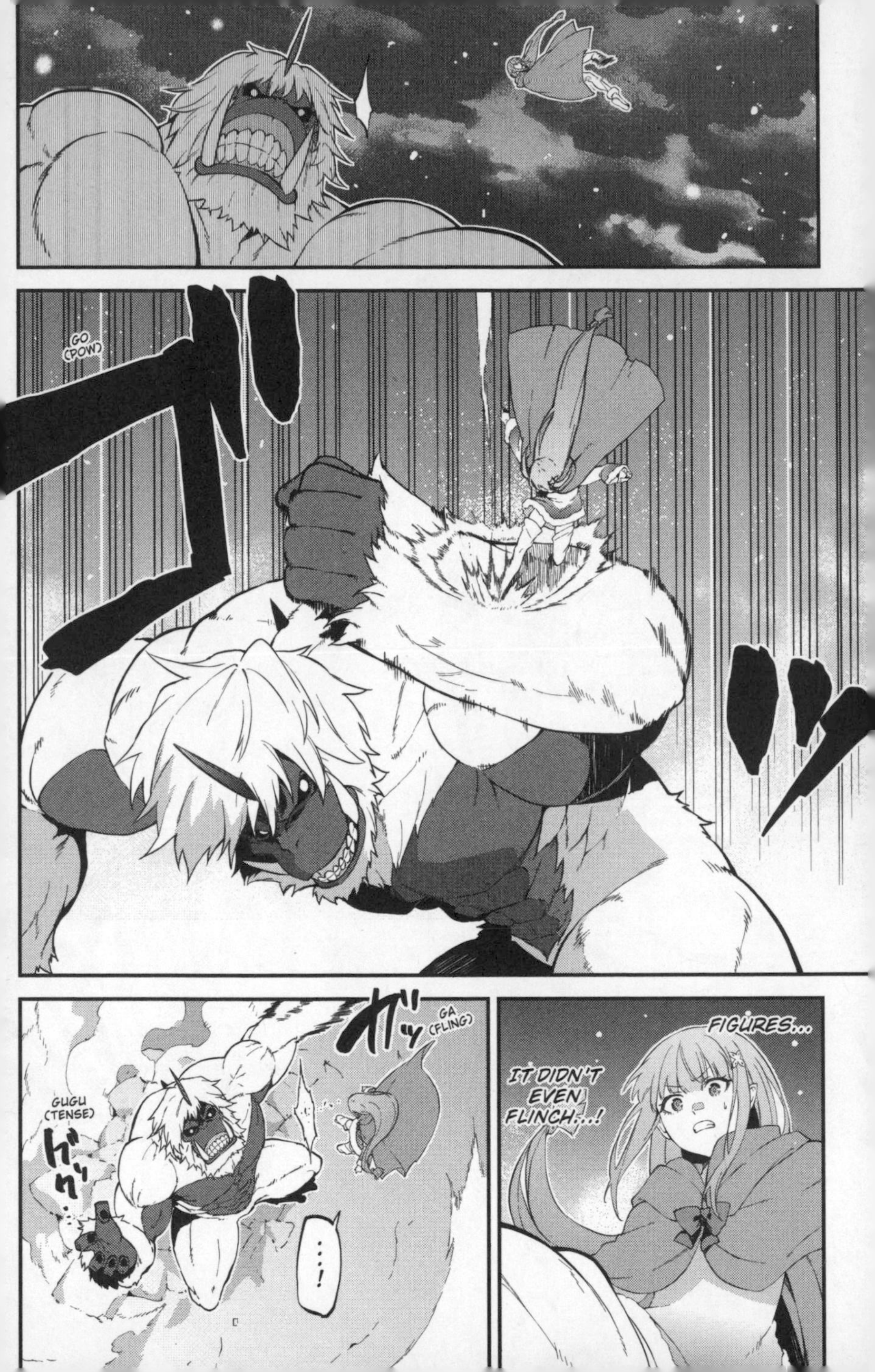
GO (POW)
FIGURES...
IT DIDN'T EVEN FLINCH...!
GA (FLING)
GUGU (TENSE)
...!

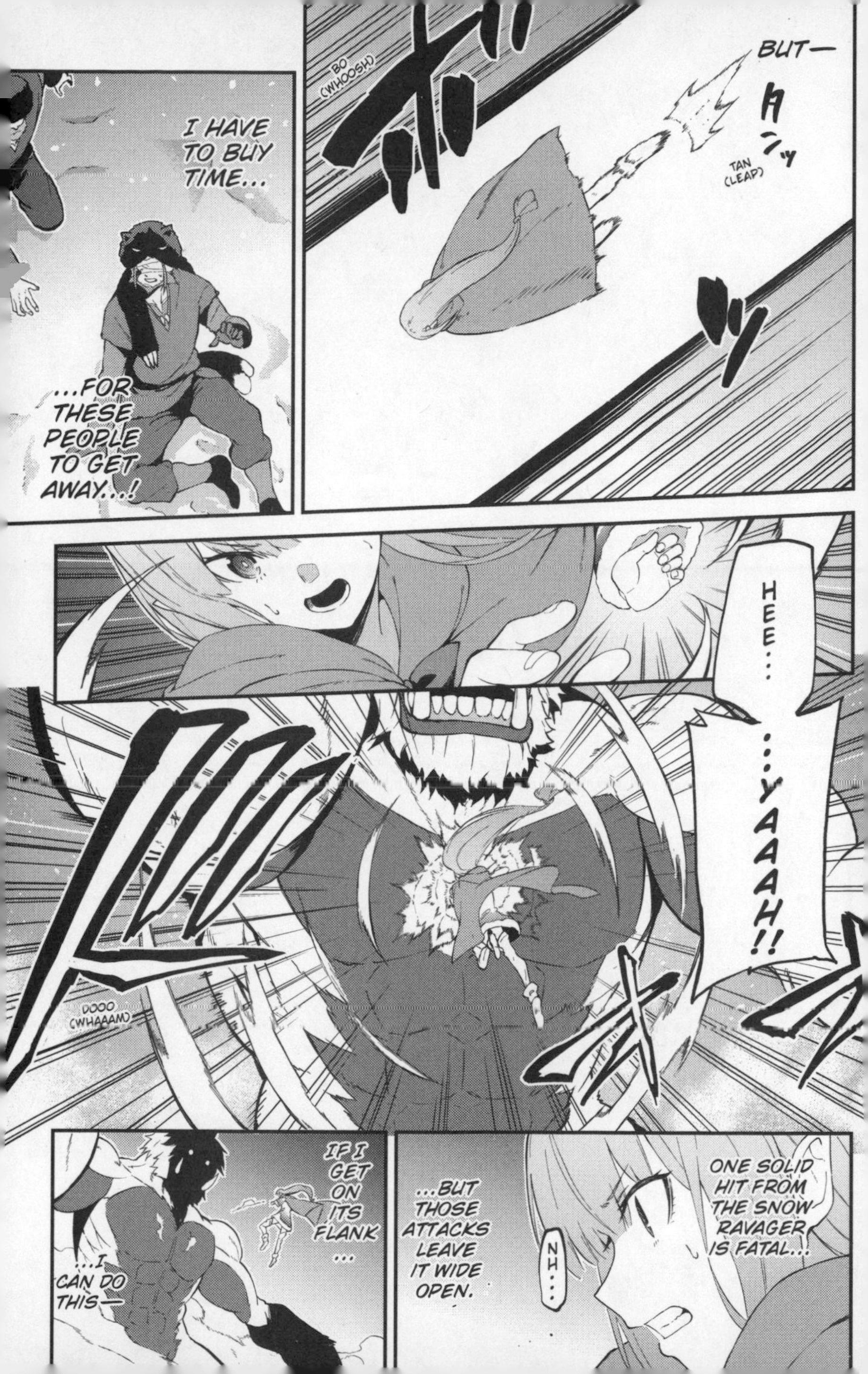
BO (WHOOSH)
BUT—
TAN (LEAP)
I HAVE TO BUY TIME...
...FOR THESE PEOPLE TO GET AWAY...!
HEE...
...YAAAAH!!
DOOO (WHAAAM)
ONE SOLID HIT FROM THE SNOW RAVAGER IS FATAL...
NH...
...BUT THOSE ATTACKS LEAVE IT WIDE OPEN.
IF I GET ON ITS FLANK...
...I CAN DO THIS—

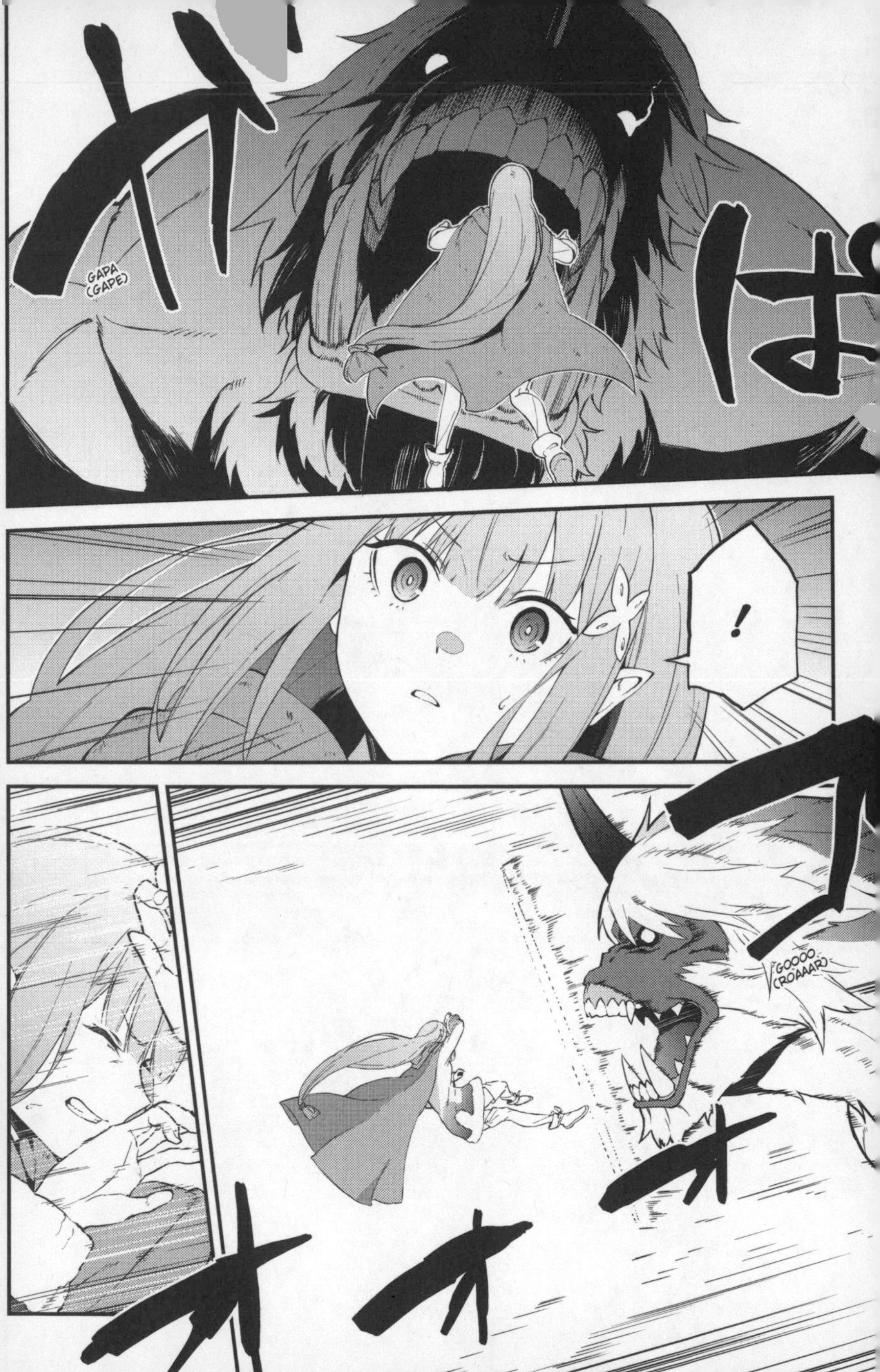
GAPA
(GAPE)
!
GOOOO
(ROAAAR)

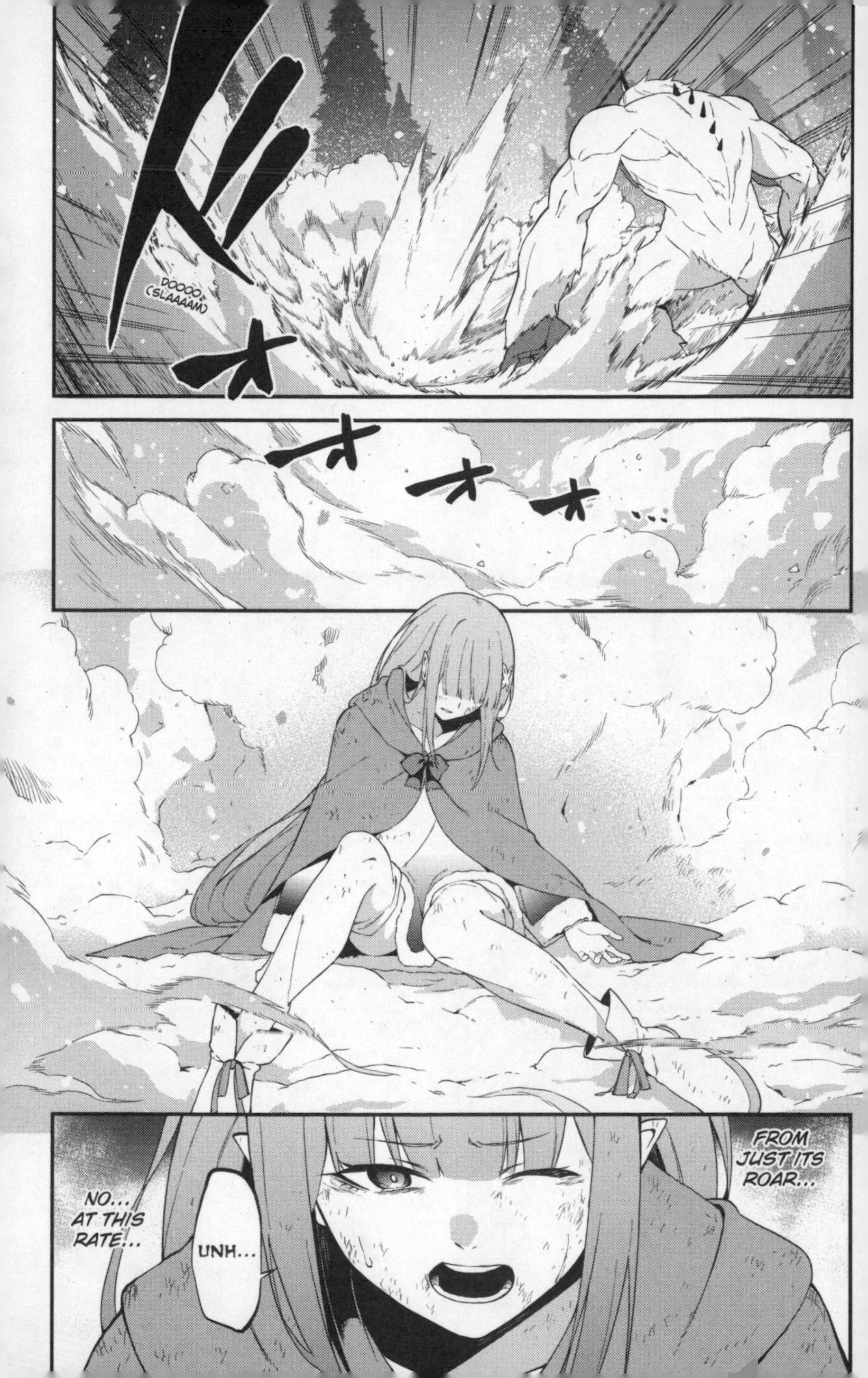
DOOOOO (SLAAAAM)
FROM JUST ITS ROAR...
UNH...
NO... AT THIS RATE...

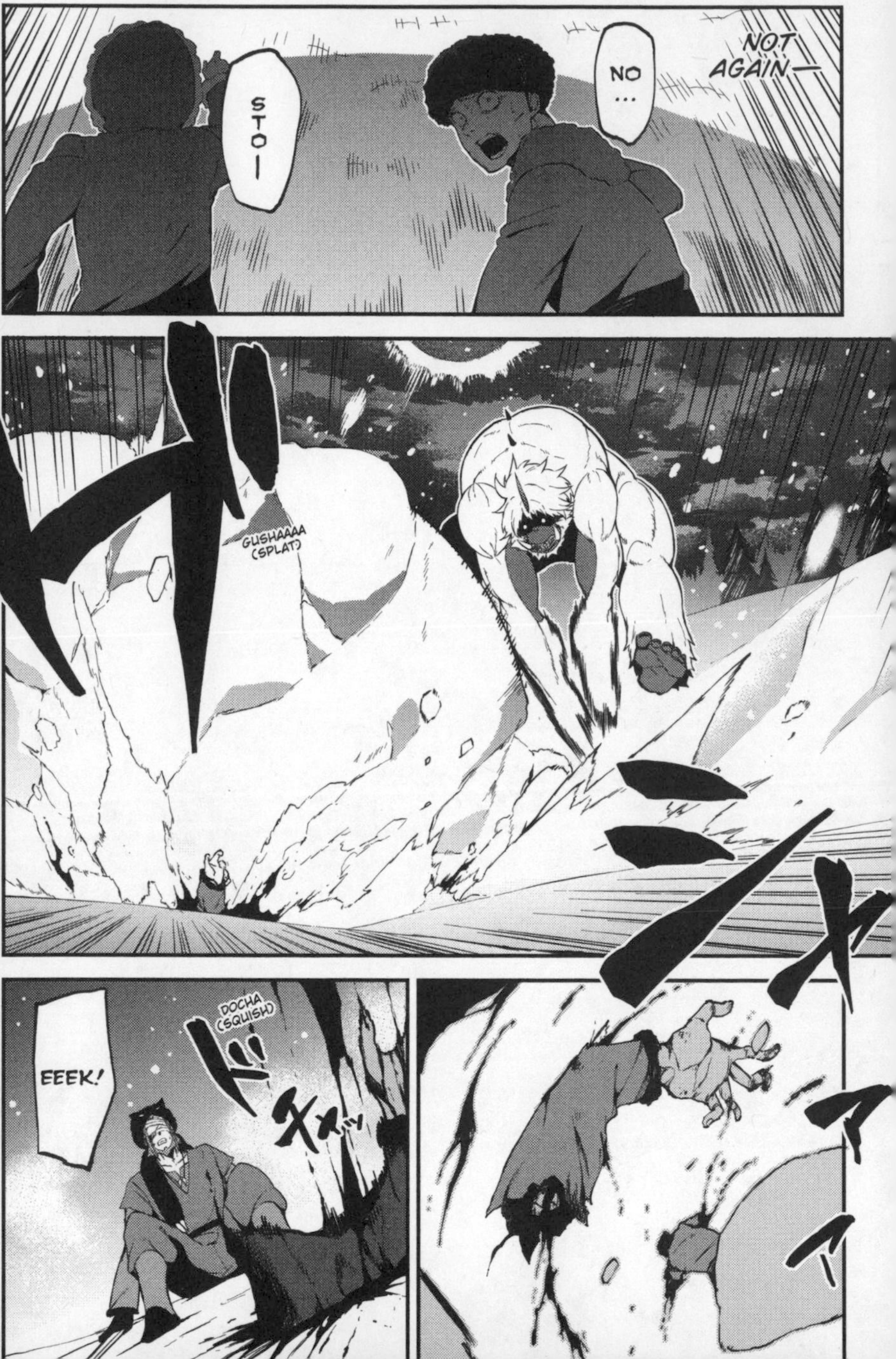
NOT AGAIN—
NO ...
STO—
GUSHAAAA (SPLAT)
DOCHA (SQUISH)
EEEK!

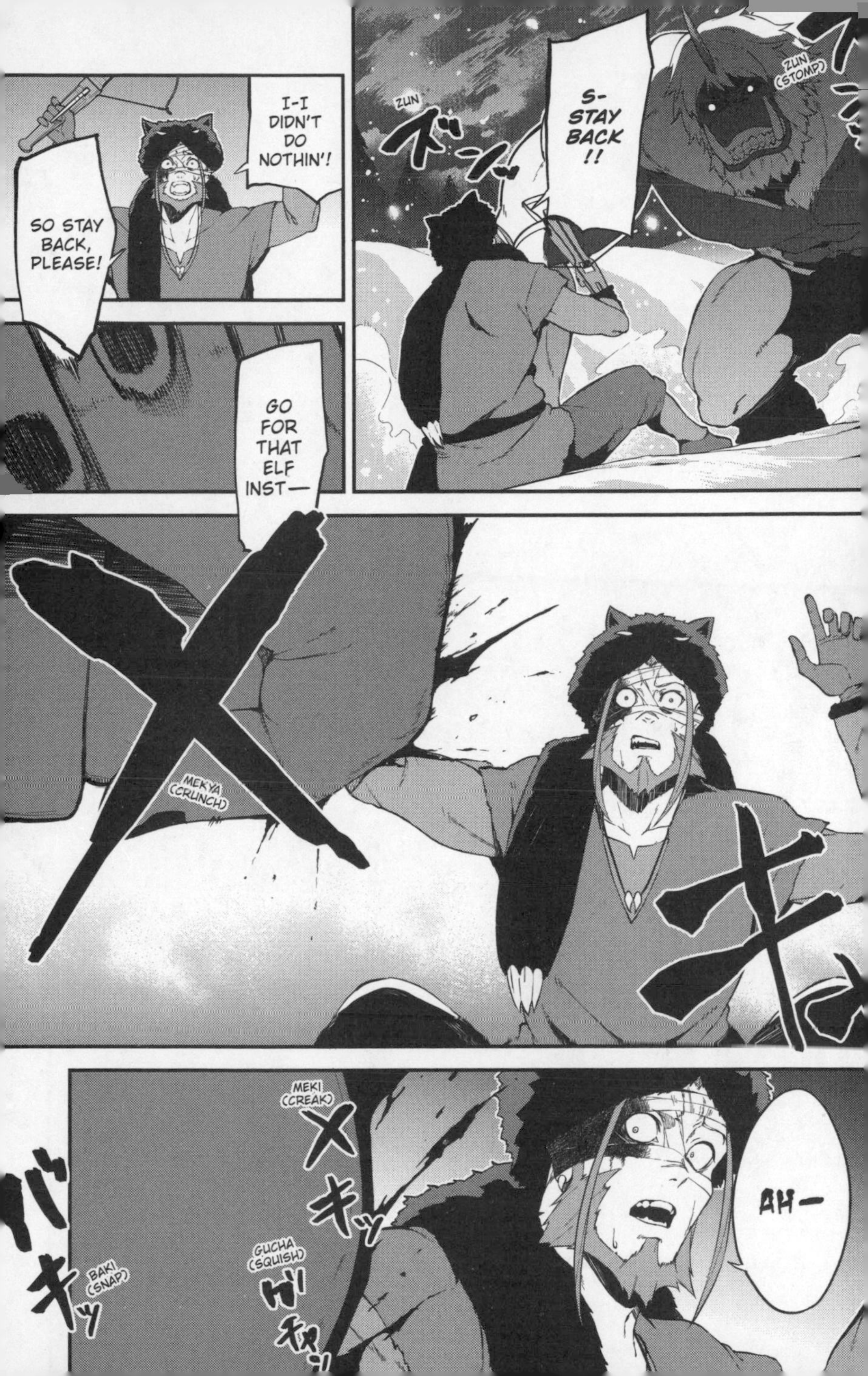
ZUN (STOMP)
S-STAY BACK!!
ZUN
I-I DIDN'T DO NOTHIN'!
SO STAY BACK, PLEASE!
GO FOR THAT ELF INST—
MEKYA (CRUNCH)
AH—
MEKI (CREAK)
GUCHA (SQUISH)
BAKI (SNAP)

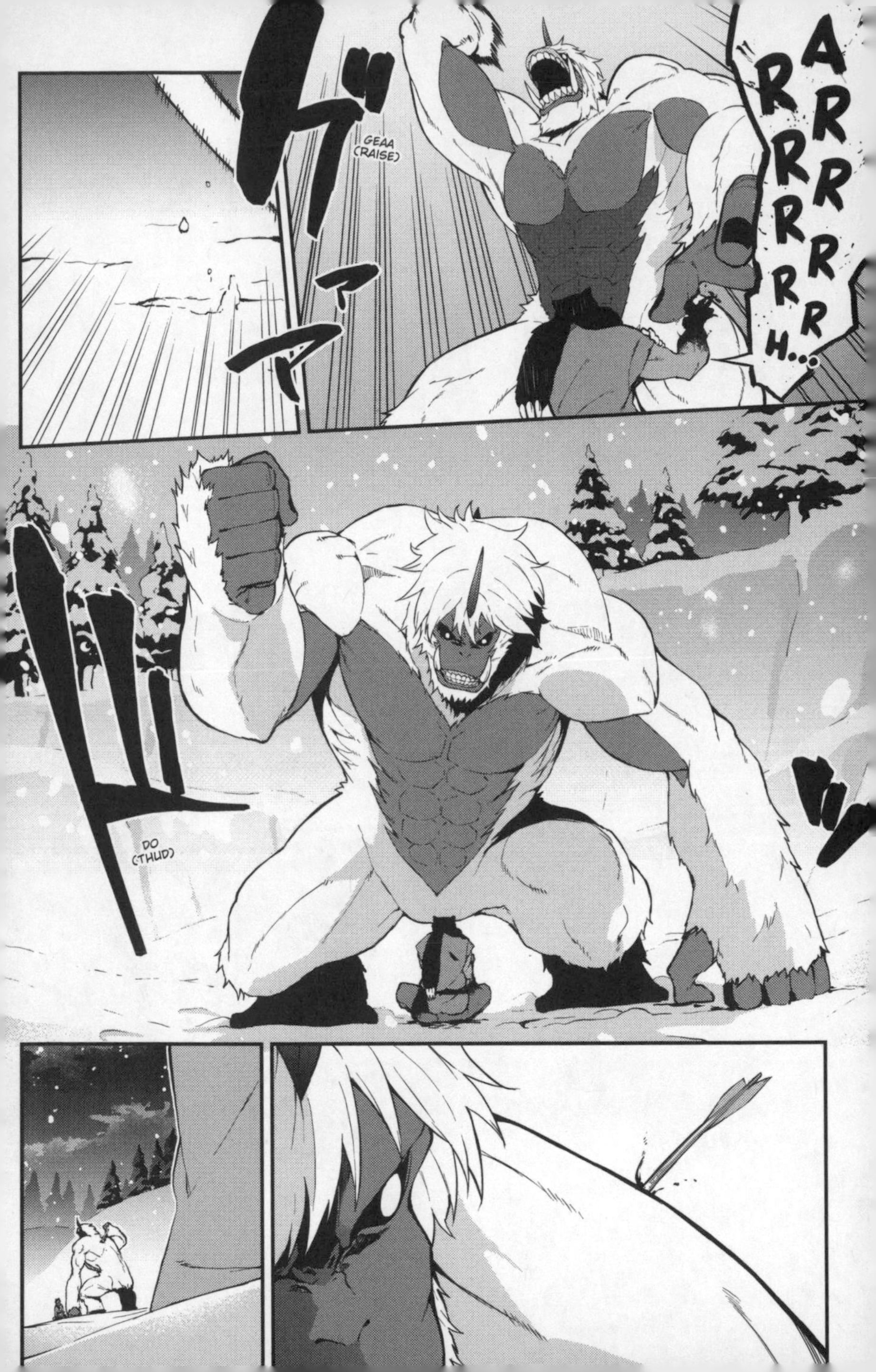
ARRRRRRRRH...
GEAA (RAISE)
DO (THUD)

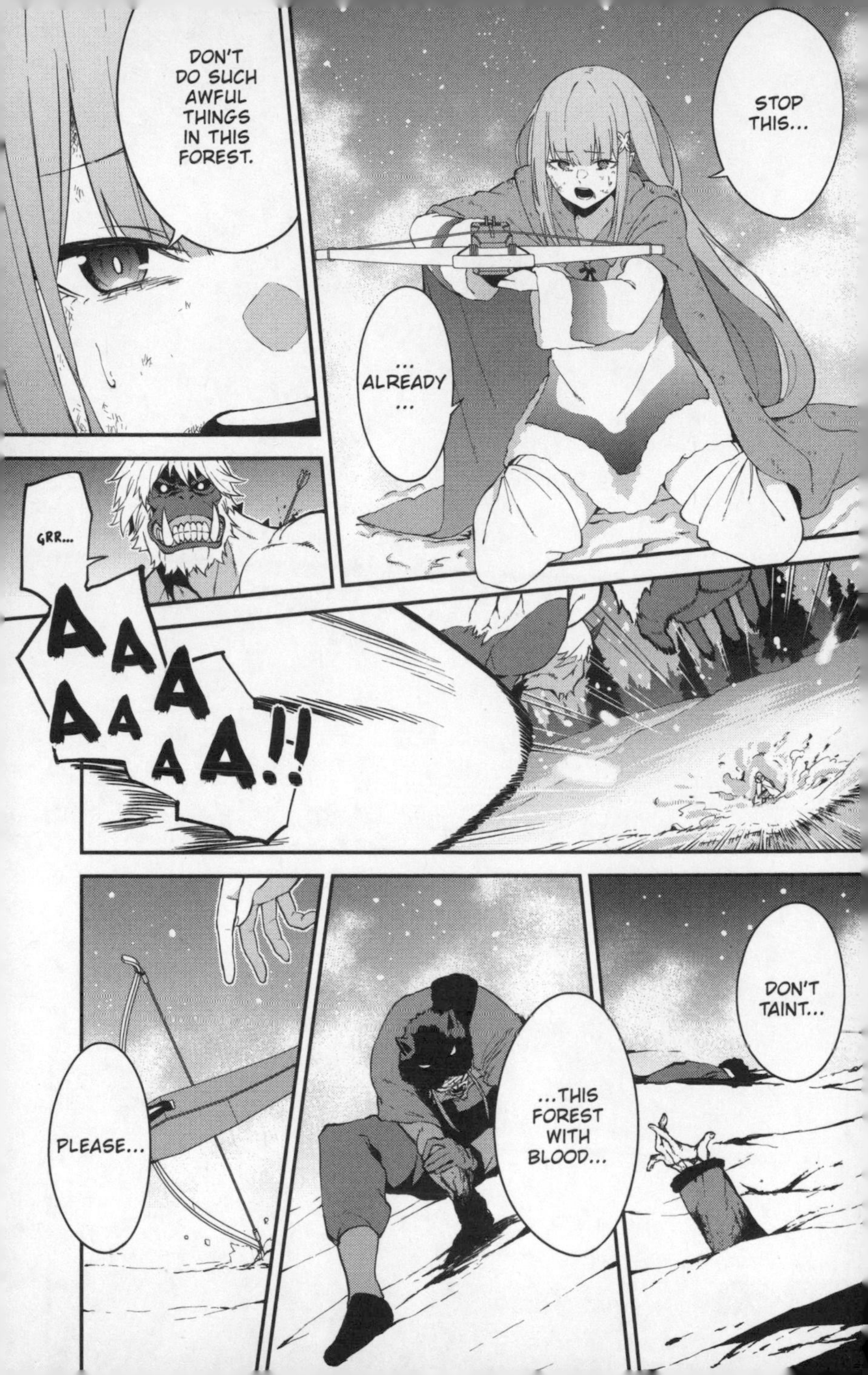
STOP THIS...
...ALREADY...
DON'T DO SUCH AWFUL THINGS IN THIS FOREST.
GRR...
AAAAAAA!!
DON'T TAINT...
...THIS FOREST WITH BLOOD...
PLEASE...

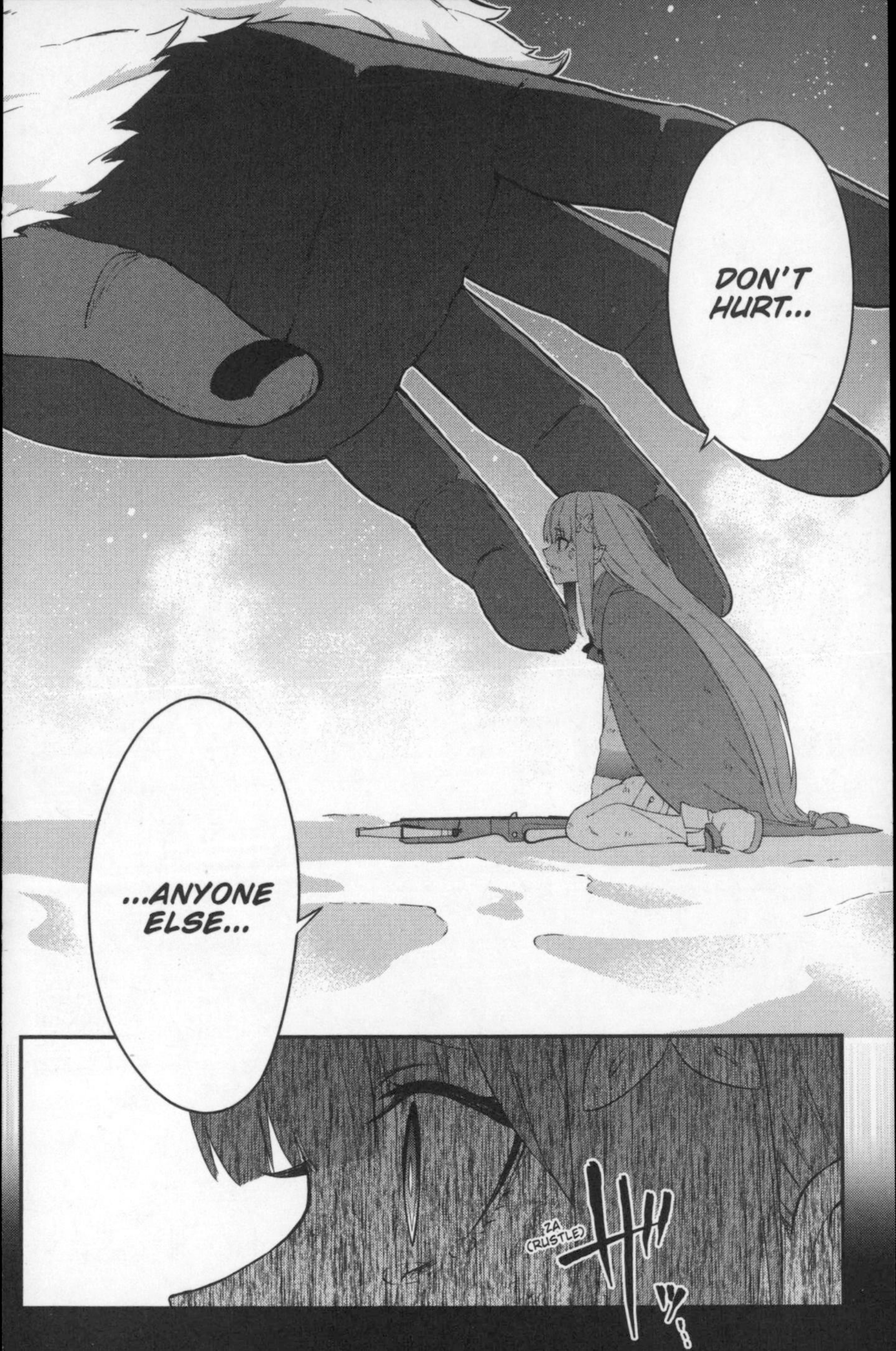
DON'T HURT...
...ANYONE ELSE...
ZA (RUSTLE)

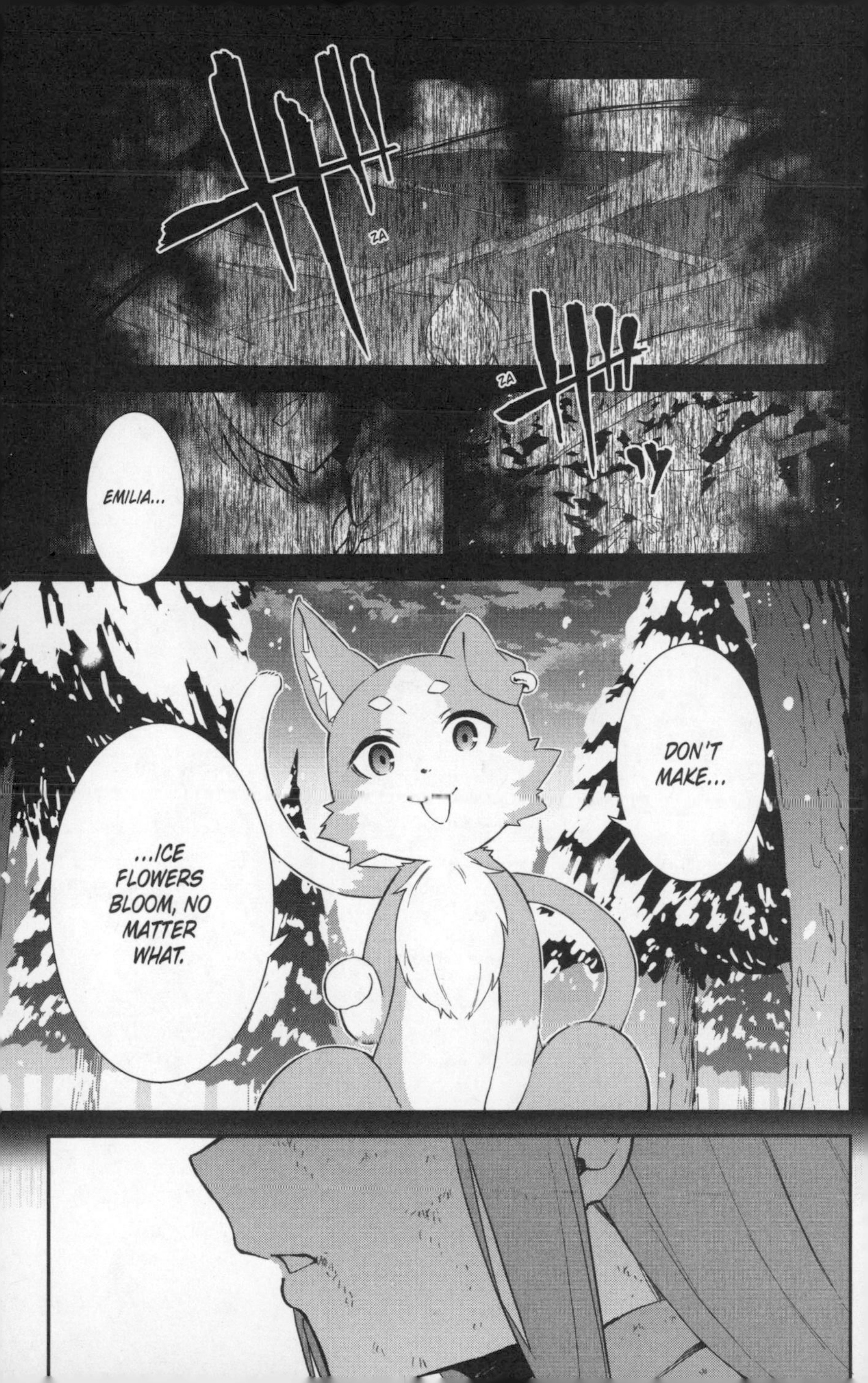
ZA
ZA
EMILIA...
DON'T MAKE...
...ICE FLOWERS BLOOM, NO MATTER WHAT.

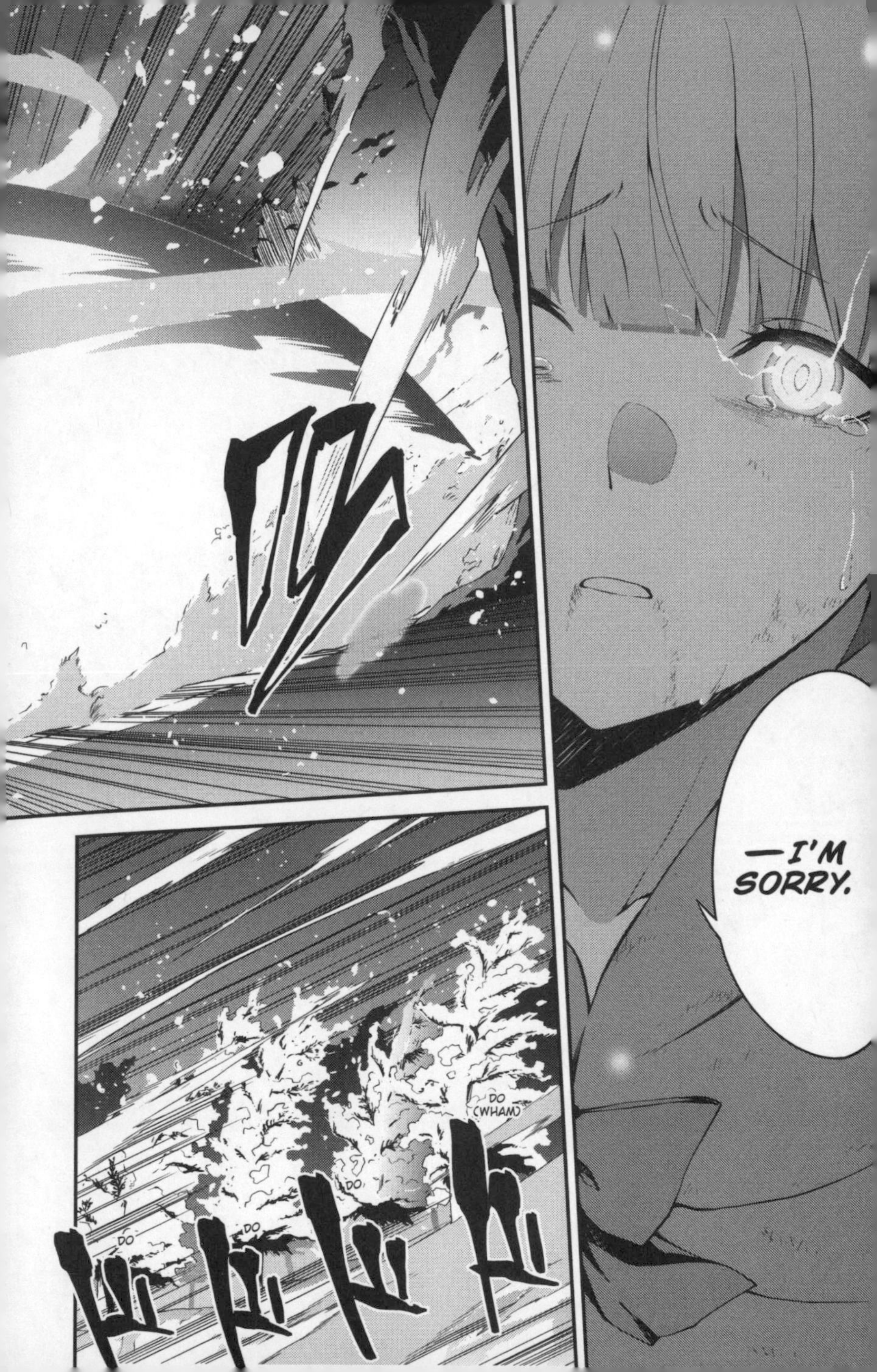
—I'M
SORRY.
DO
(WHAM)
DO
DO
DO

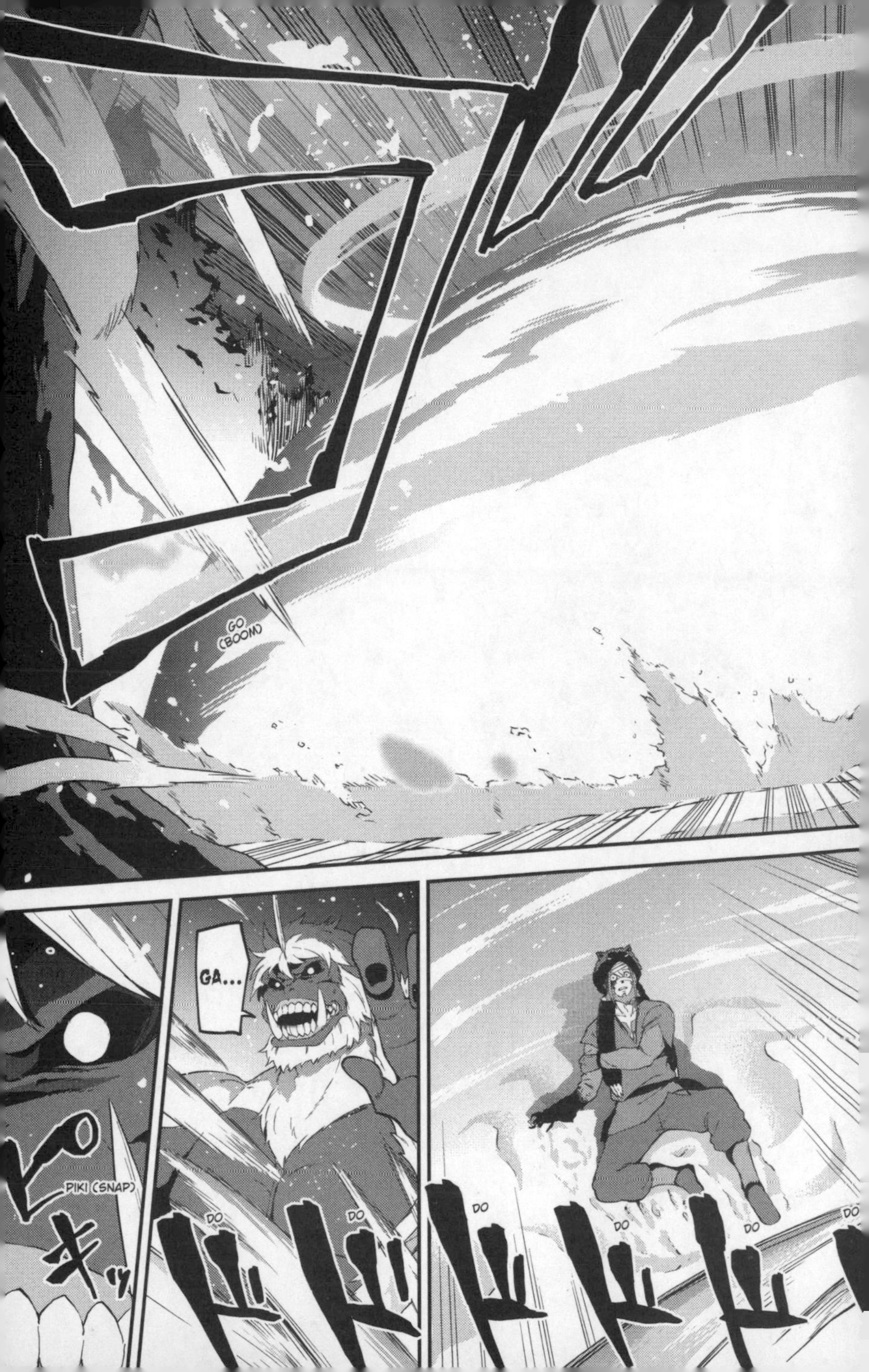
GO (BOOM)
DO
DO
DO
DO
GA...
DO
DO
PIKI (SNAP)

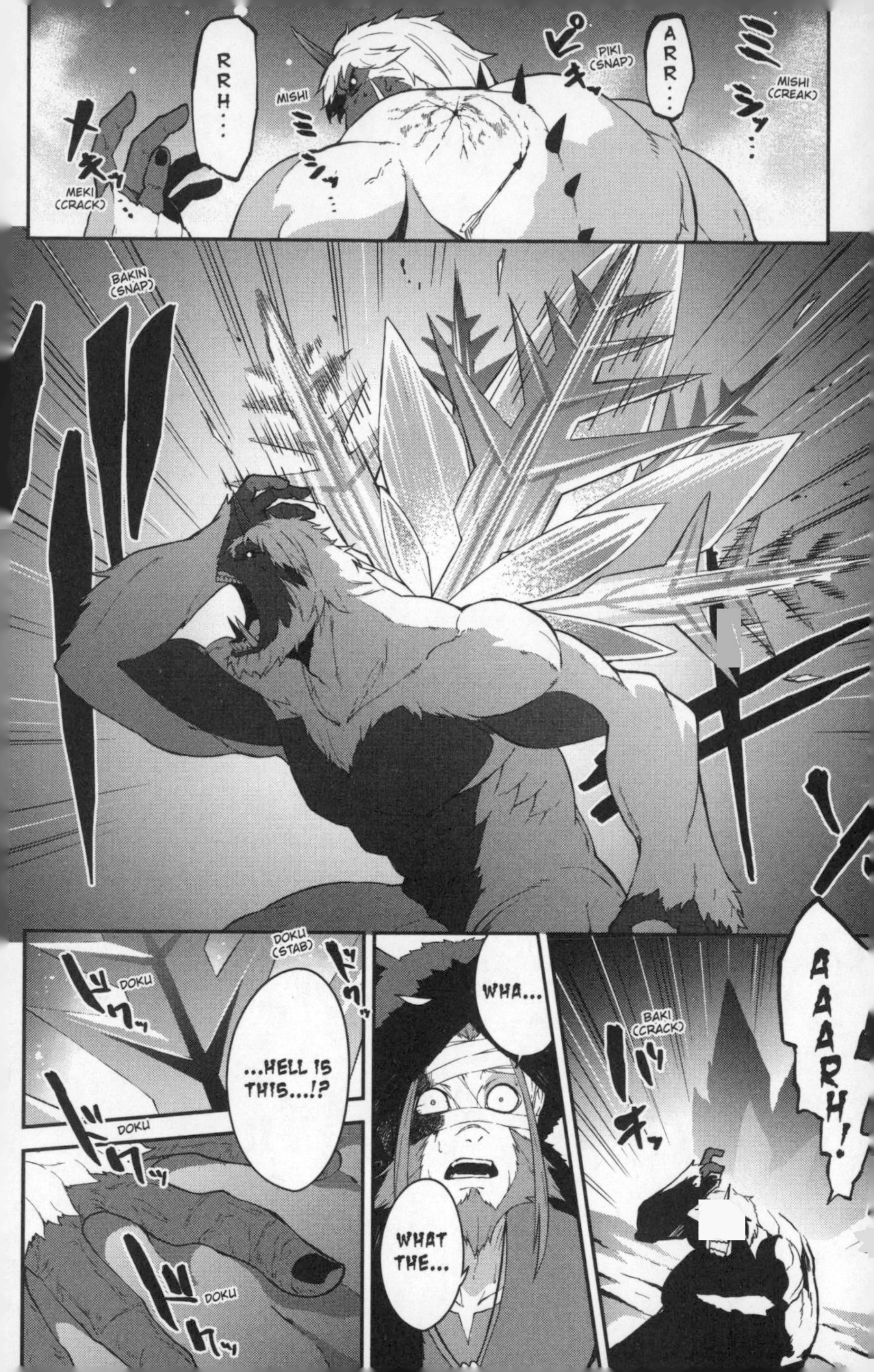
MISHI (CREAK)
ARR...
PIKI (SNAP)
MISHI
RRH...
MEKI (CRACK)
BAKIN (SNAP)
AAAARH!
BAKI (CRACK)
WHA...
WHAT THE...
DOKU (STAB)
DOKU
...HELL IS THIS...!?
DOKU
DOKU

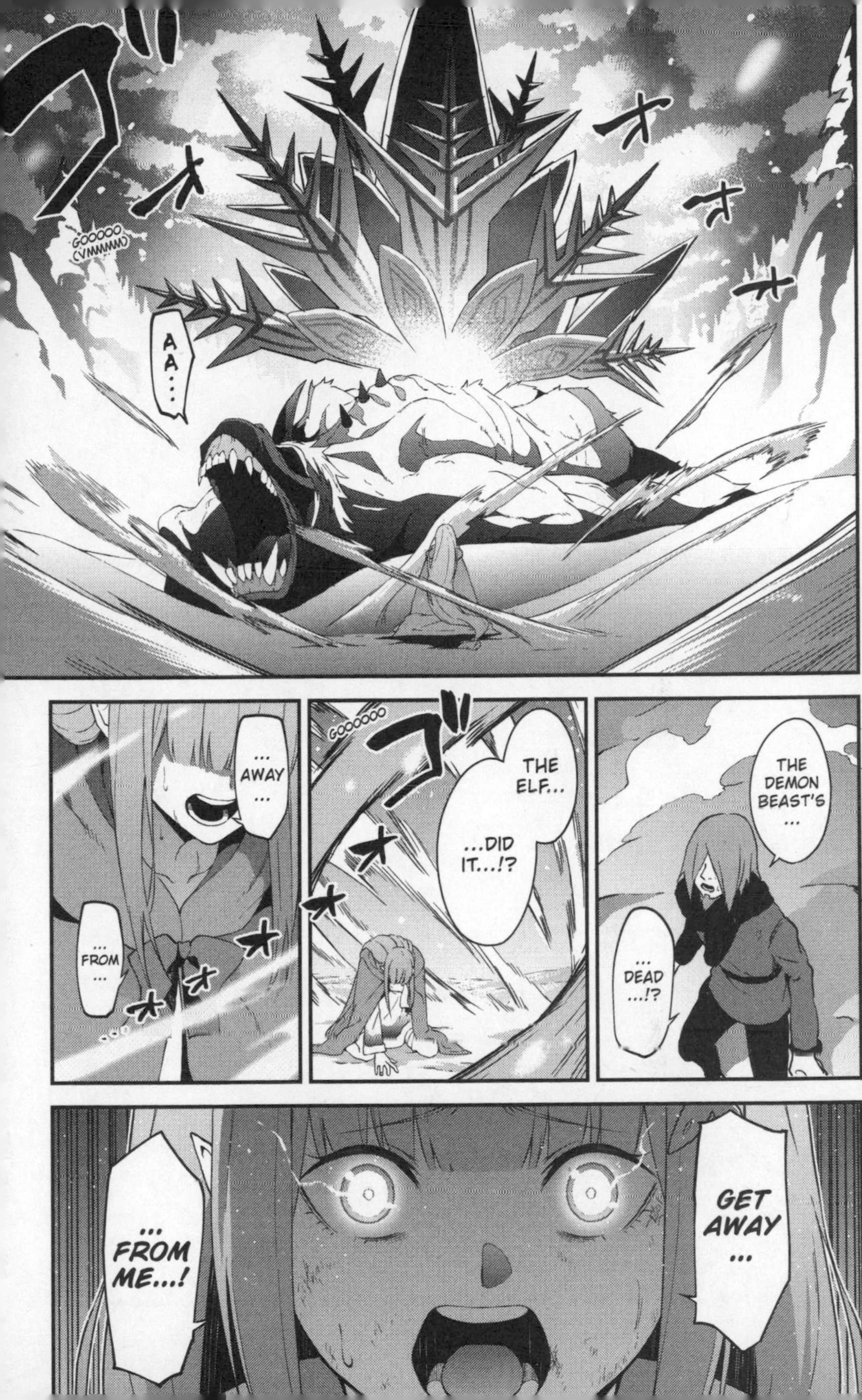
GOOOOO (VMMMMM)
AA...
THE DEMON BEAST'S ...
... DEAD ...!?
GOOOOOO
THE ELF...
...DID IT...!?
... AWAY ...
... FROM ...
GET AWAY ...
... FROM ME...!

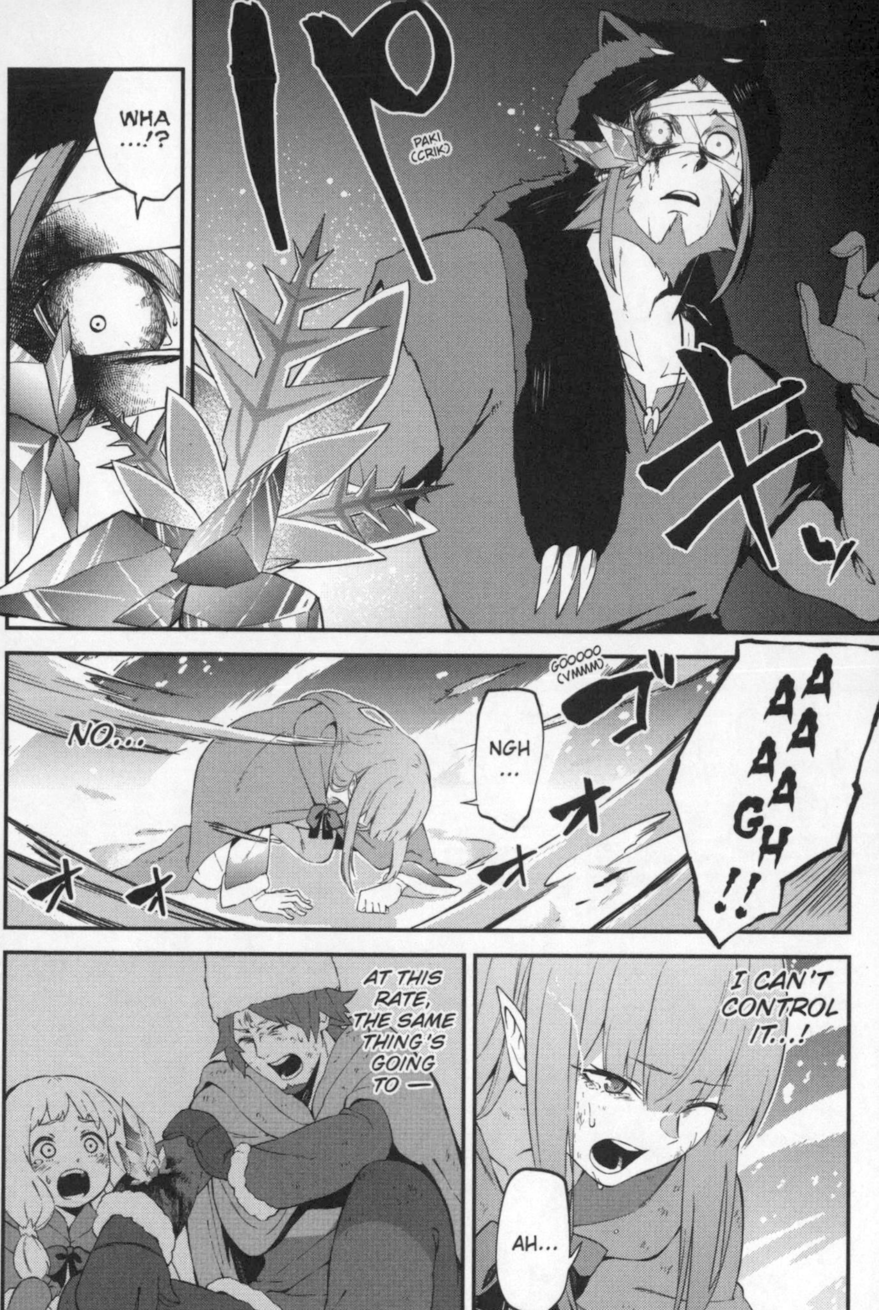
PAKI (CRIK)
WHA ...!?
AAAAAAGH!!
GOOOOO (VMMMM)
NGH ...
NO...
I CAN'T CONTROL IT...!
AH...
AT THIS RATE, THE SAME THING'S GOING TO —

PLEASE! WAIT!

OOOOO (BLOOOW)

I-I APOLO- GIZE!

I'M SORRY, SO PLEEE- ASE!!

NO...

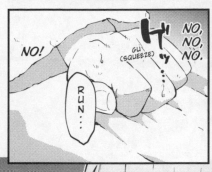

NO, NO, NO.

NO!

GU (SQUEEZE)

RUN...

—NO.

PLEASE ...

PAKI

I CAN'T ...

...TAKE ANY MORE LIVES—

I DON'T WANT TO...

SOME- BODY...

SAVE ME...

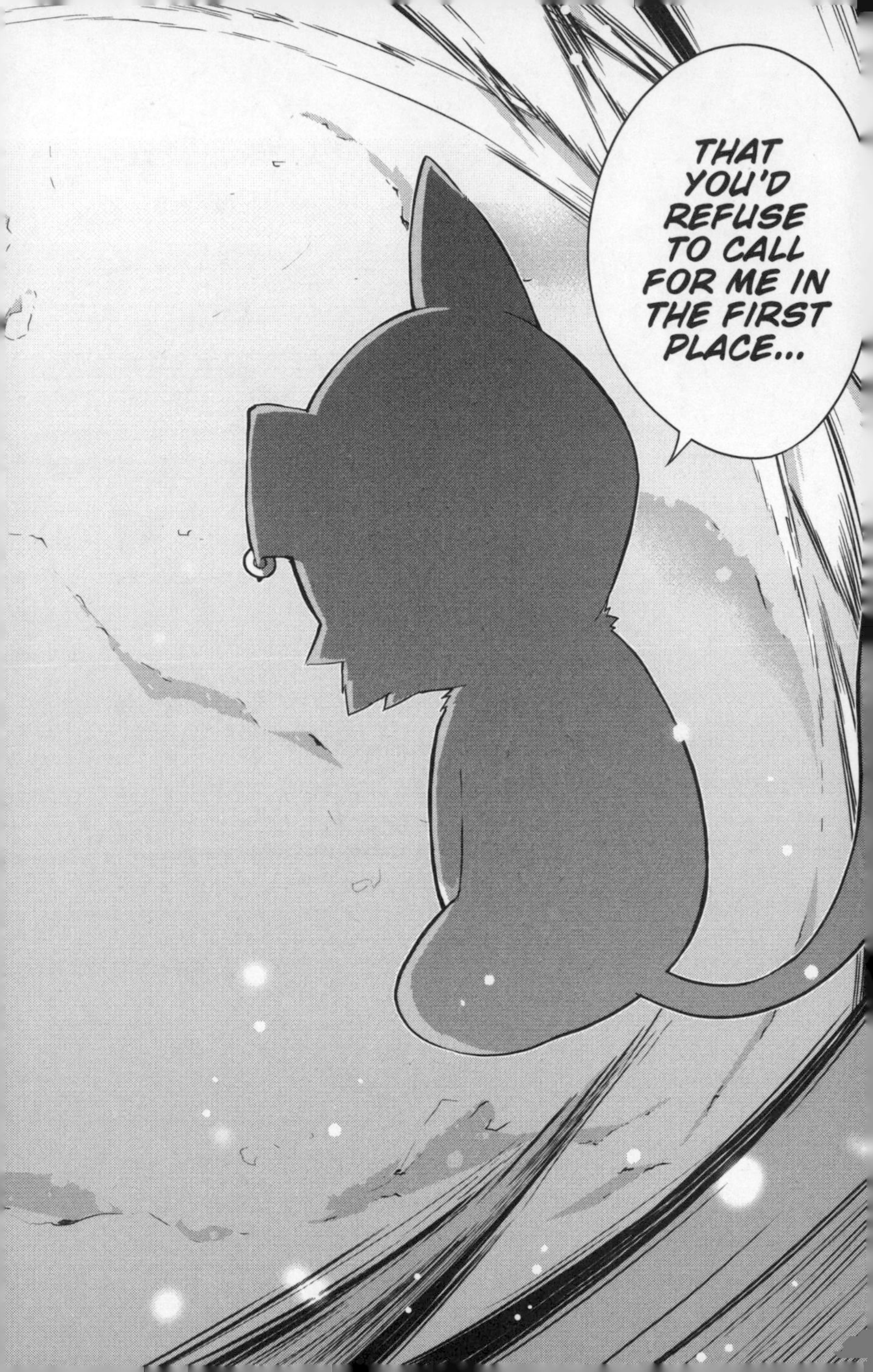
THAT YOU'D REFUSE TO CALL FOR ME IN THE FIRST PLACE...

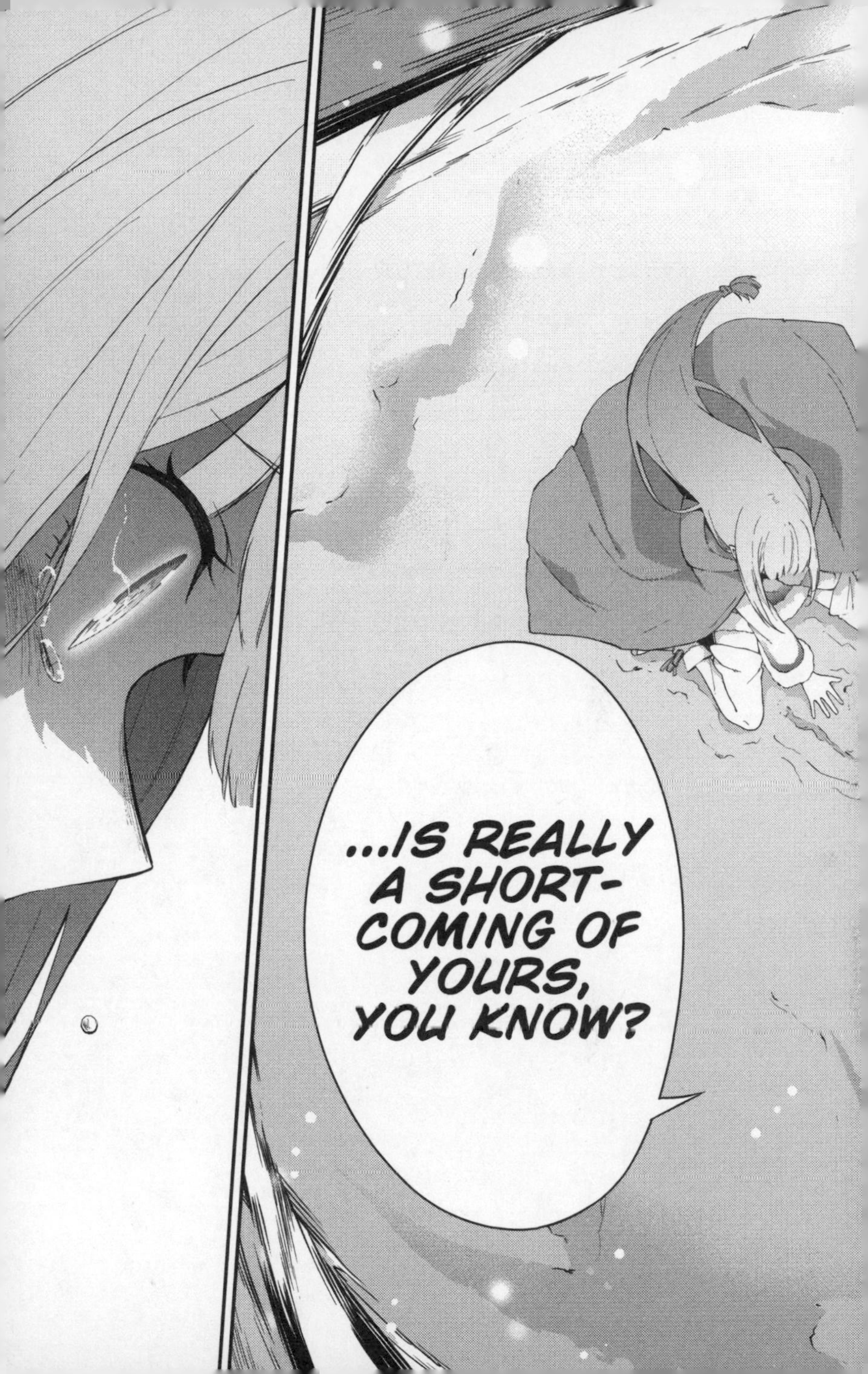
...IS REALLY A SHORT-COMING OF YOURS, YOU KNOW?

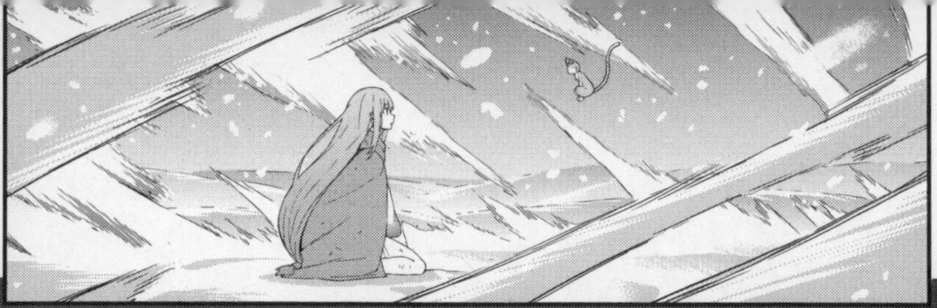

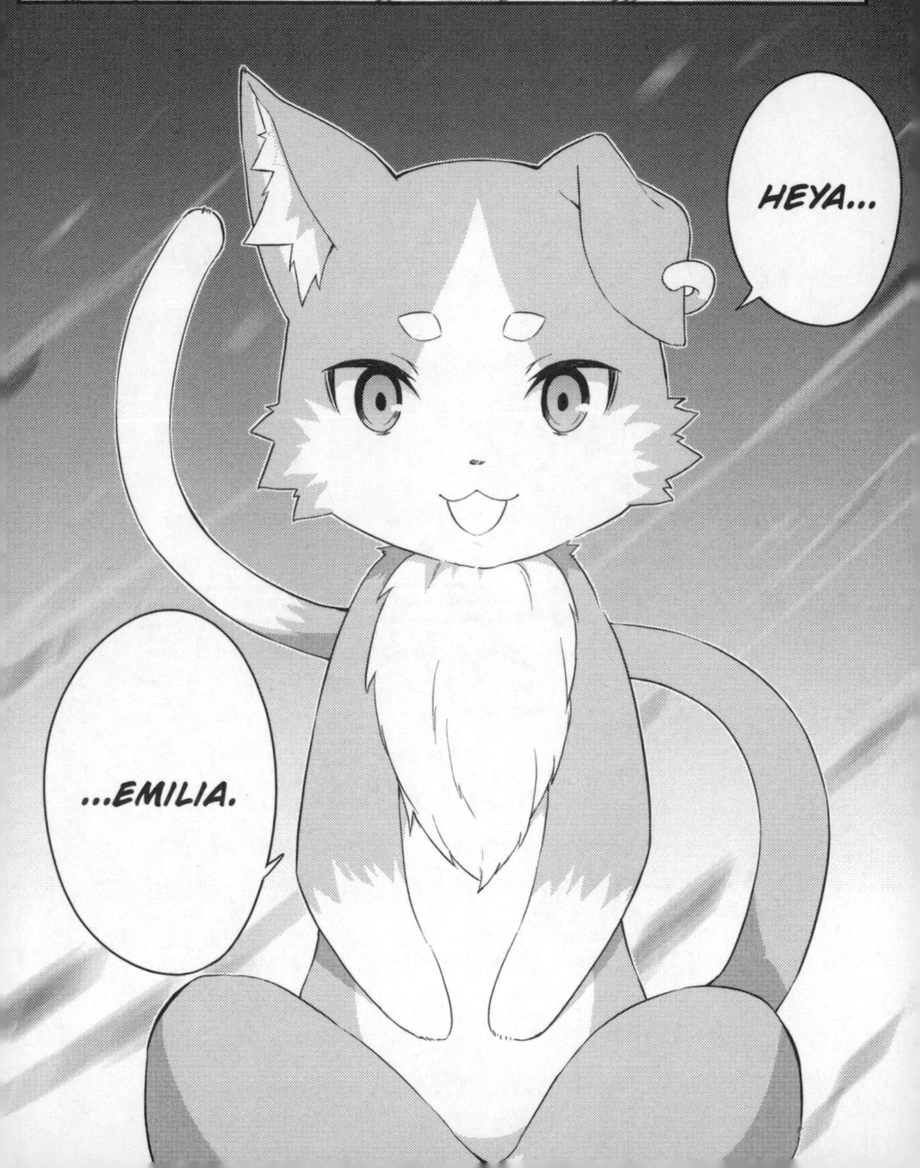
HEYA...
...EMILIA.

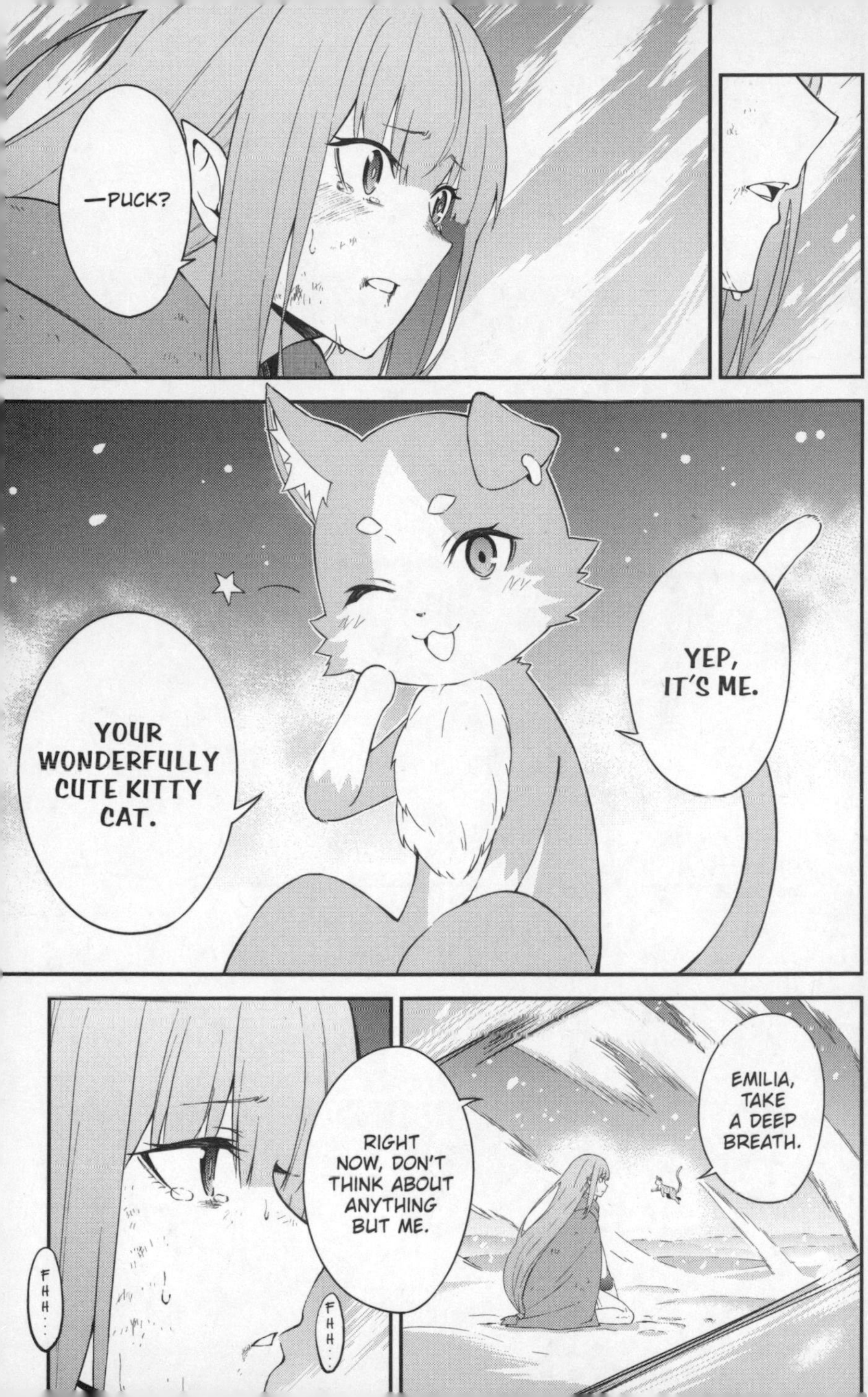
—PUCK?
YEP, IT'S ME.
YOUR WONDERFULLY CUTE KITTY CAT.
EMILIA, TAKE A DEEP BREATH.
RIGHT NOW, DON'T THINK ABOUT ANYTHING BUT ME.
FHH...
FHH...

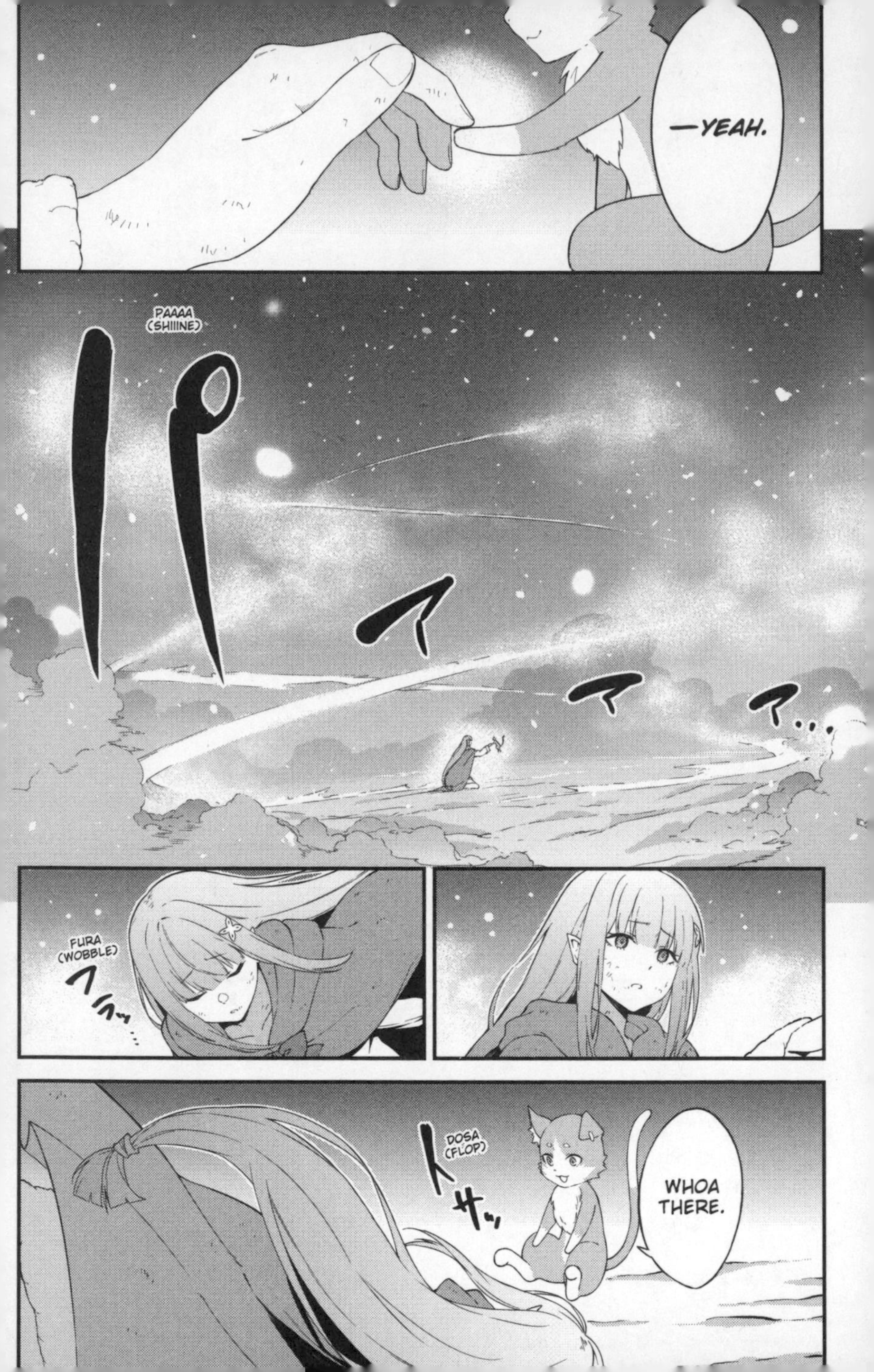
—YEAH.
PAAAA (SHIIINE)
パァァァ...
FURA (WOBBLE)
WHOA THERE.
DOSA (FLOP)
ドサッ

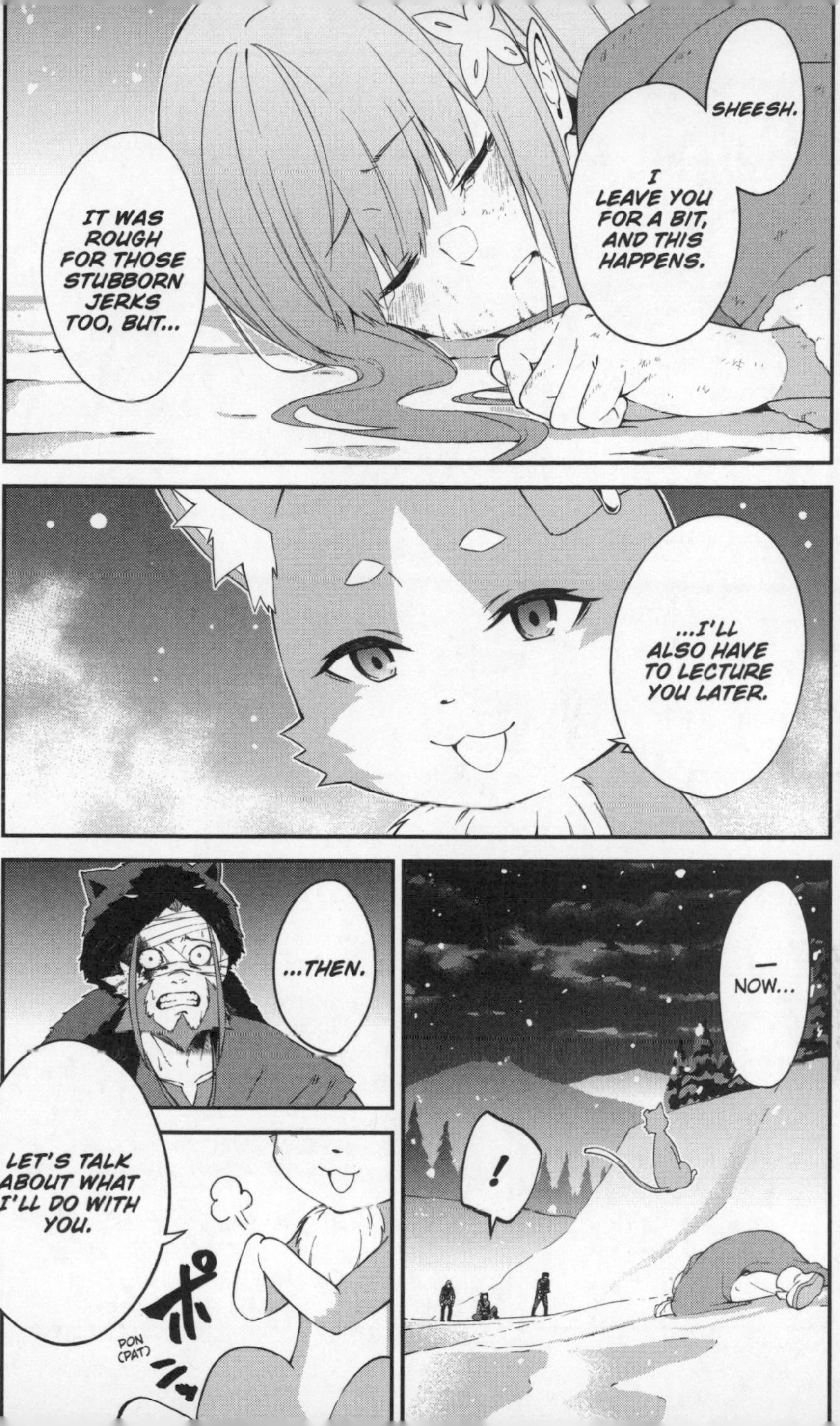
SHEESH.
I LEAVE YOU FOR A BIT, AND THIS HAPPENS.
IT WAS ROUGH FOR THOSE STUBBORN JERKS TOO, BUT...
...I'LL ALSO HAVE TO LECTURE YOU LATER.
—NOW...
!
...THEN.
LET'S TALK ABOUT WHAT I'LL DO WITH YOU.
PON (PAT)

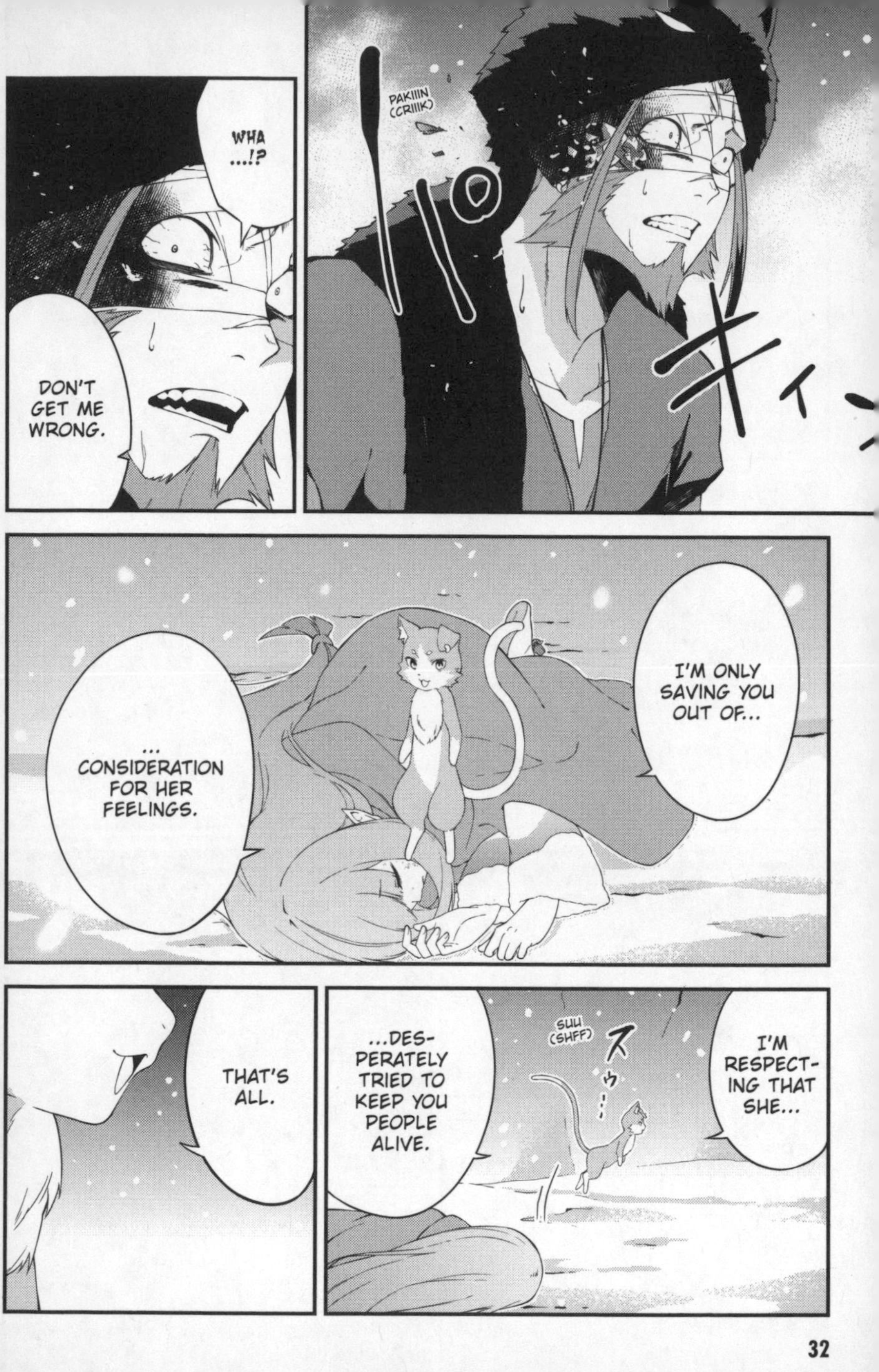
PAKIIIN (CRIIIK)
WHA ...!?
DON'T GET ME WRONG.
I'M ONLY SAVING YOU OUT OF...
... CONSIDERATION FOR HER FEELINGS.
I'M RESPECT- ING THAT SHE...
SUU (SHFF)
スゥ…
...DES- PERATELY TRIED TO KEEP YOU PEOPLE ALIVE.
THAT'S ALL.

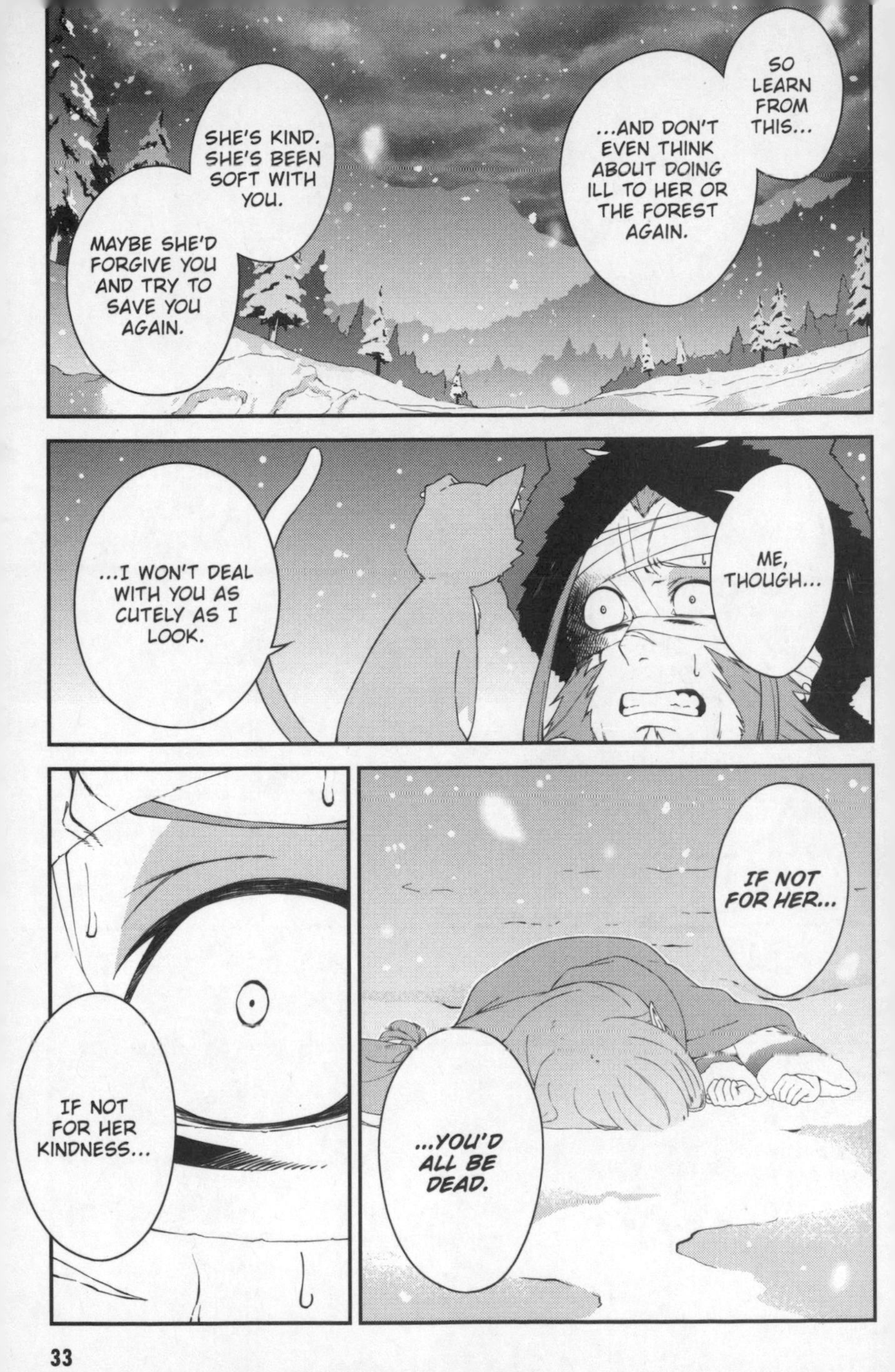
SO LEARN FROM THIS...
...AND DON'T EVEN THINK ABOUT DOING ILL TO HER OR THE FOREST AGAIN.
SHE'S KIND. SHE'S BEEN SOFT WITH YOU.
MAYBE SHE'D FORGIVE YOU AND TRY TO SAVE YOU AGAIN.
ME, THOUGH...
...I WON'T DEAL WITH YOU AS CUTELY AS I LOOK.
IF NOT FOR HER...
...YOU'D ALL BE DEAD.
IF NOT FOR HER KINDNESS...

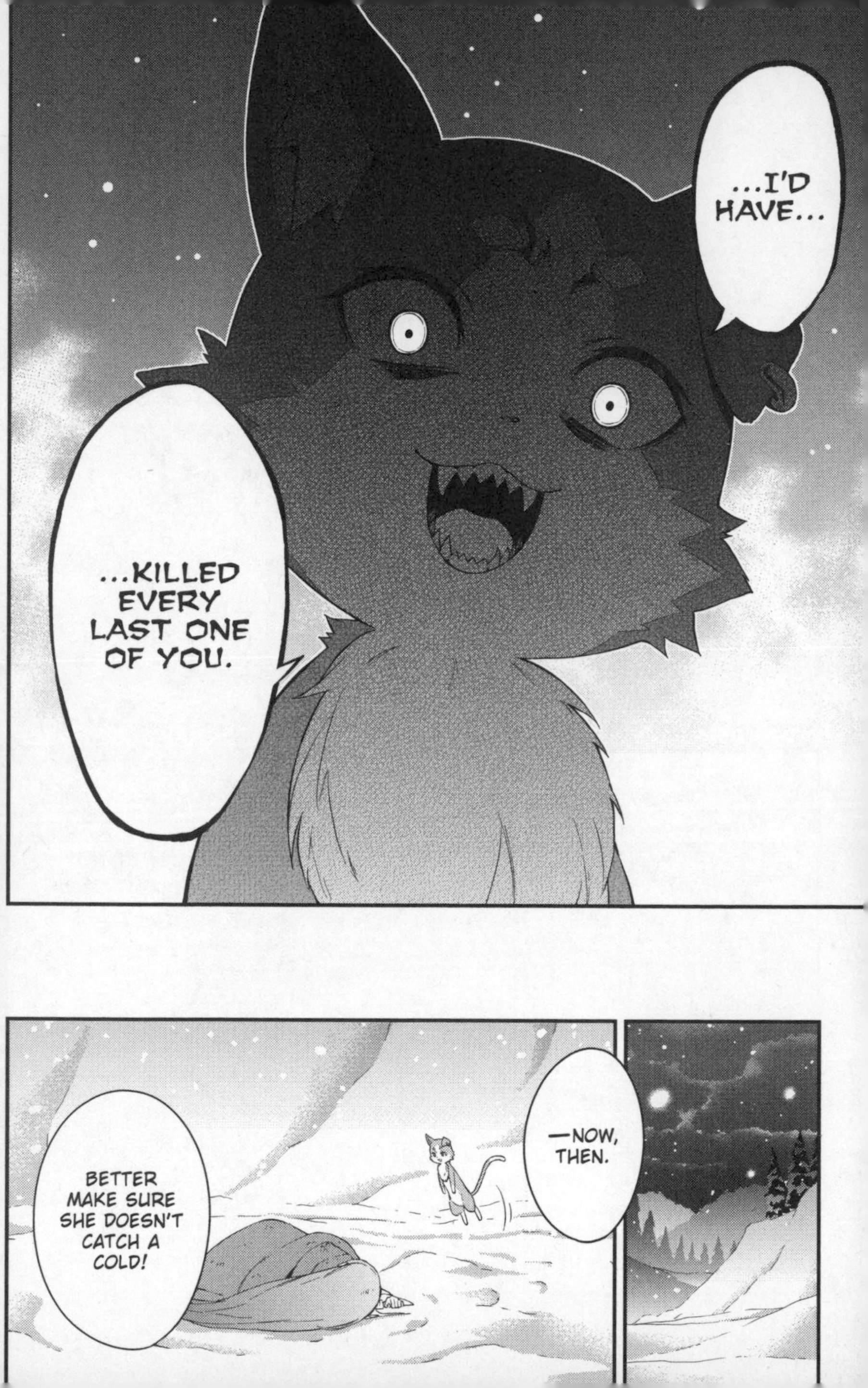
...I'D HAVE...
...KILLED EVERY LAST ONE OF YOU.
—NOW, THEN.
BETTER MAKE SURE SHE DOESN'T CATCH A COLD!

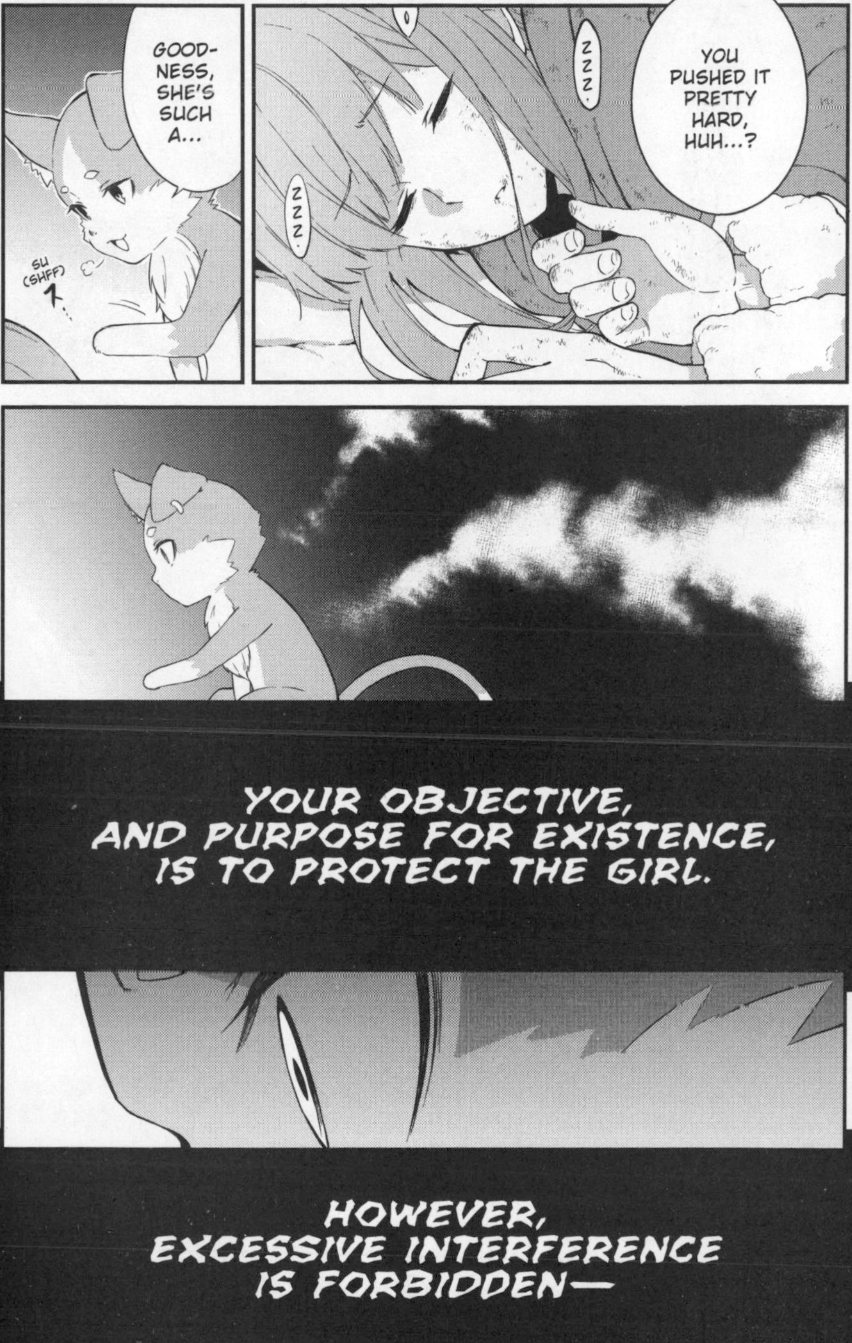
YOU PUSHED IT PRETTY HARD, HUH...?
ZZZ.
ZZZ.
GOOD-NESS, SHE'S SUCH A...
SU (SHFF)
YOUR OBJECTIVE, AND PURPOSE FOR EXISTENCE, IS TO PROTECT THE GIRL.
HOWEVER, EXCESSIVE INTERFERENCE IS FORBIDDEN—

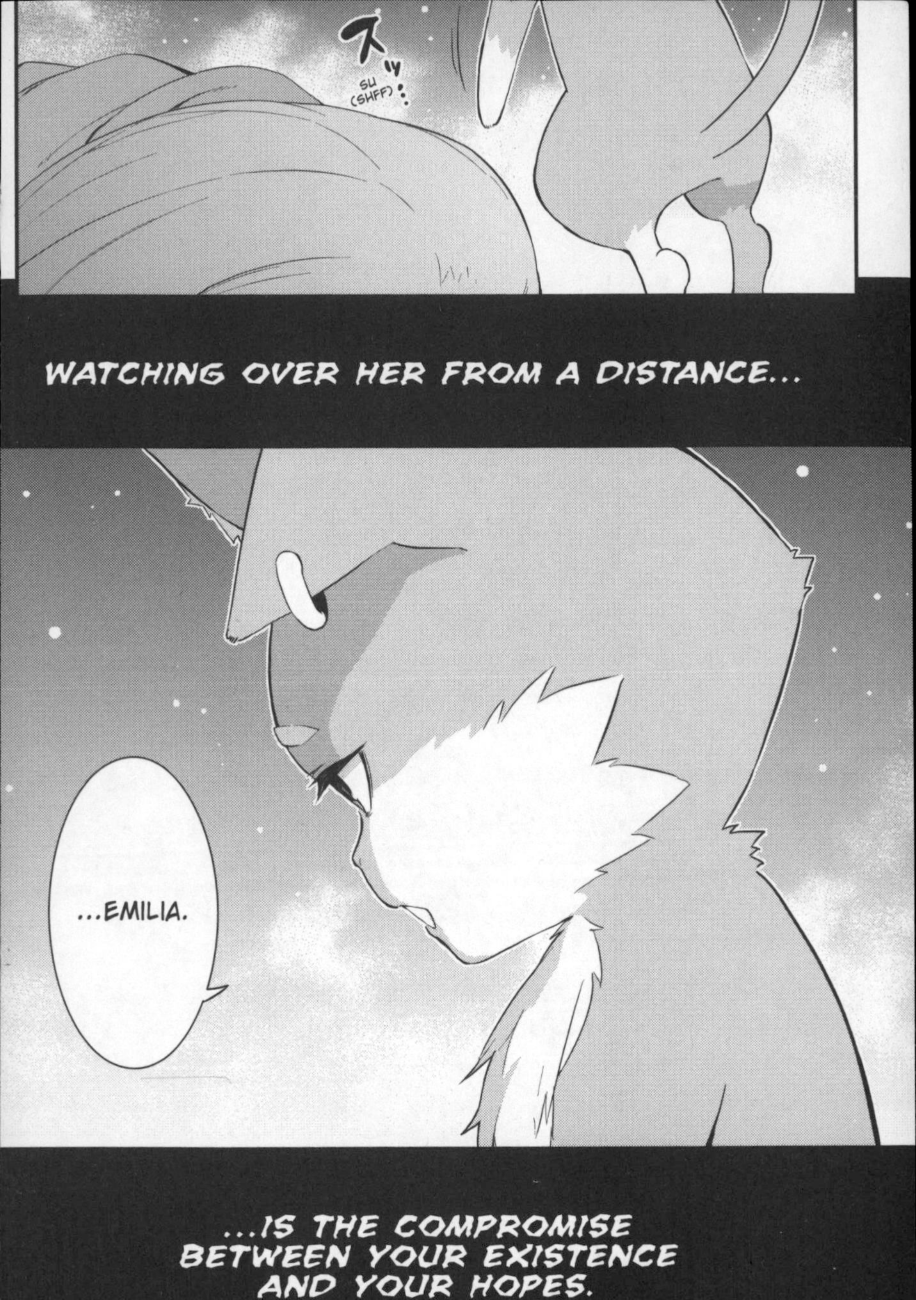
スッ
SU (SHFF)
WATCHING OVER HER FROM A DISTANCE...
...EMILIA.
...IS THE COMPROMISE BETWEEN YOUR EXISTENCE AND YOUR HOPES.

Re:ZERO

-Starting Life in Another World-

The Frozen Bond

The only ability Subaru Natsuki gets when he's
summoned to another world is time travel via his own death.
But to save her, he'll die as many times as it takes.

Re:ZERO

-Starting Life in Another World-
The Frozen Bond

Minori Tsukahara

Tappei Nagatsuki, Shinichirou Otsuka

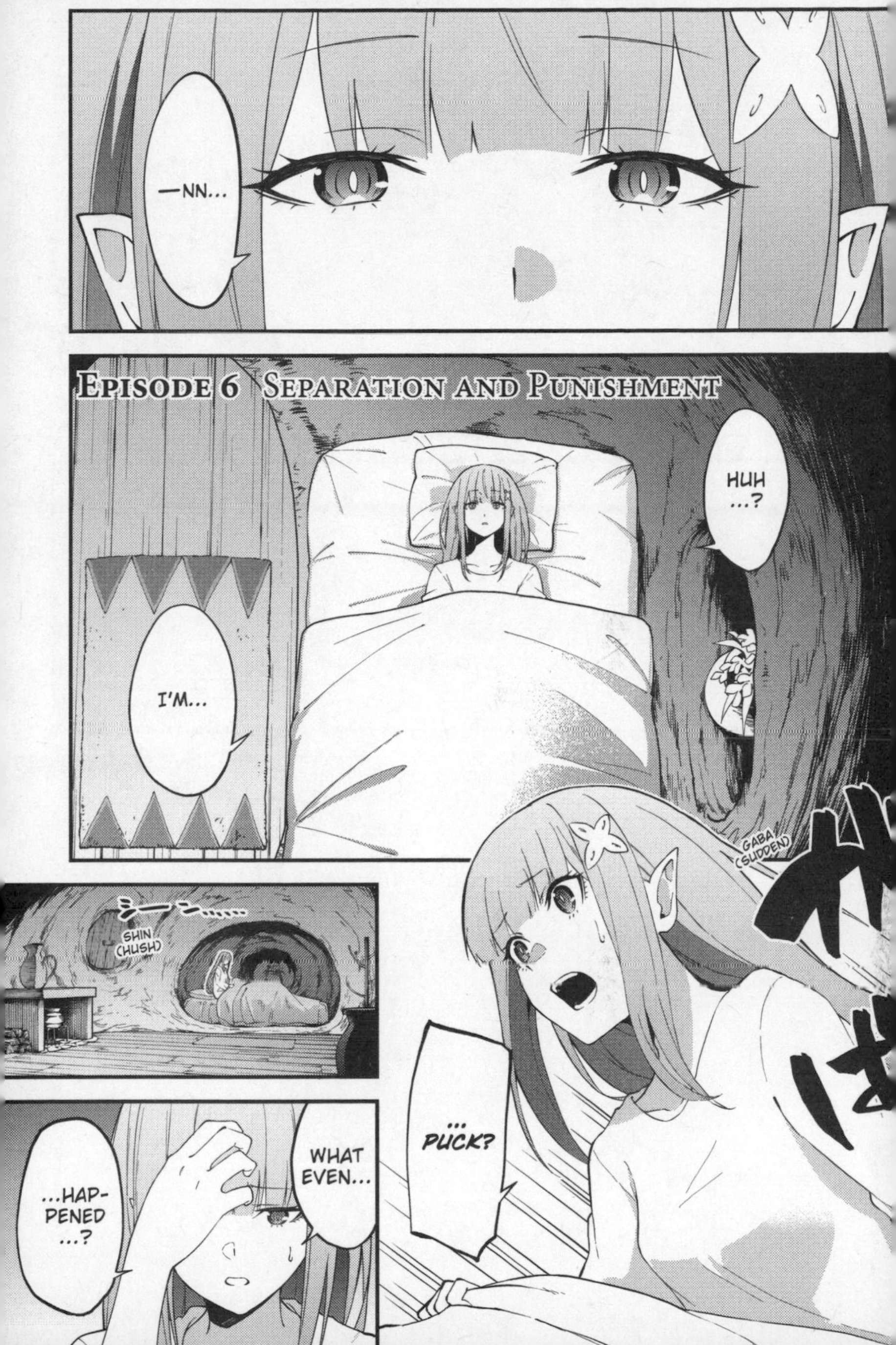
—NN...
EPISODE 6 SEPARATION AND PUNISHMENT
HUH ...?
I'M...
GABA (SUDDEN)
... PUCK?
SHIN (HUSH)
WHAT EVEN...
...HAP-PENED ...?

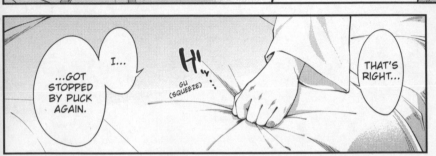

...GOT STOPPED BY PUCK AGAIN.

I...

HI!...

GU (SQUEEZE)

THAT'S RIGHT...

!!

THAT'S RIGHT!

I BROKE MY PROMISE, BUT HE HELPED ME AGAIN...

IF PUCK HADN'T STOPPED ME, NOT JUST THE FOREST, BUT THE VILLAGE—

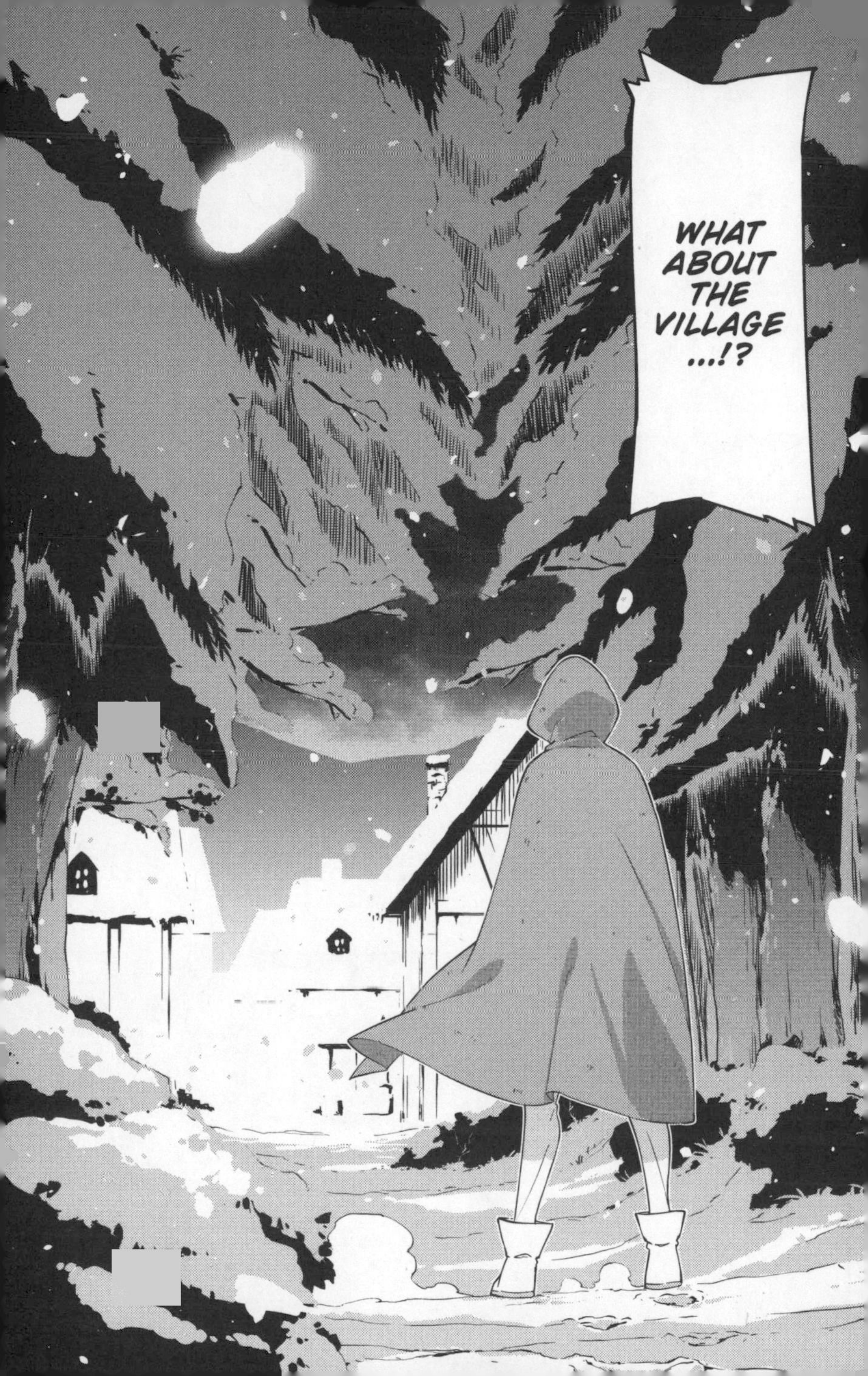
WHAT ABOUT THE VILLAGE ...!?

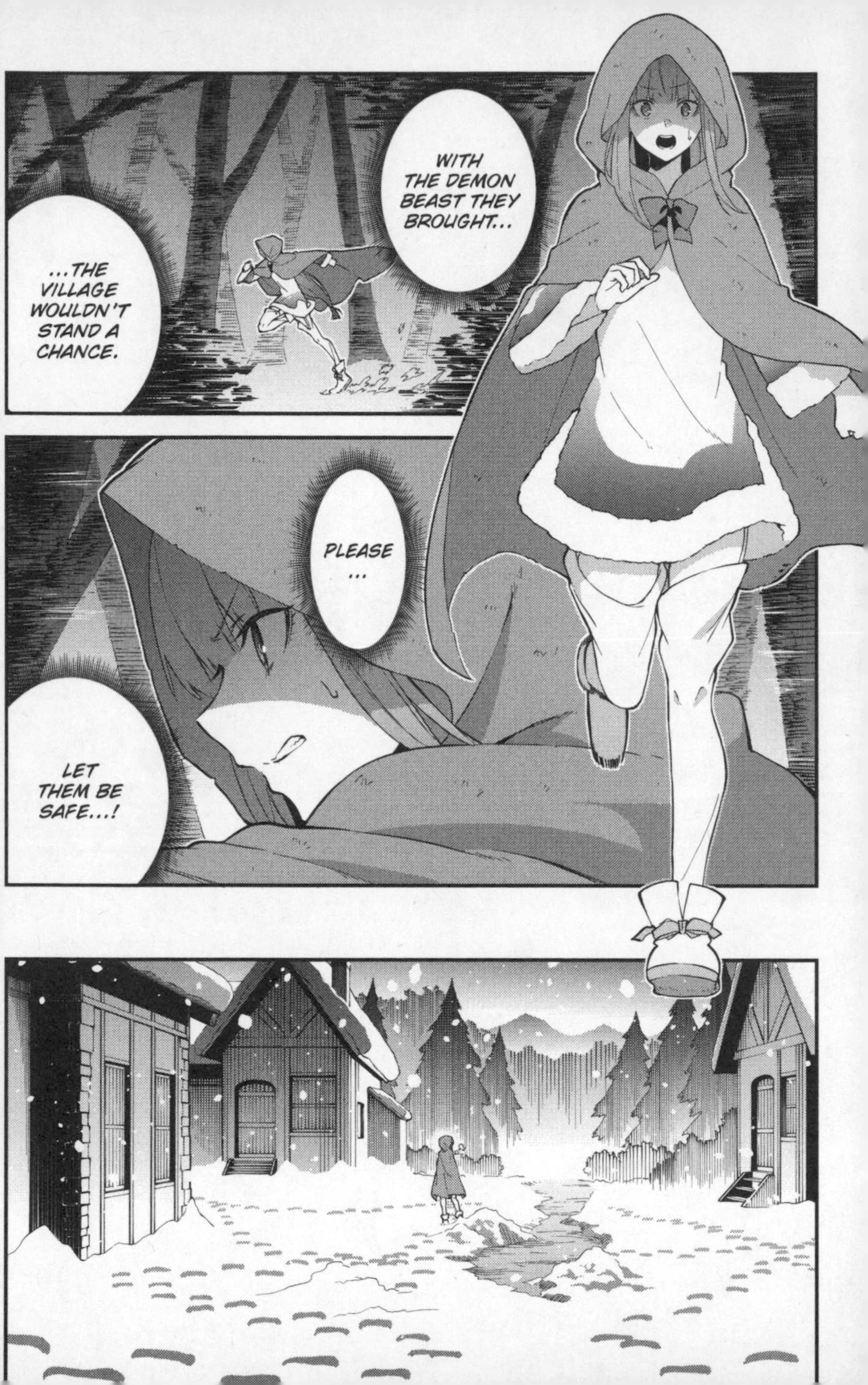
WITH THE DEMON BEAST THEY BROUGHT...
...THE VILLAGE WOULDN'T STAND A CHANCE.
PLEASE ...
LET THEM BE SAFE...!

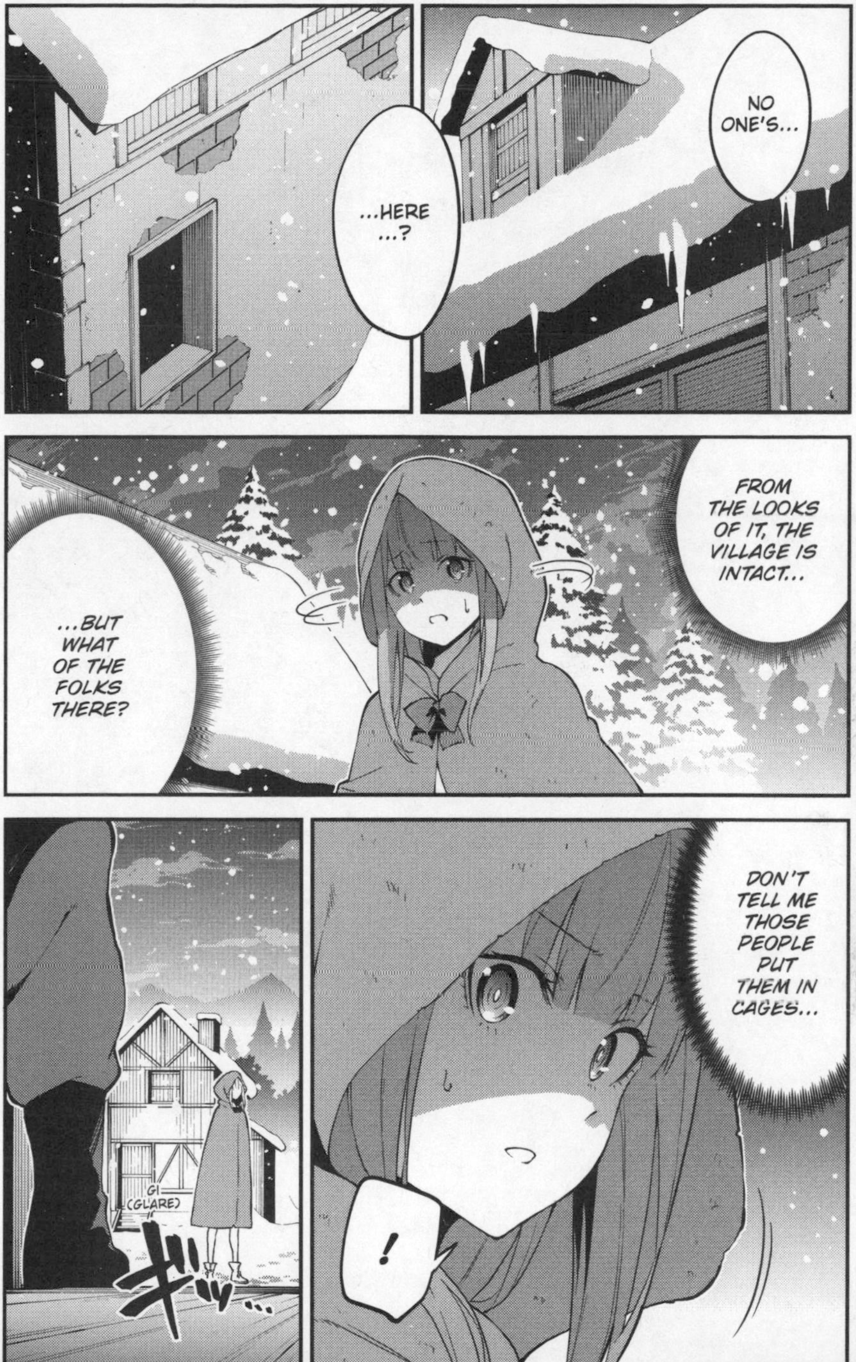
NO ONE'S...
...HERE ...?
FROM THE LOOKS OF IT, THE VILLAGE IS INTACT...
...BUT WHAT OF THE FOLKS THERE?
DON'T TELL ME THOSE PEOPLE PUT THEM IN CAGES...
!
GI (GLARE)
ギッ...

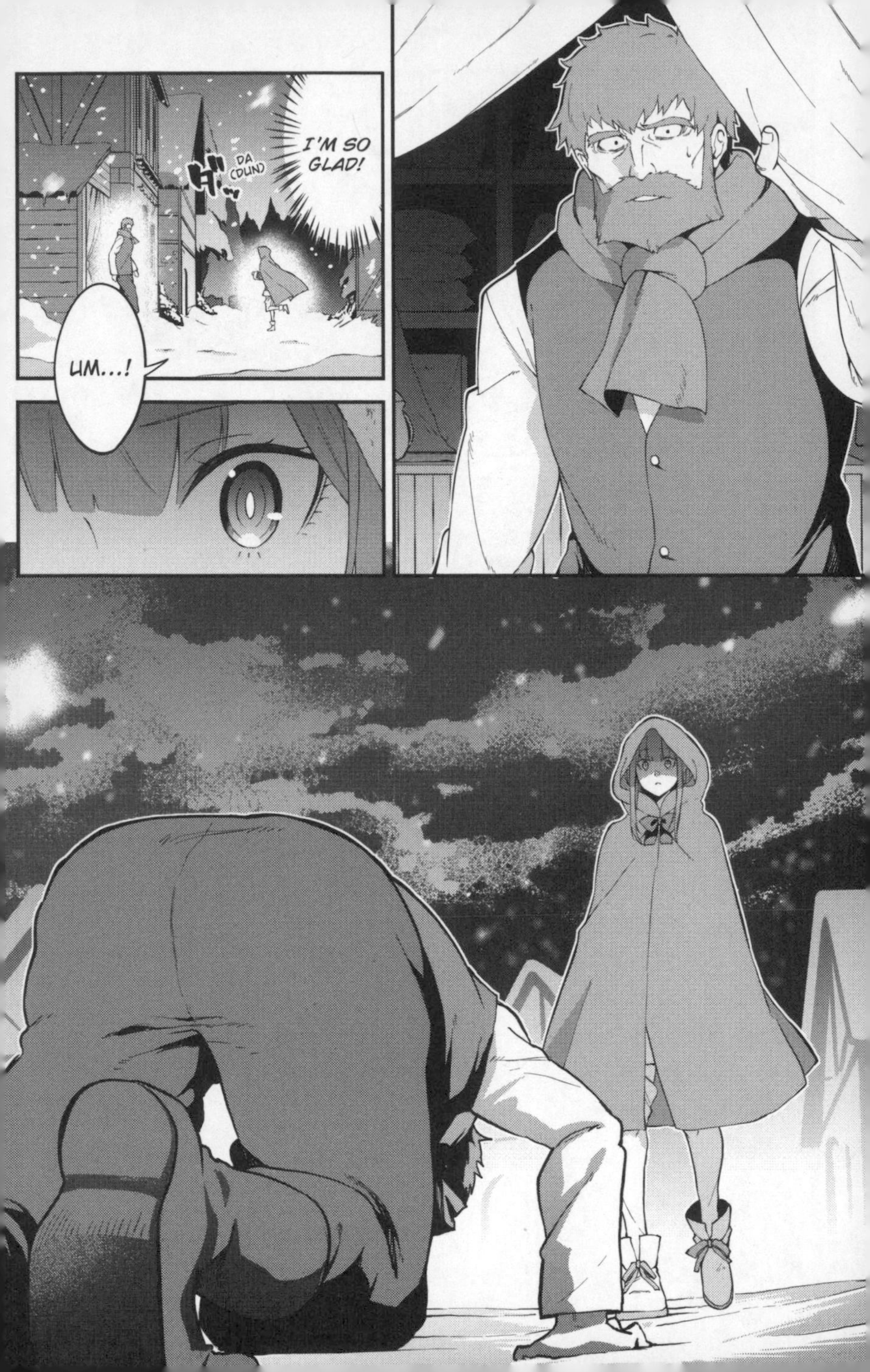
I'M SO GLAD!
DA (DUN)
UM...!

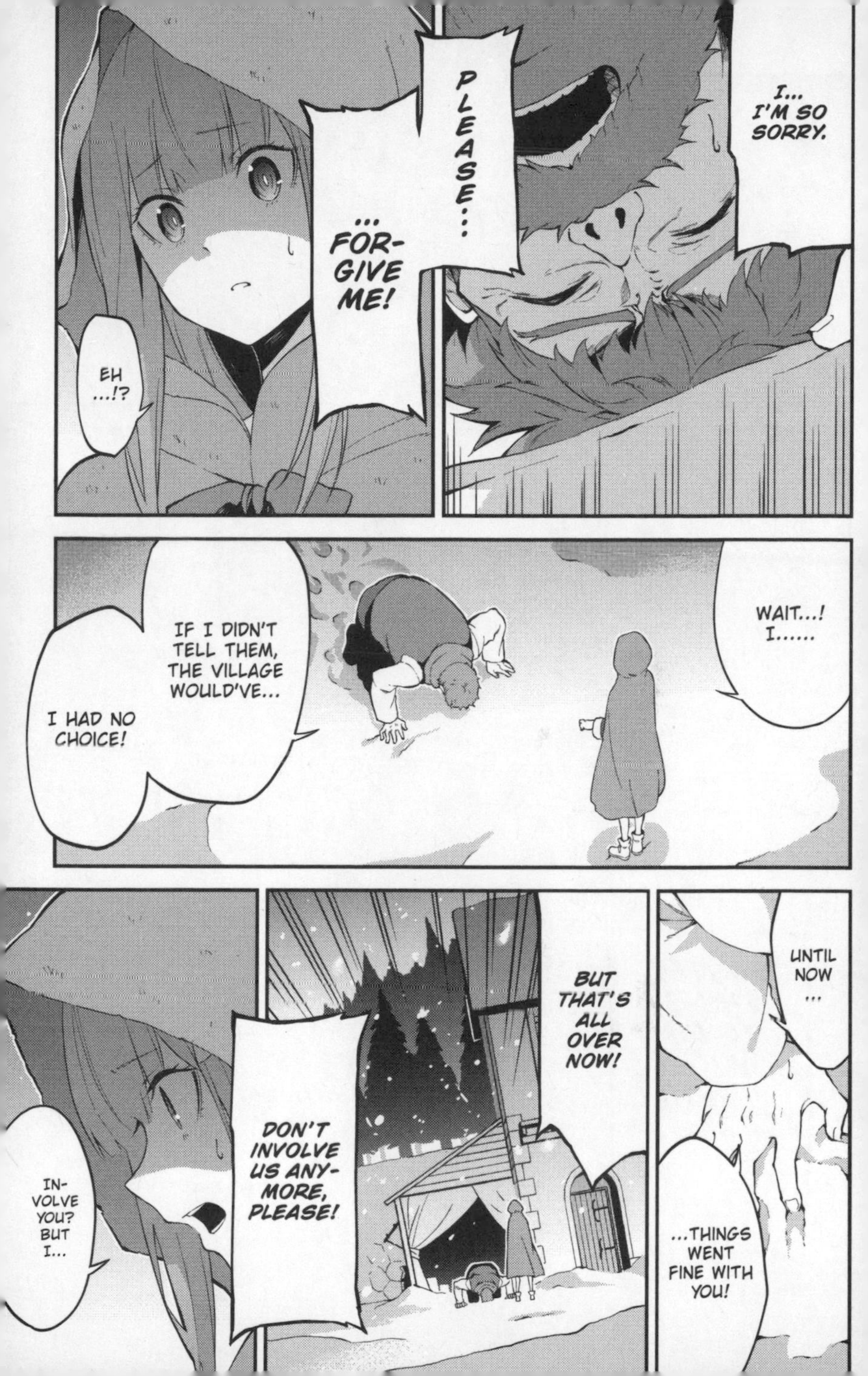
I... I'M SO SORRY.
PLEASE...
...FOR-GIVE ME!
EH ...!?
WAIT...! I......
IF I DIDN'T TELL THEM, THE VILLAGE WOULD'VE...
I HAD NO CHOICE!
UNTIL NOW ...
...THINGS WENT FINE WITH YOU!
BUT THAT'S ALL OVER NOW!
DON'T INVOLVE US ANY-MORE, PLEASE!
IN-VOLVE YOU? BUT I...

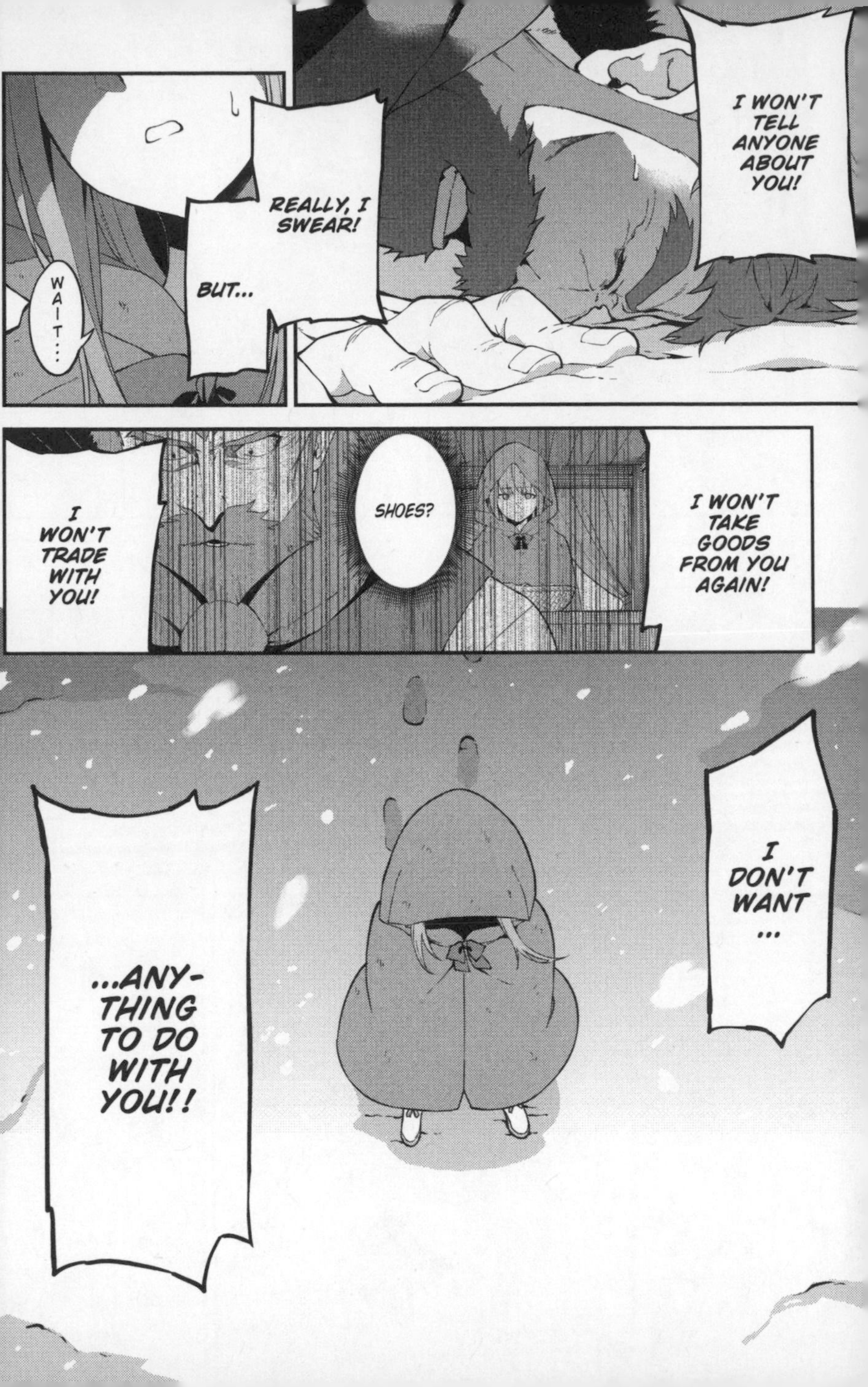
I WON'T TELL ANYONE ABOUT YOU!
REALLY, I SWEAR!
BUT...
WAIT...
I WON'T TAKE GOODS FROM YOU AGAIN!
SHOES?
I WON'T TRADE WITH YOU!
I DON'T WANT...
...ANY-THING TO DO WITH YOU!!

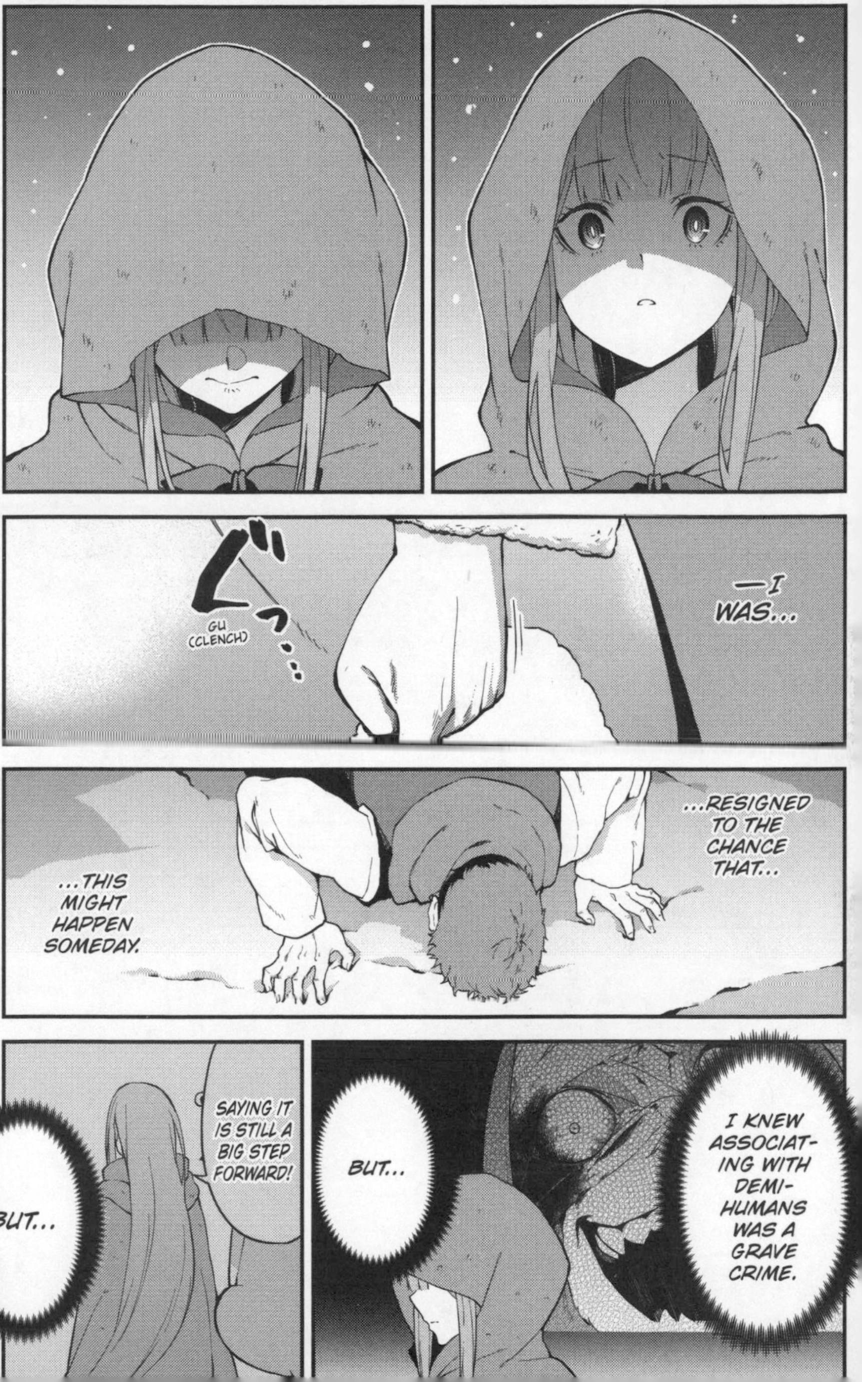
—I WAS...
ぐっ
GU (CLENCH)
...RESIGNED TO THE CHANCE THAT...
...THIS MIGHT HAPPEN SOMEDAY.
I KNEW ASSOCIATING WITH DEMI-HUMANS WAS A GRAVE CRIME.
BUT...
SAYING IT IS STILL A BIG STEP FORWARD!
BUT...

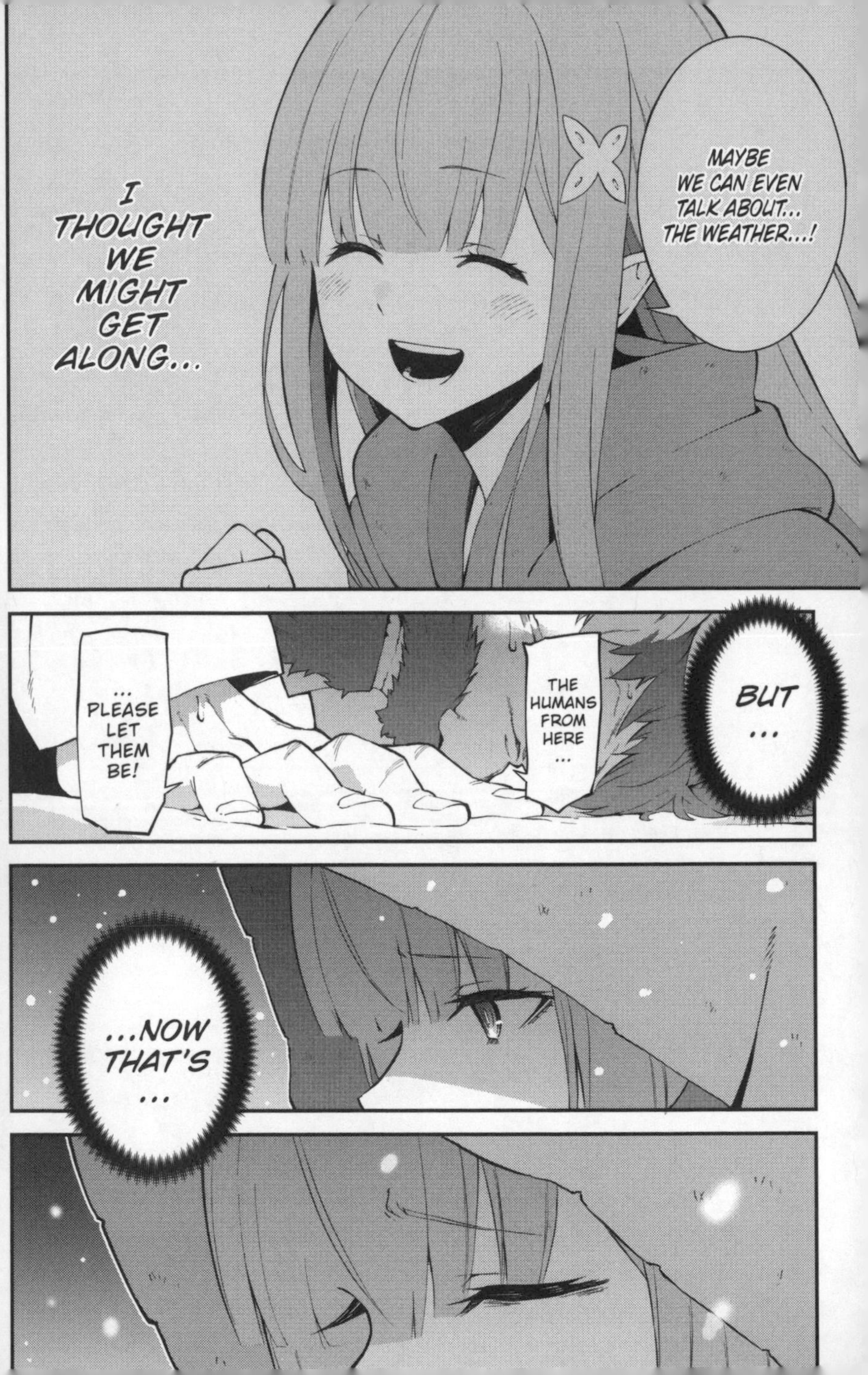
MAYBE WE CAN EVEN TALK ABOUT... THE WEATHER...!
I THOUGHT WE MIGHT GET ALONG...
BUT...
THE HUMANS FROM HERE...
...PLEASE LET THEM BE!
...NOW THAT'S...

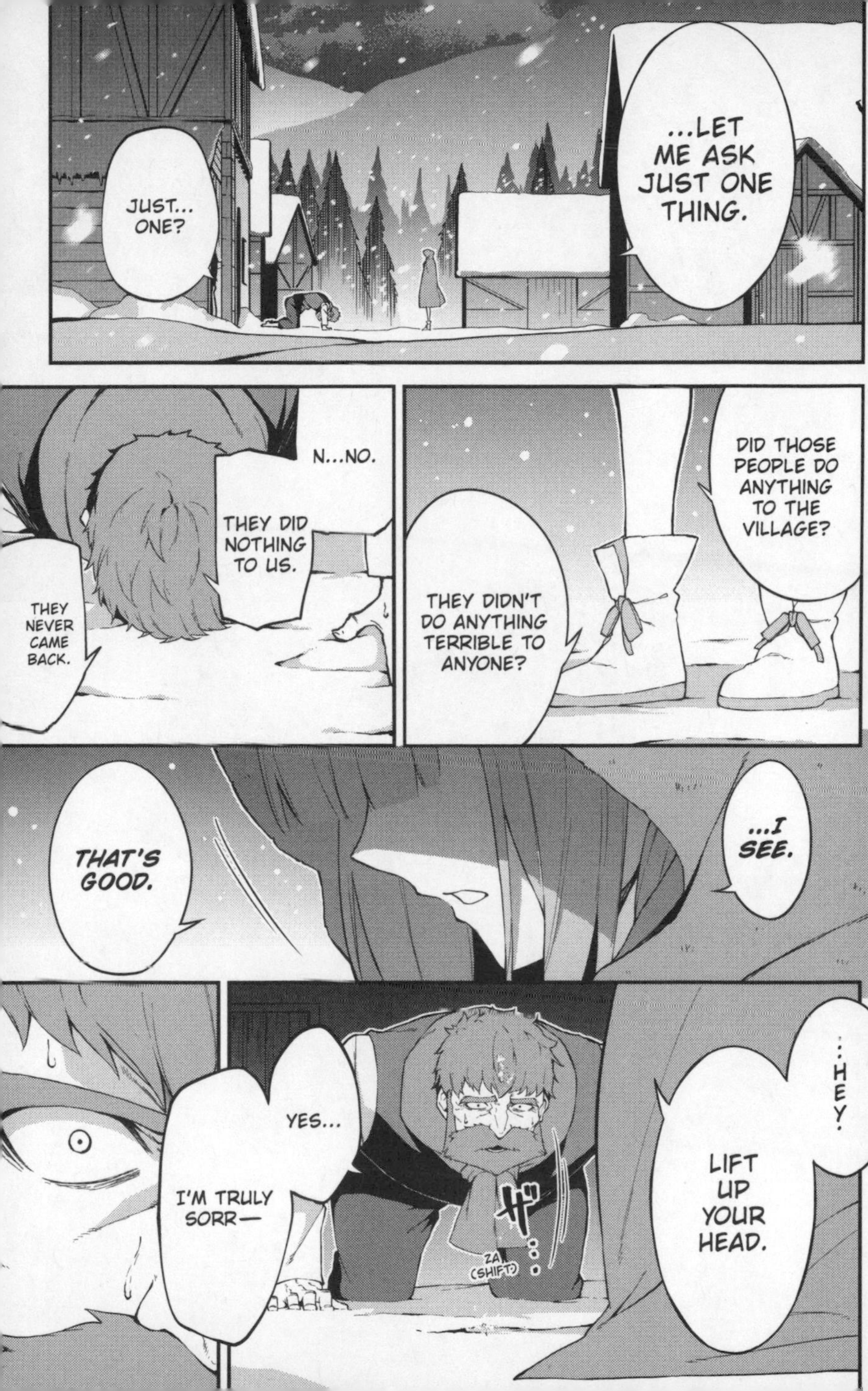
...LET ME ASK JUST ONE THING.
JUST... ONE?
DID THOSE PEOPLE DO ANYTHING TO THE VILLAGE?
THEY DIDN'T DO ANYTHING TERRIBLE TO ANYONE?
N...NO.
THEY DID NOTHING TO US.
THEY NEVER CAME BACK.
...I SEE.
THAT'S GOOD.
...HEY.
LIFT UP YOUR HEAD.
ZA (SHIFT)
YES...
I'M TRULY SORR—

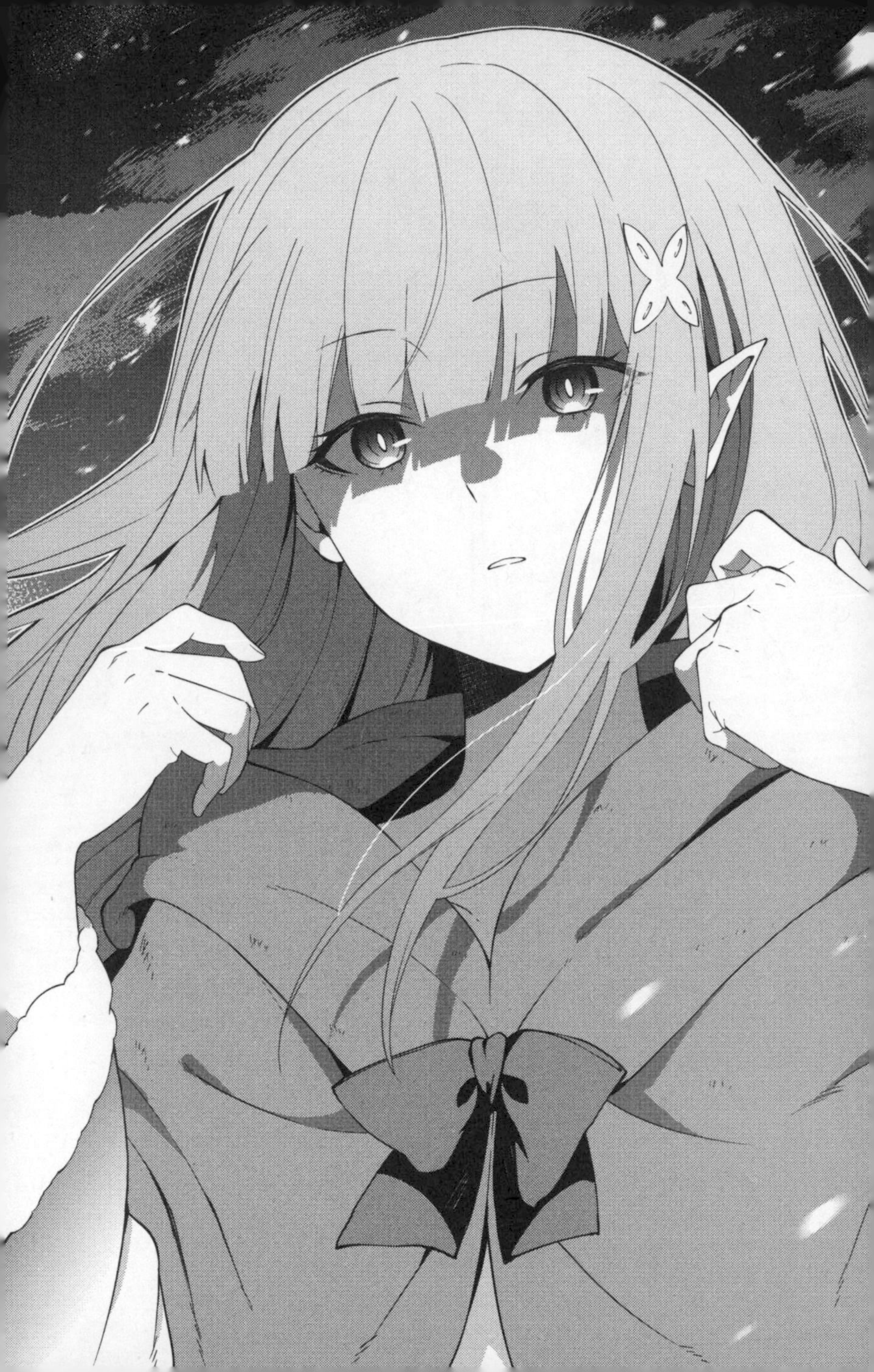

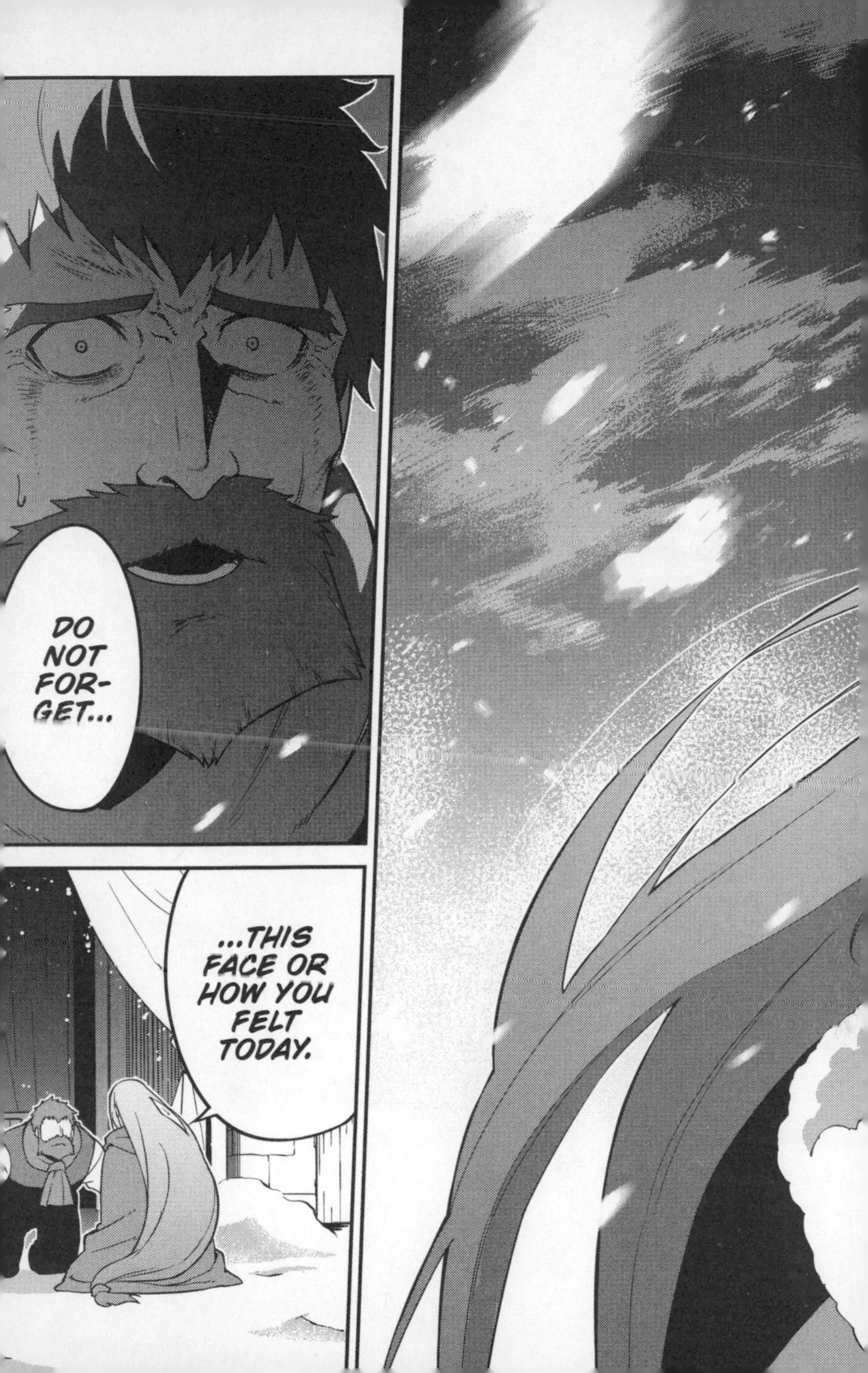
DO NOT FOR-GET...
...THIS FACE OR HOW YOU FELT TODAY.

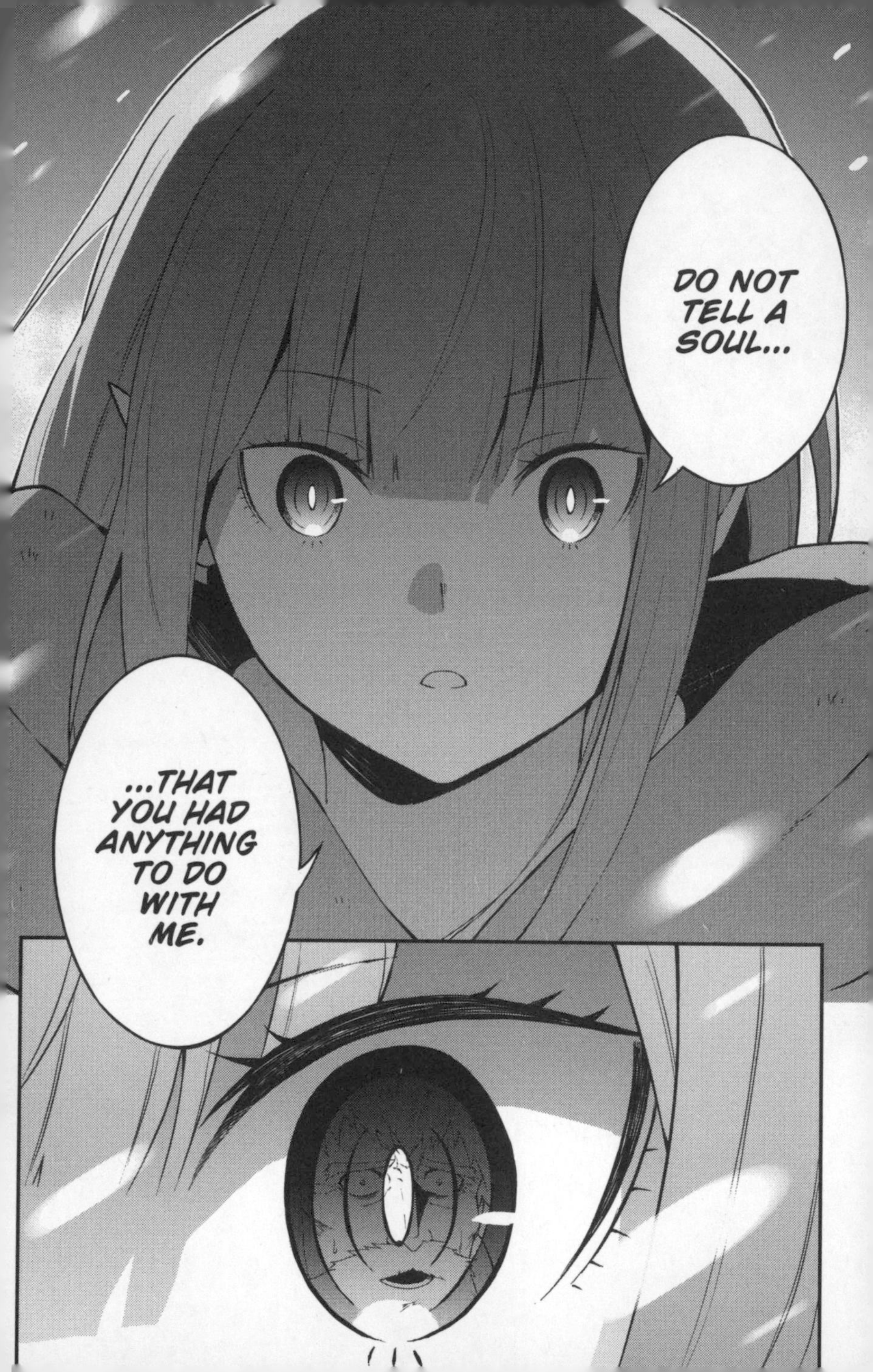
DO NOT TELL A SOUL...
...THAT YOU HAD ANYTHING TO DO WITH ME.

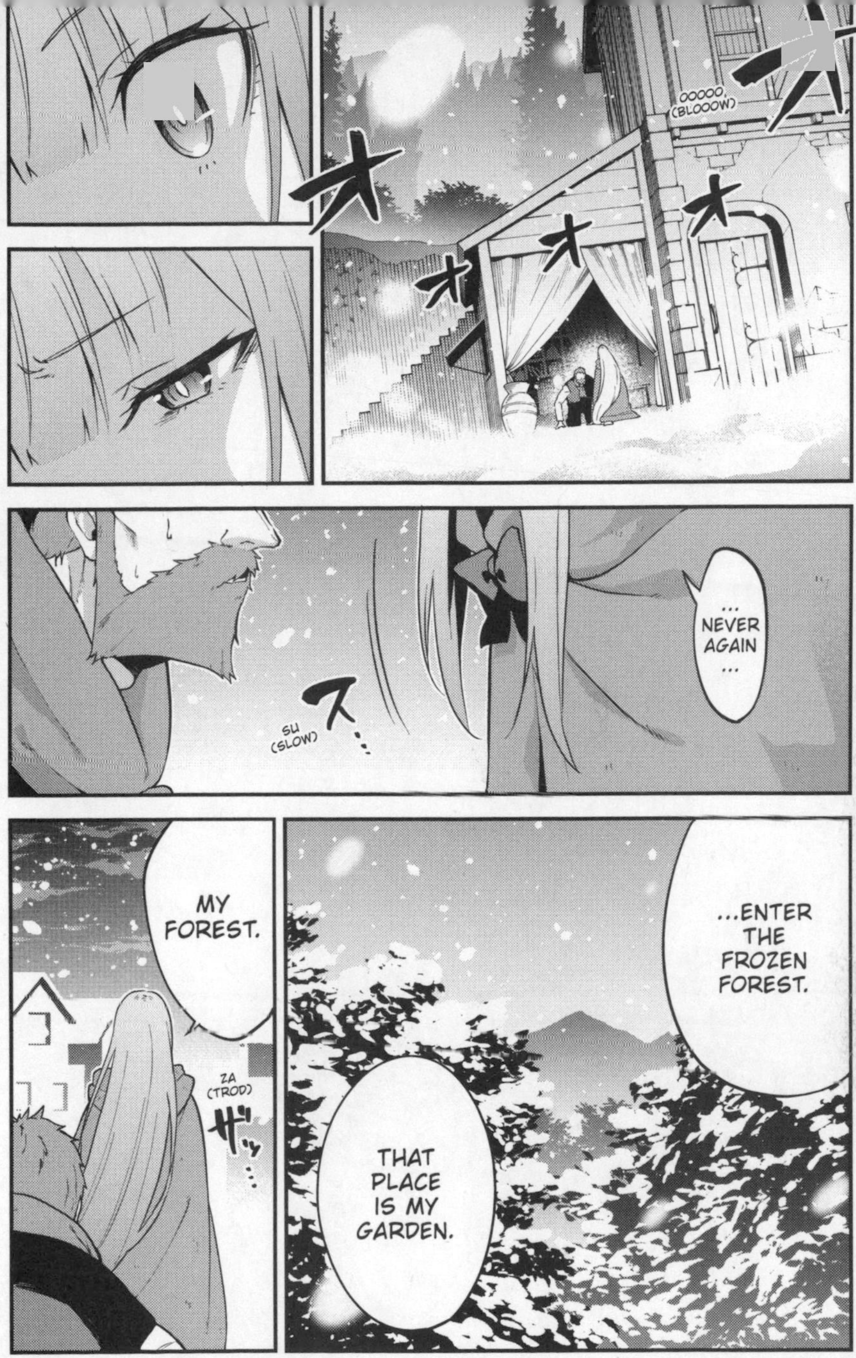
OOOOO
(BLOOOW)
...
NEVER
AGAIN
...
SU
(SLOW)
...ENTER THE FROZEN FOREST.
THAT PLACE IS MY GARDEN.
MY FOREST.
ZA
(TROD)

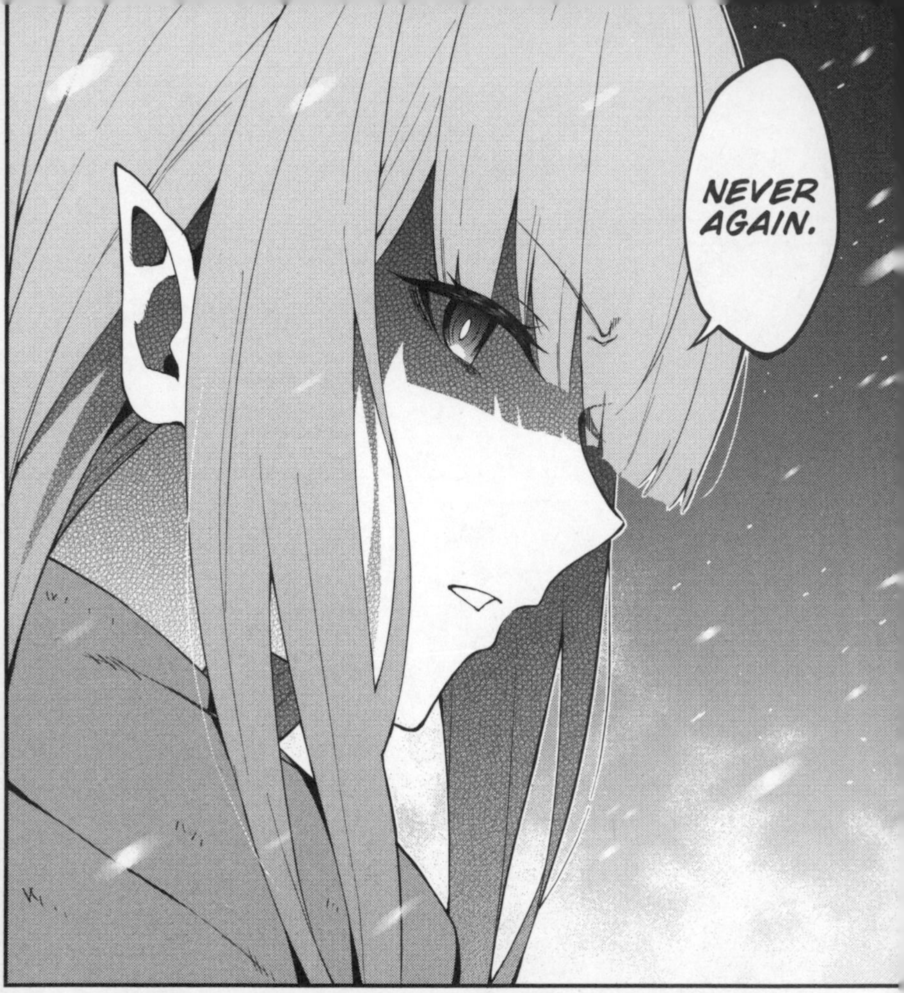
NEVER AGAIN.
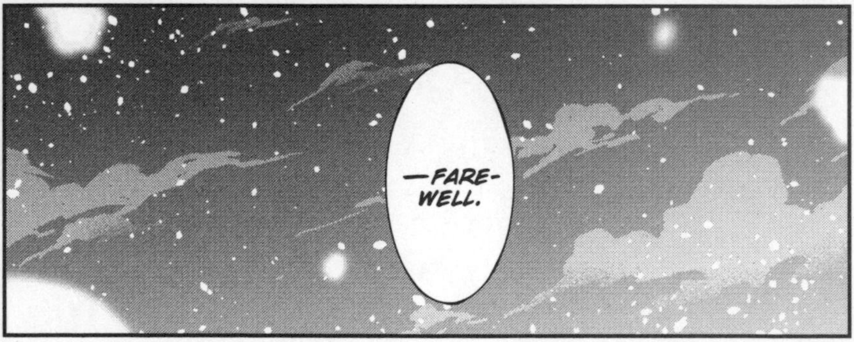
—FARE-WELL.

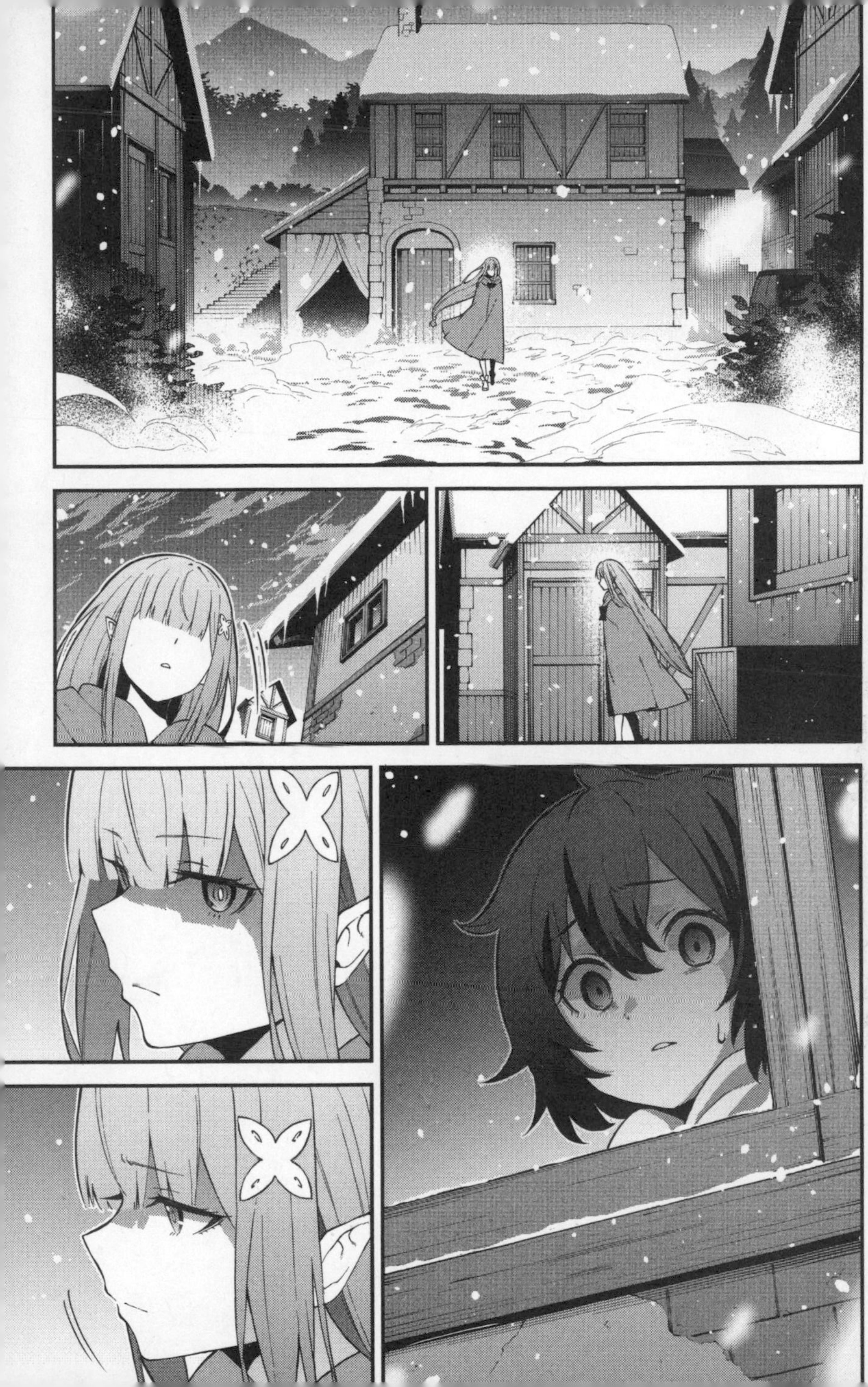

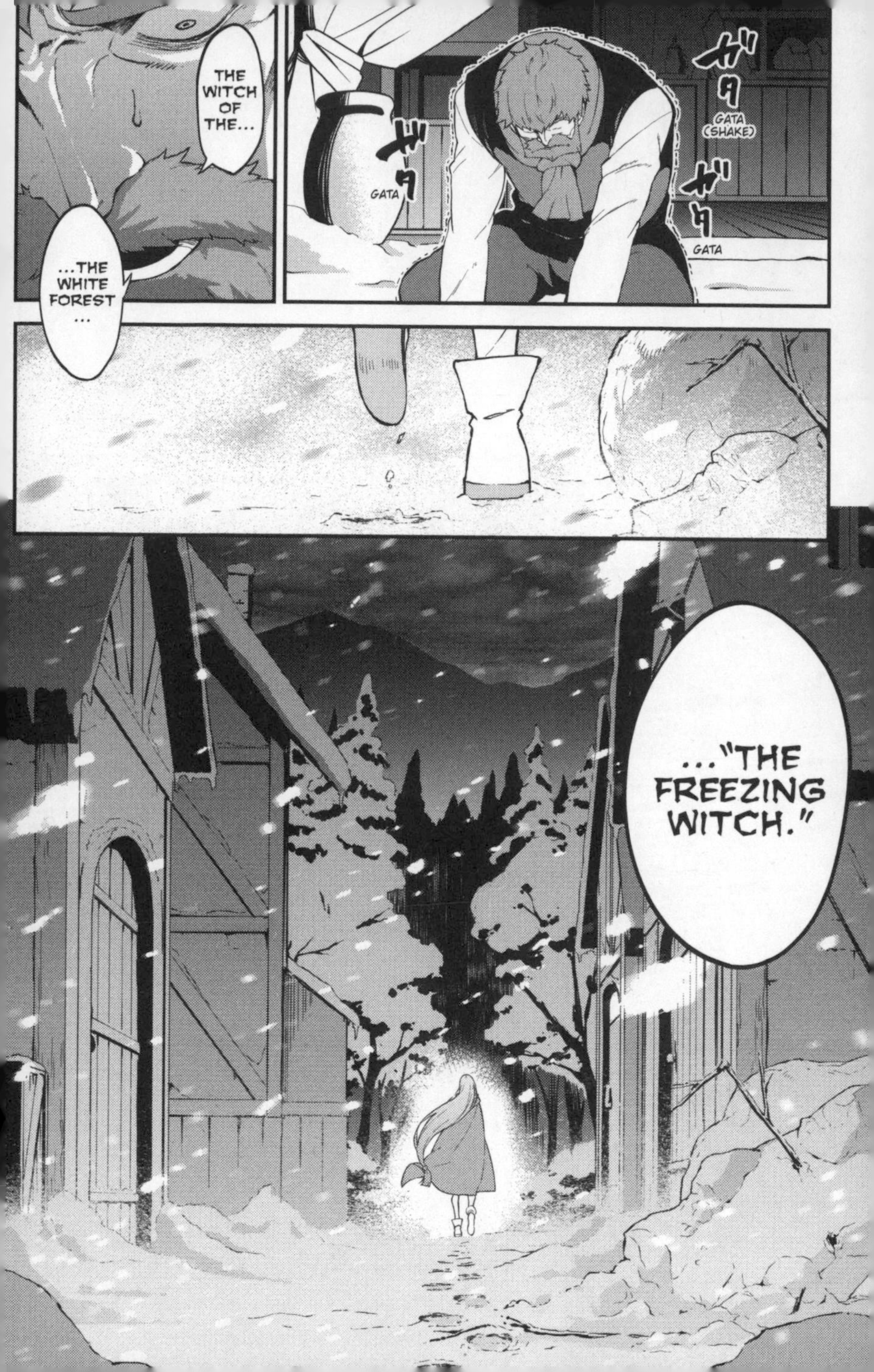
ガタ
GATA (SHAKE)
ガタ
GATA
ガタ
GATA
THE WITCH OF THE...
...THE WHITE FOREST...
..."THE FREEZING WITCH."

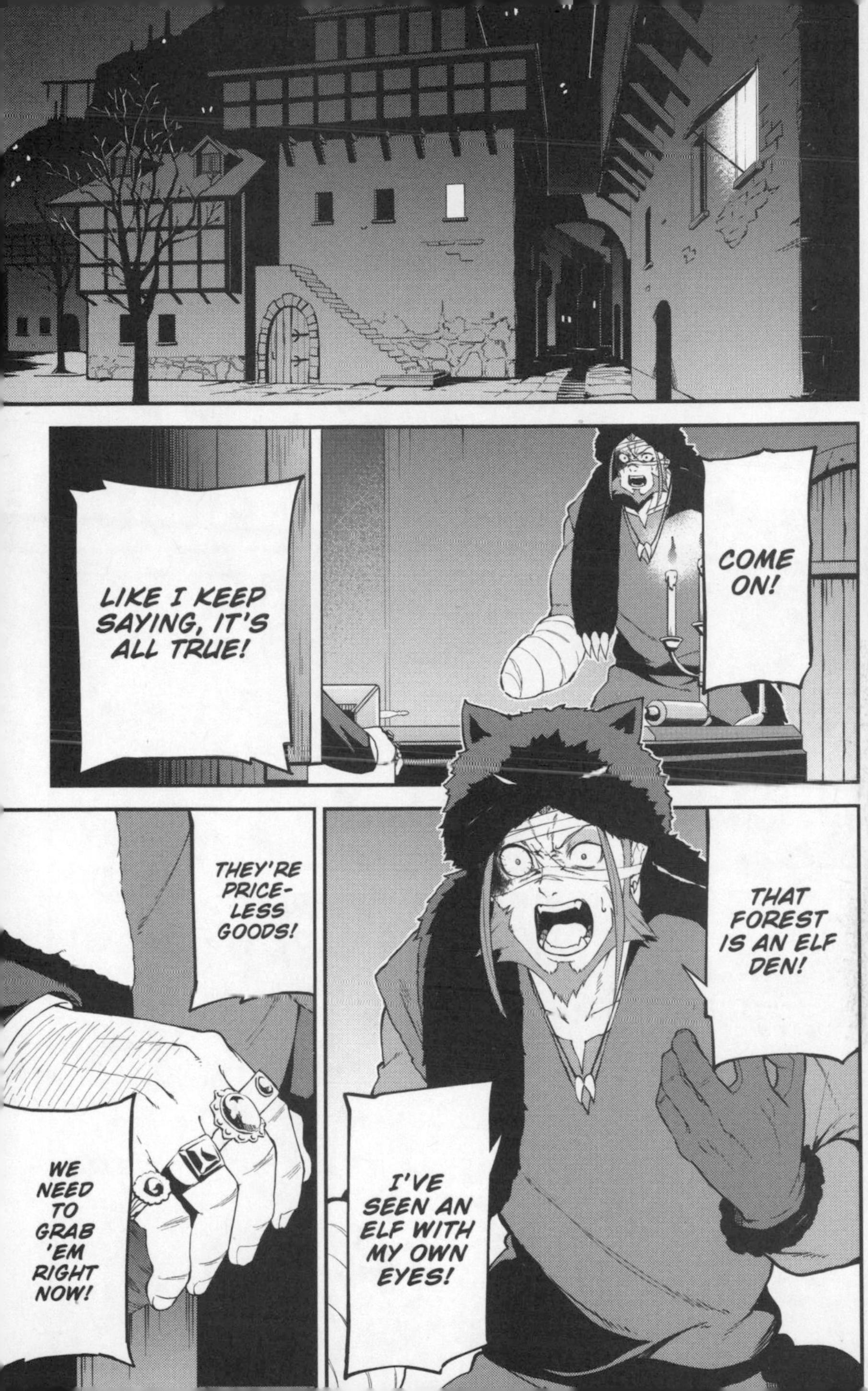
COME ON!
LIKE I KEEP SAYING, IT'S ALL TRUE!
THAT FOREST IS AN ELF DEN!
I'VE SEEN AN ELF WITH MY OWN EYES!
THEY'RE PRICE-LESS GOODS!
WE NEED TO GRAB 'EM RIGHT NOW!

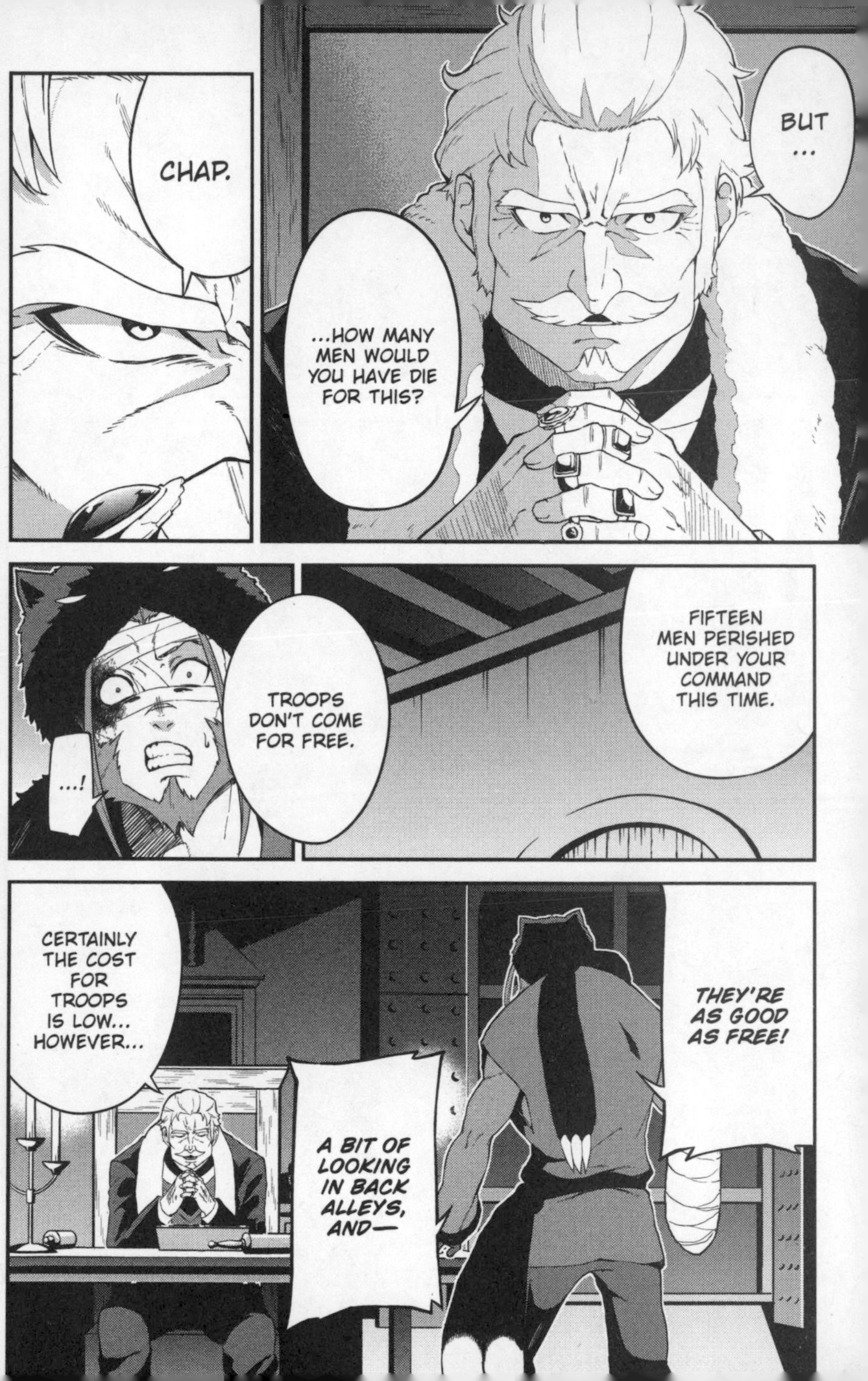
BUT ...
...HOW MANY MEN WOULD YOU HAVE DIE FOR THIS?
CHAP.
FIFTEEN MEN PERISHED UNDER YOUR COMMAND THIS TIME.
TROOPS DON'T COME FOR FREE.
...!
THEY'RE AS GOOD AS FREE!
A BIT OF LOOKING IN BACK ALLEYS, AND—
CERTAINLY THE COST FOR TROOPS IS LOW... HOWEVER...

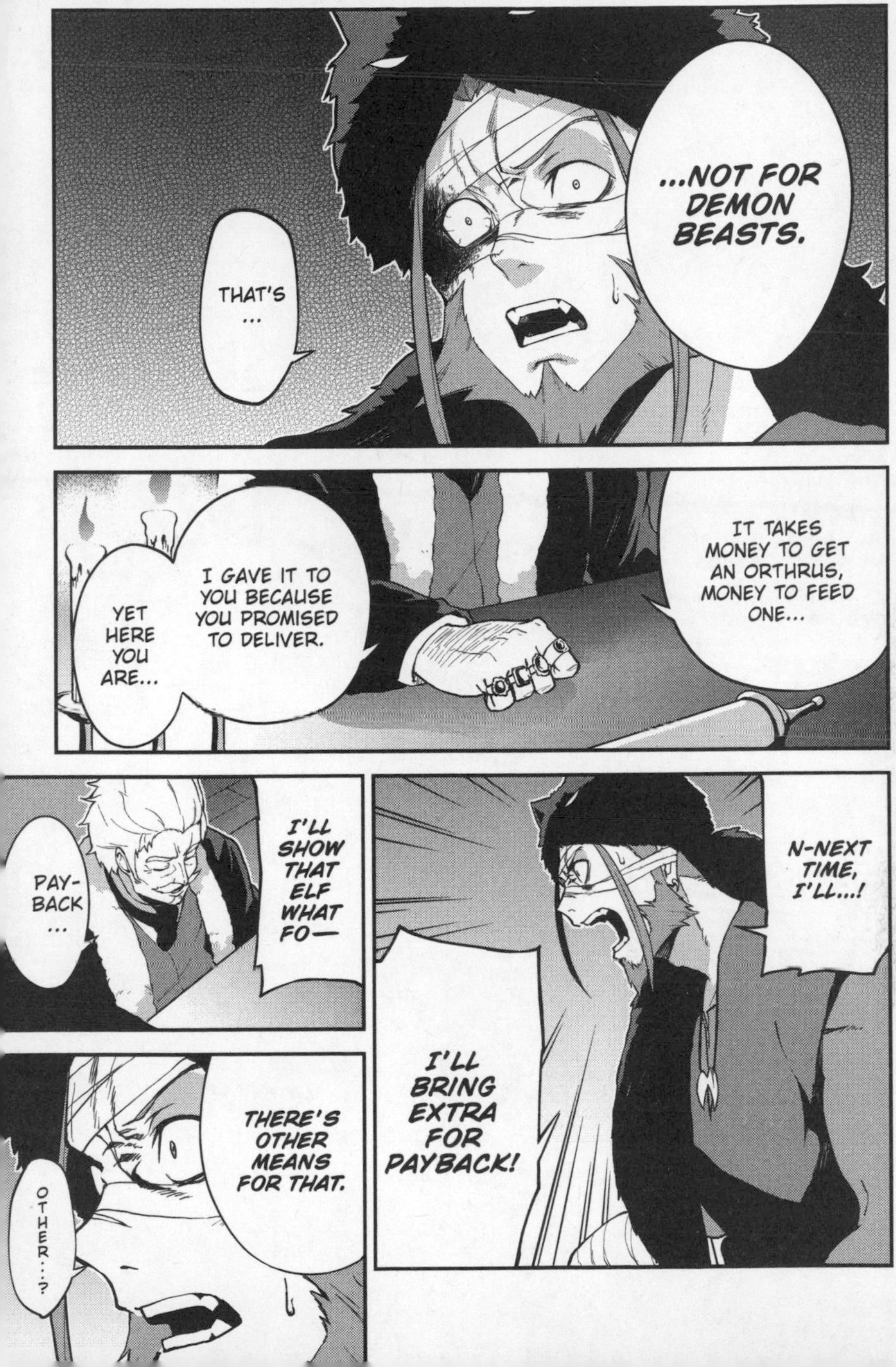
...NOT FOR DEMON BEASTS.
THAT'S ...
IT TAKES MONEY TO GET AN ORTHRUS, MONEY TO FEED ONE...
I GAVE IT TO YOU BECAUSE YOU PROMISED TO DELIVER.
YET HERE YOU ARE...
N-NEXT TIME, I'LL...!
I'LL BRING EXTRA FOR PAYBACK!
I'LL SHOW THAT ELF WHAT FO—
PAY-BACK ...
THERE'S OTHER MEANS FOR THAT.
OTHER...?

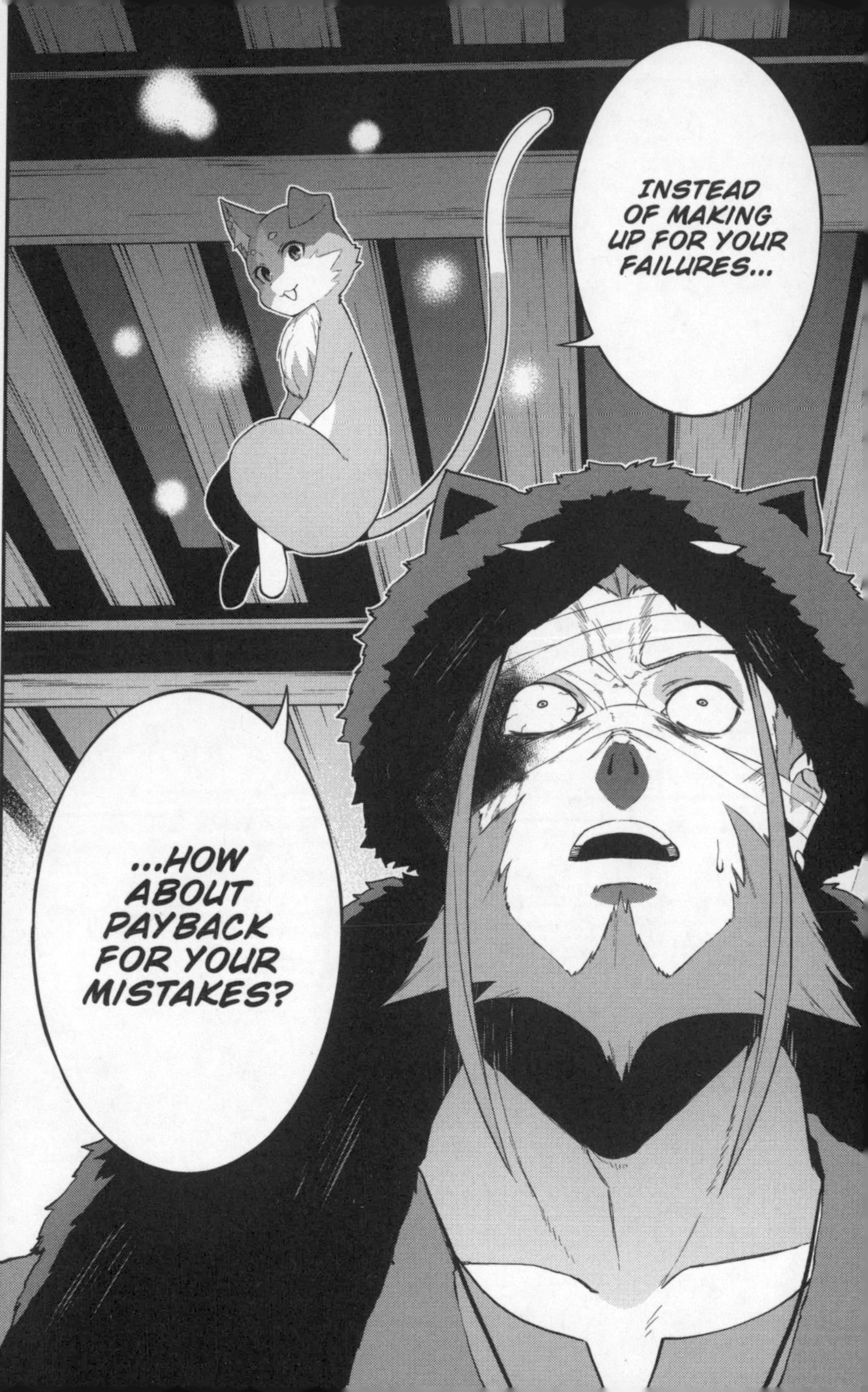
INSTEAD OF MAKING UP FOR YOUR FAILURES...
...HOW ABOUT PAYBACK FOR YOUR MISTAKES?

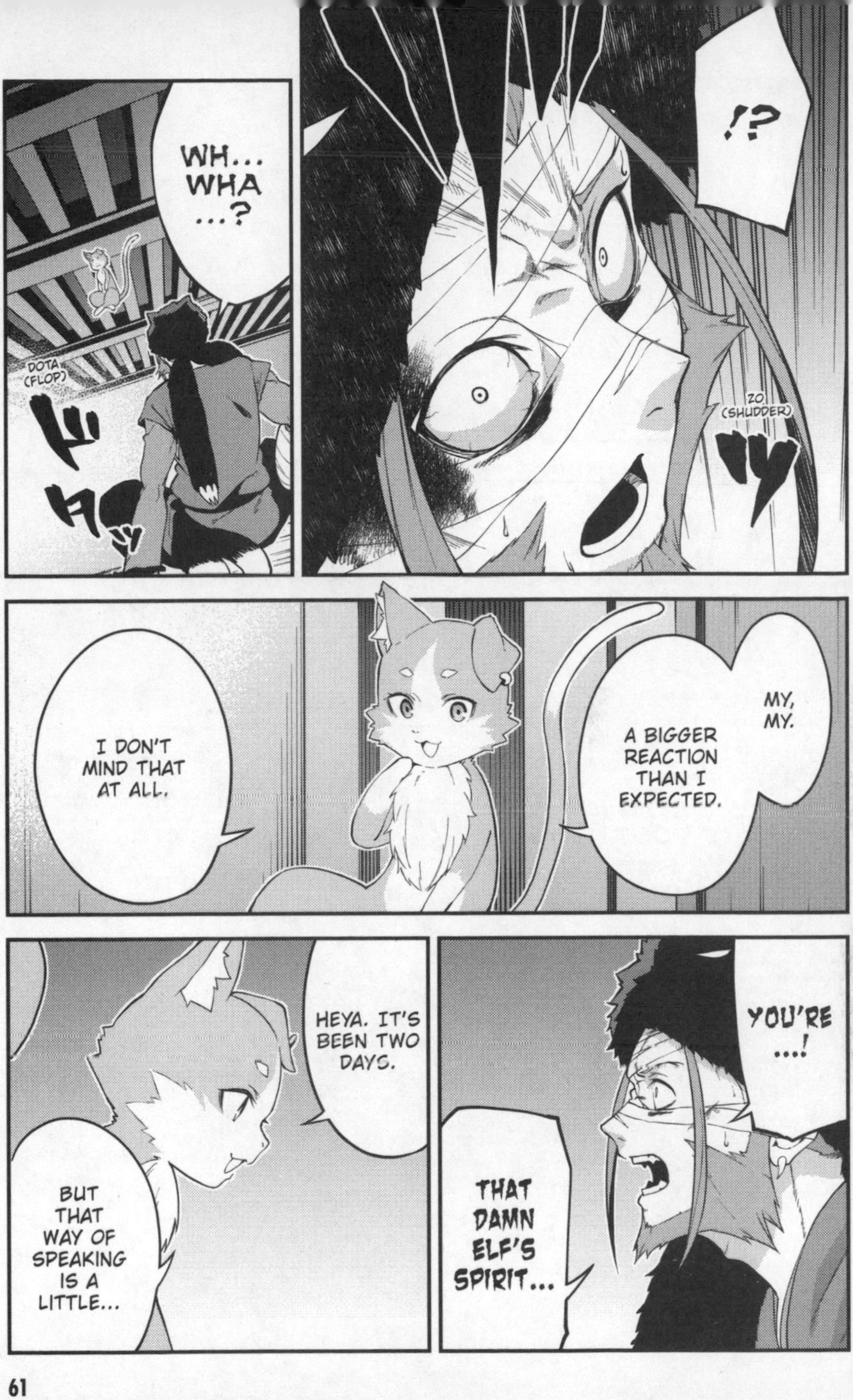
!?
ZO
(SHUDDER)
WH... WHA ...?
DOTA
(FLOP)
MY, MY.
A BIGGER REACTION THAN I EXPECTED.
I DON'T MIND THAT AT ALL.
YOU'RE ...!
THAT DAMN ELF'S SPIRIT...
HEYA. IT'S BEEN TWO DAYS.
BUT THAT WAY OF SPEAKING IS A LITTLE...

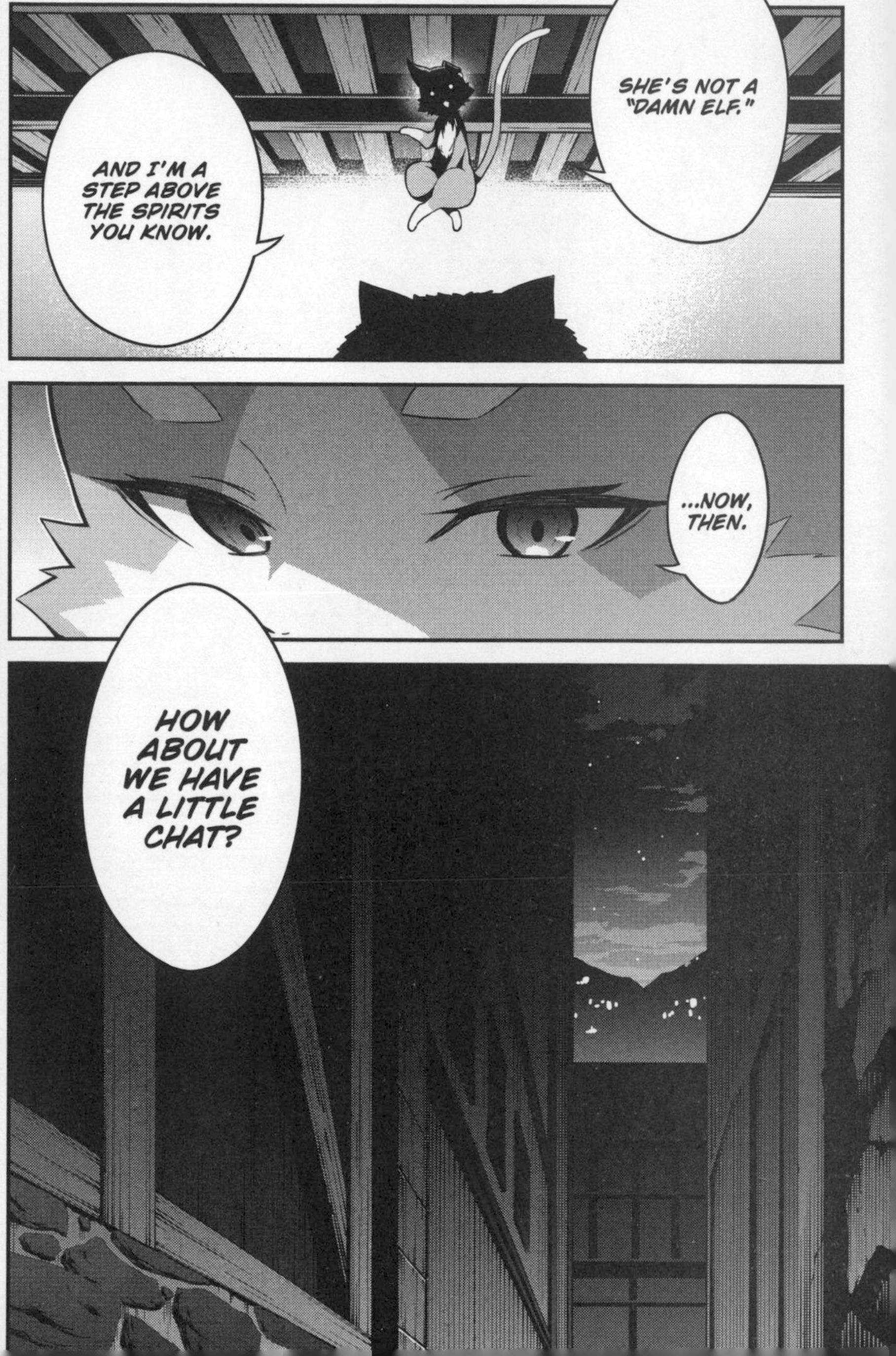
SHE'S NOT A "DAMN ELF."
AND I'M A STEP ABOVE THE SPIRITS YOU KNOW.
...NOW, THEN.
HOW ABOUT WE HAVE A LITTLE CHAT?

Re:ZERO

-Starting Life in Another World-

The Frozen Bond

The only ability Subaru Natsuki gets when he's
summoned to another world is time travel via his own death.
But to save her, he'll die as many times as it takes.

Re:ZERO

-Starting Life in Another World-
The Frozen Bond

Minori Tsukahara

Tappei Nagatsuki, Shinichirou Otsuka

Episode 7 Payback

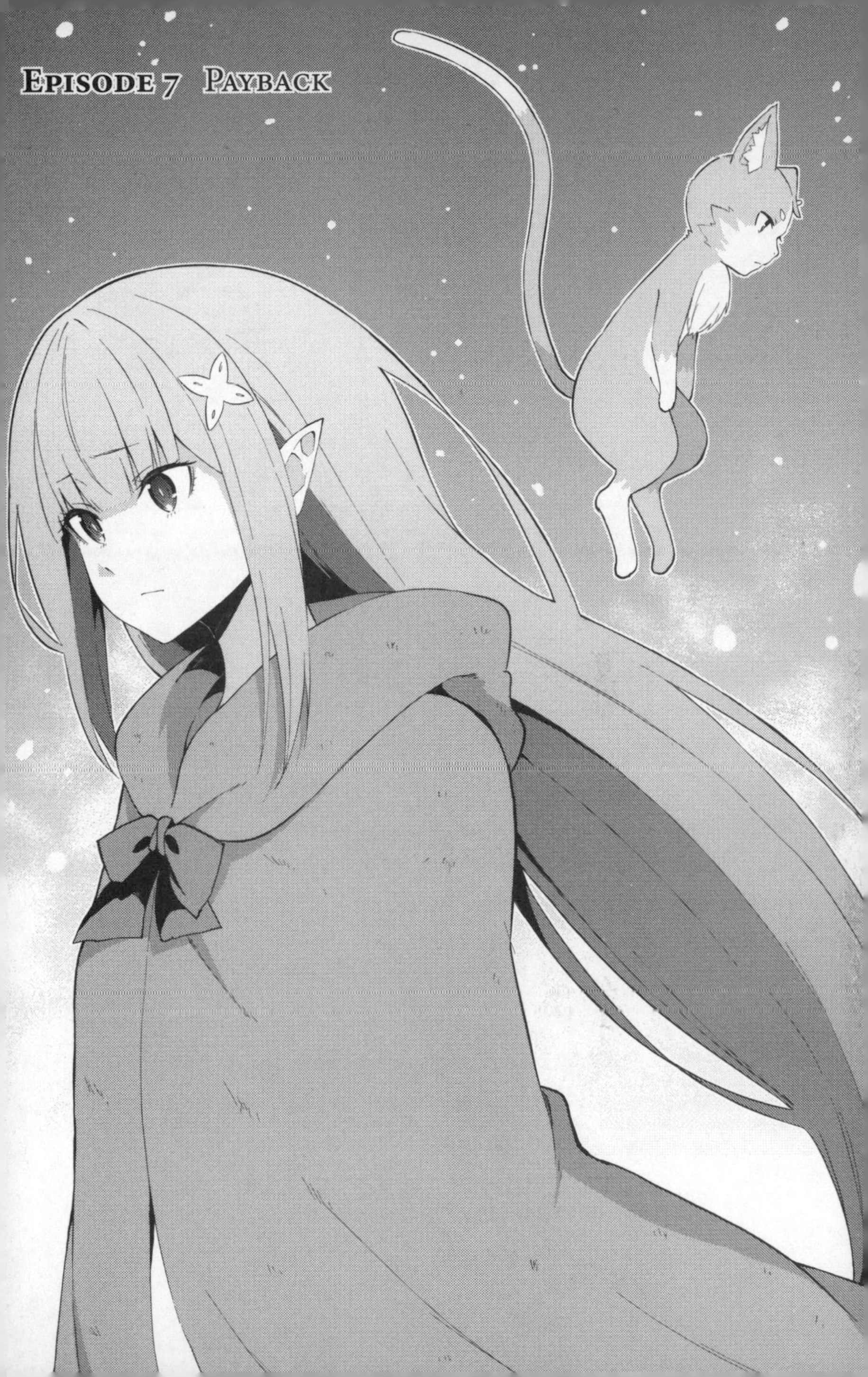

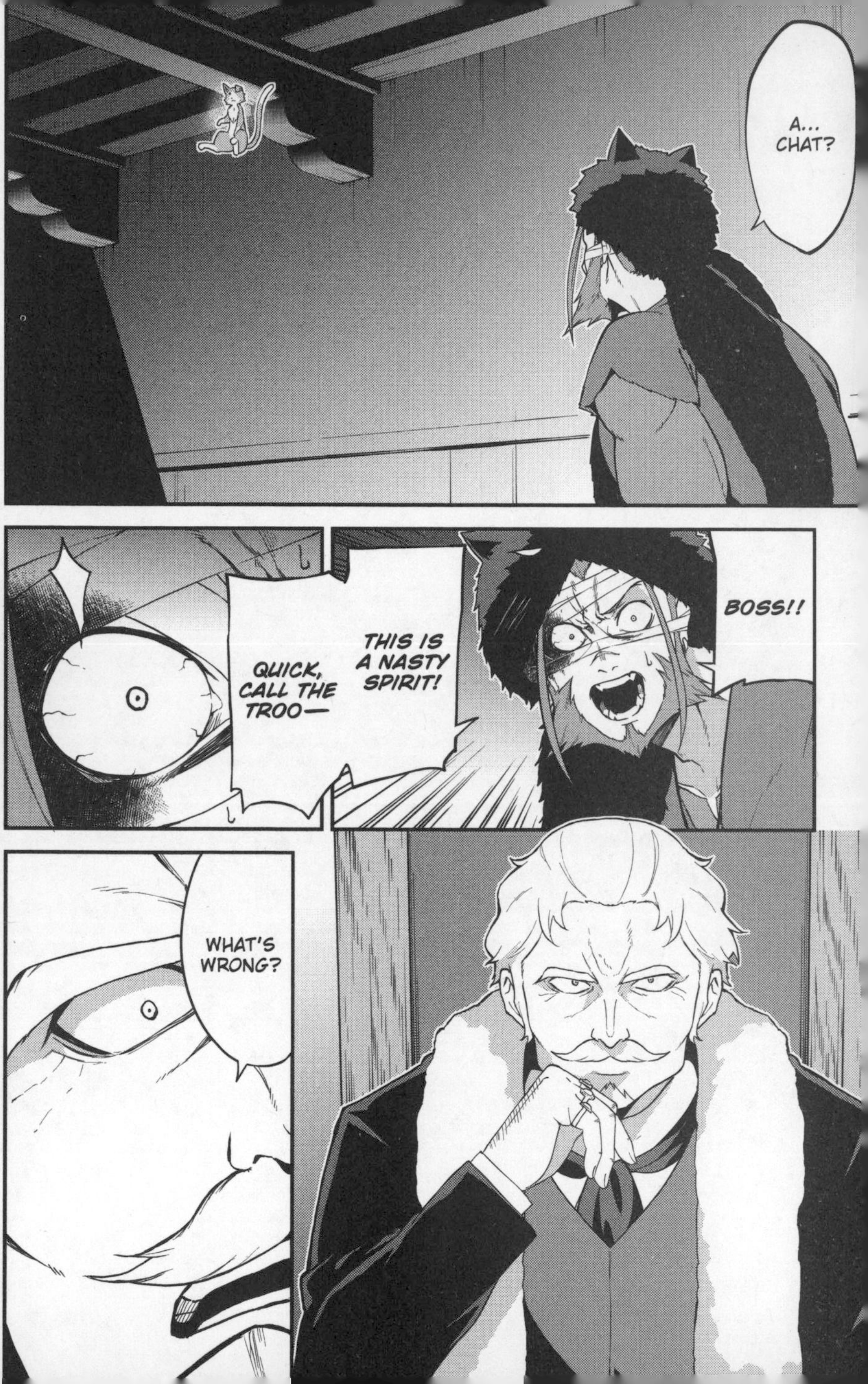
A... CHAT?
BOSS!!
THIS IS A NASTY SPIRIT!
QUICK, CALL THE TROO—
WHAT'S WRONG?

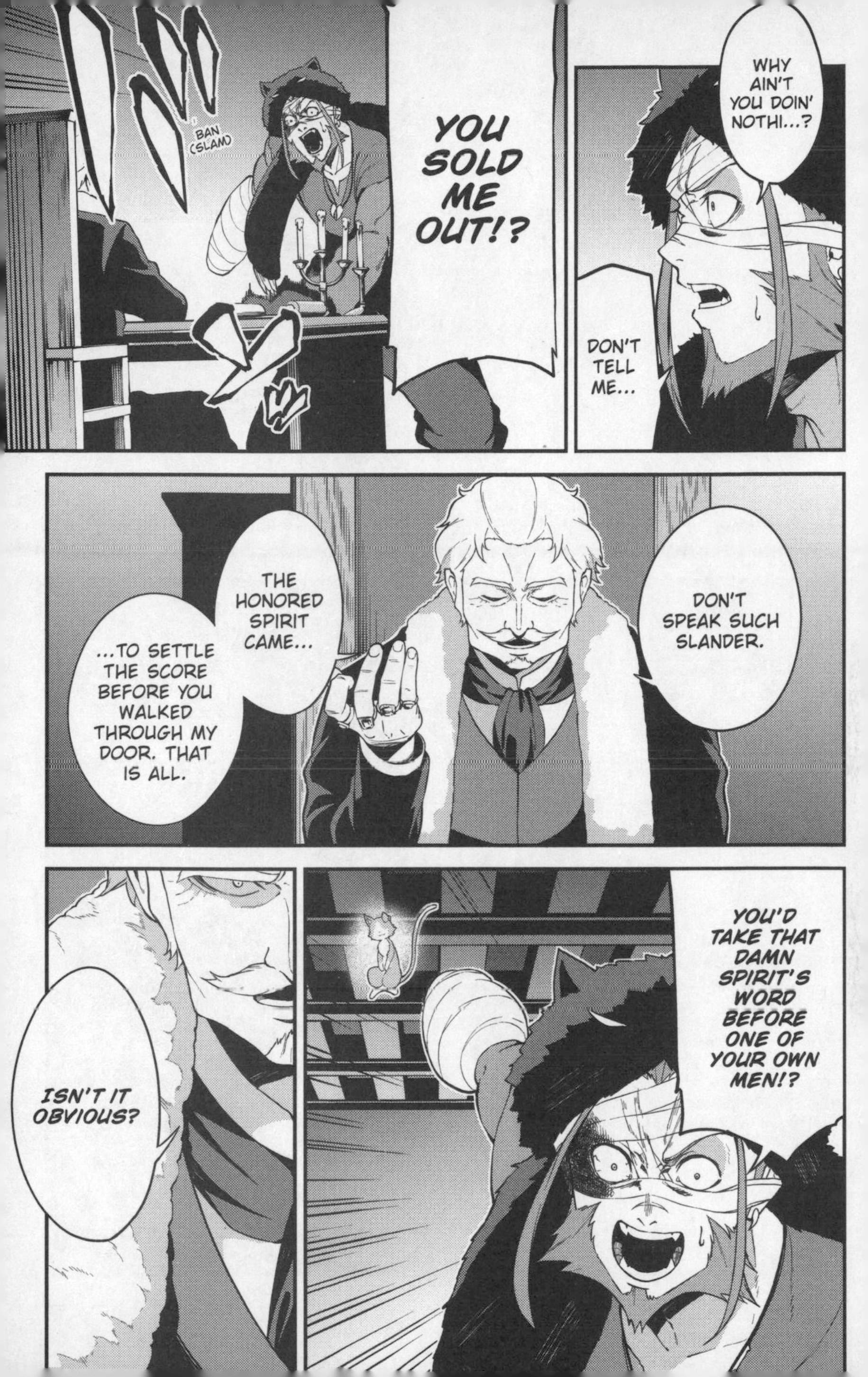
WHY AIN'T YOU DOIN' NOTHI...?
DON'T TELL ME...
YOU SOLD ME OUT!?
BAN (SLAM)
DON'T SPEAK SUCH SLANDER.
THE HONORED SPIRIT CAME...
...TO SETTLE THE SCORE BEFORE YOU WALKED THROUGH MY DOOR. THAT IS ALL.
YOU'D TAKE THAT DAMN SPIRIT'S WORD BEFORE ONE OF YOUR OWN MEN!?
ISN'T IT OBVIOUS?

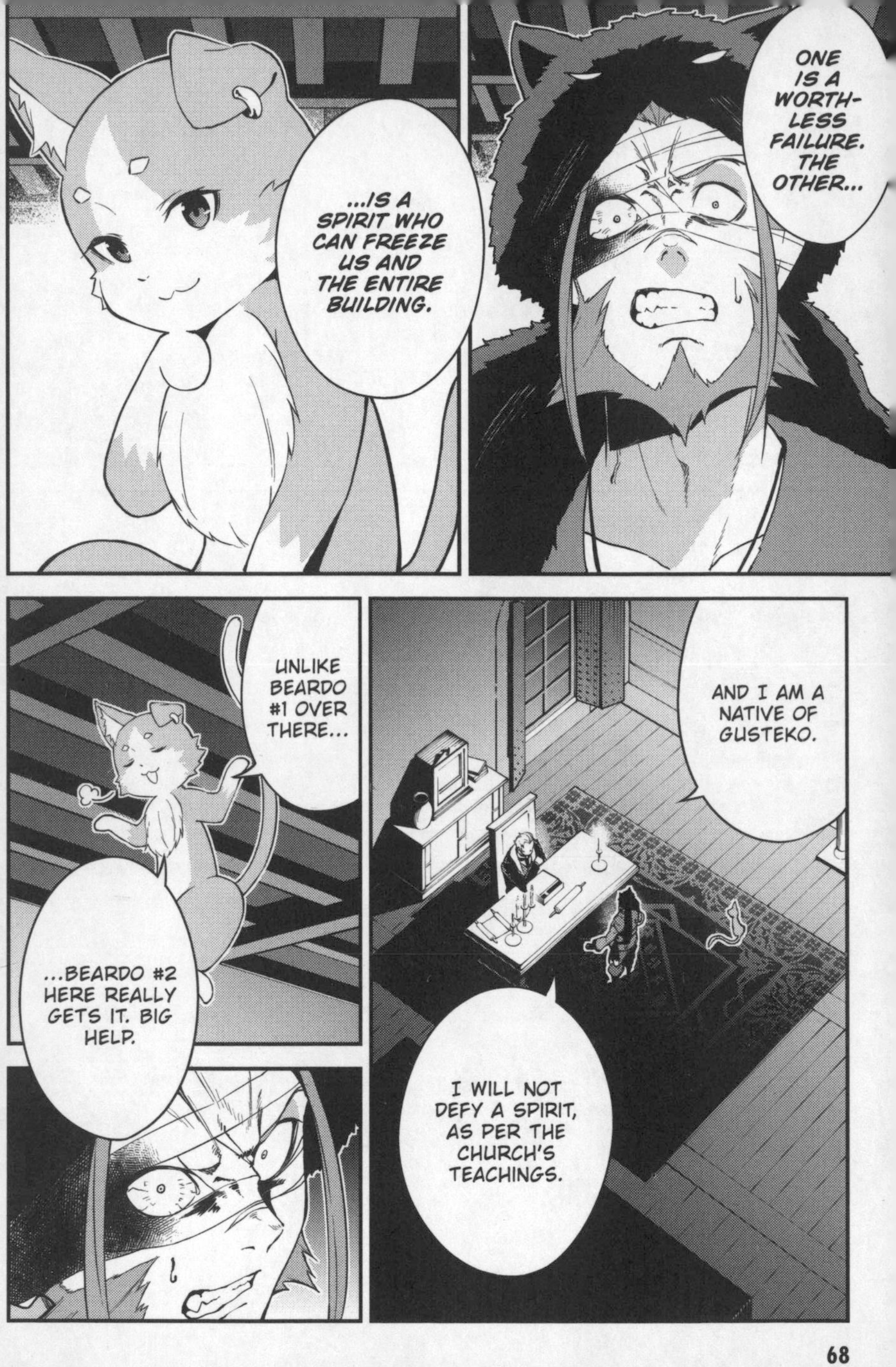
ONE IS A WORTHLESS FAILURE. THE OTHER...
...IS A SPIRIT WHO CAN FREEZE US AND THE ENTIRE BUILDING.
AND I AM A NATIVE OF GUSTEKO.
I WILL NOT DEFY A SPIRIT, AS PER THE CHURCH'S TEACHINGS.
UNLIKE BEARDO #1 OVER THERE...
...BEARDO #2 HERE REALLY GETS IT. BIG HELP.

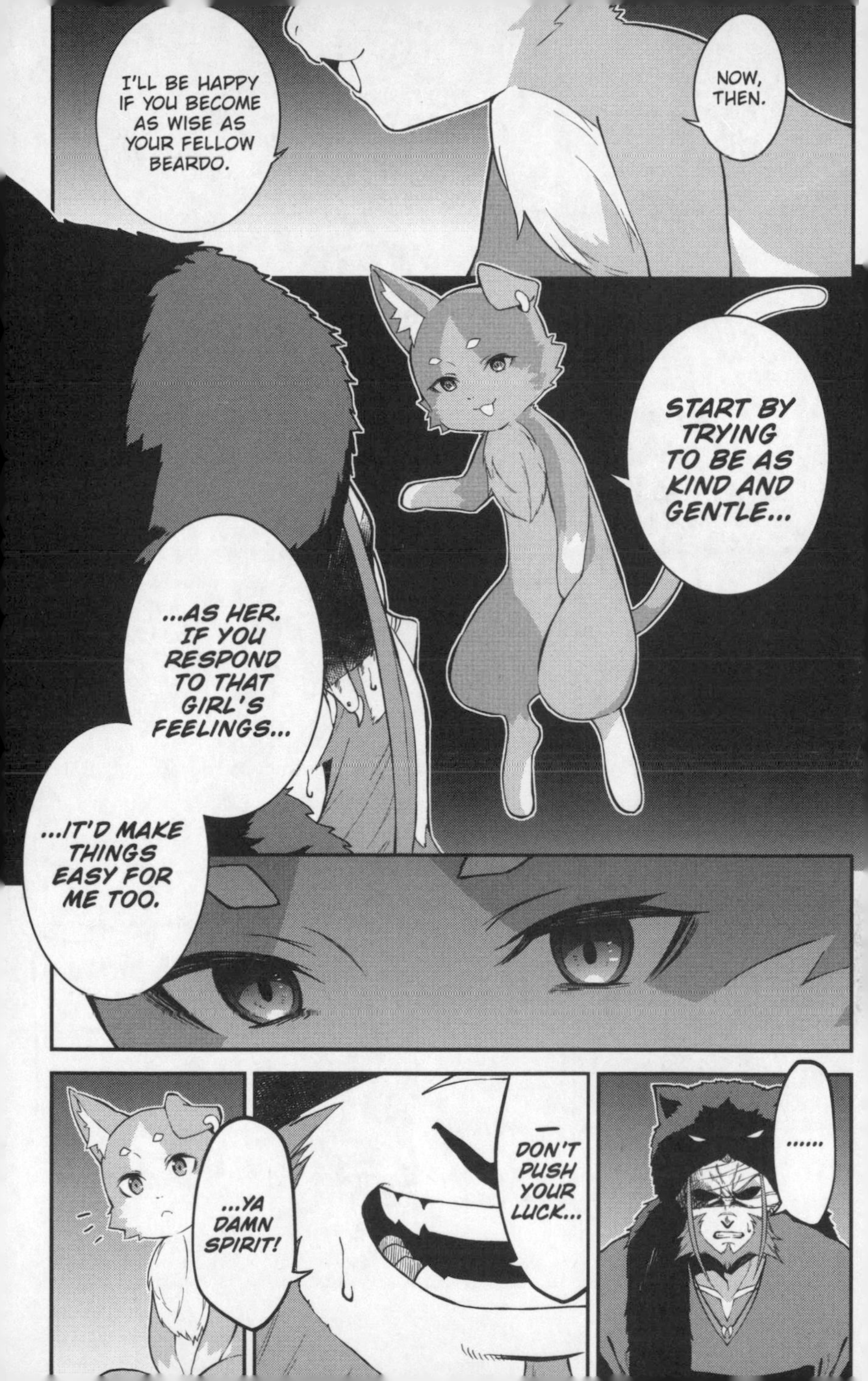
NOW, THEN.
I'LL BE HAPPY IF YOU BECOME AS WISE AS YOUR FELLOW BEARDO.
START BY TRYING TO BE AS KIND AND GENTLE...
...AS HER. IF YOU RESPOND TO THAT GIRL'S FEELINGS...
...IT'D MAKE THINGS EASY FOR ME TOO.
......
—DON'T PUSH YOUR LUCK...
...YA DAMN SPIRIT!

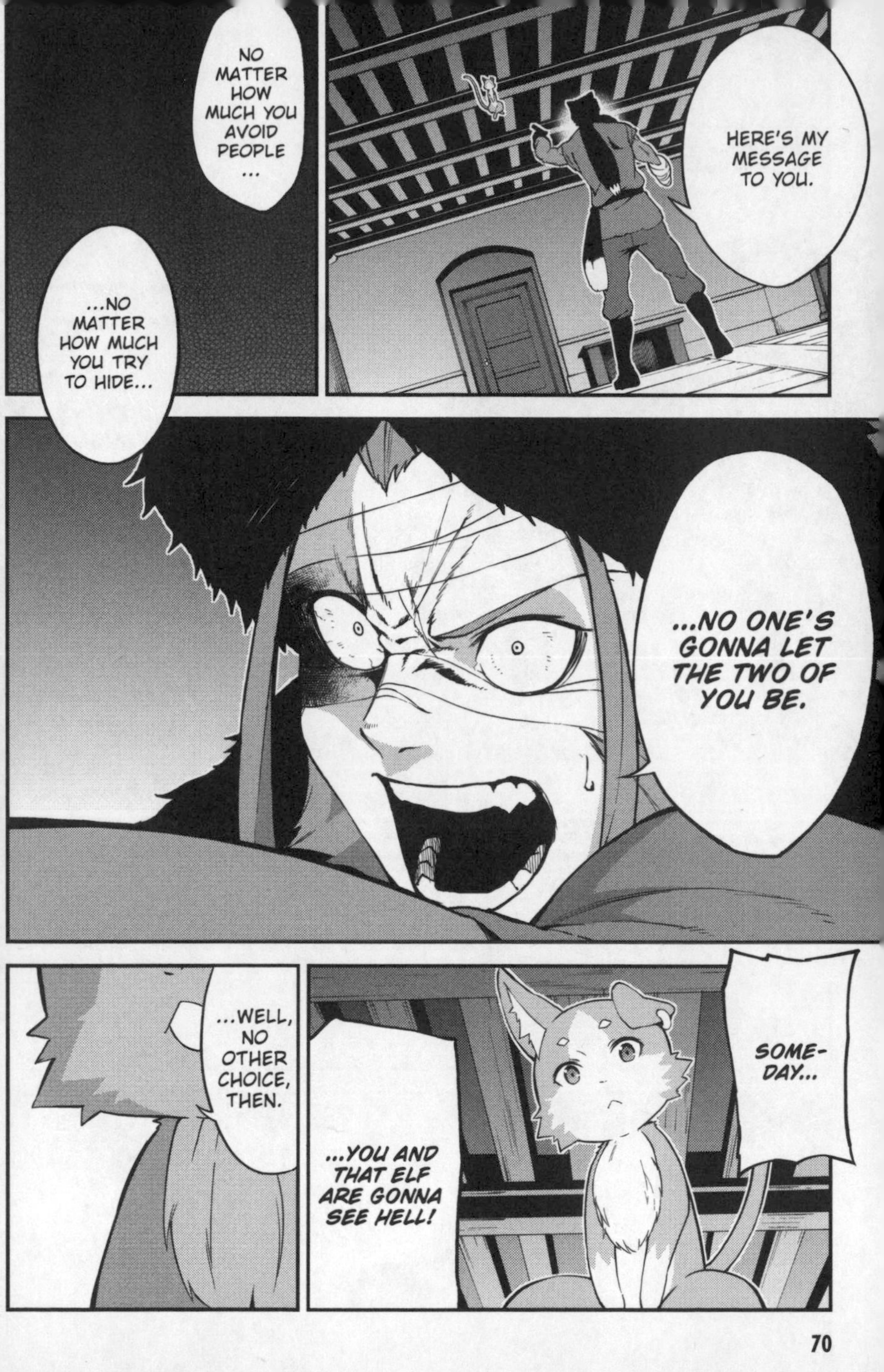
HERE'S MY MESSAGE TO YOU.
NO MATTER HOW MUCH YOU AVOID PEOPLE ...
...NO MATTER HOW MUCH YOU TRY TO HIDE...
...NO ONE'S GONNA LET THE TWO OF YOU BE.
SOME-DAY...
...YOU AND THAT ELF ARE GONNA SEE HELL!
...WELL, NO OTHER CHOICE, THEN.

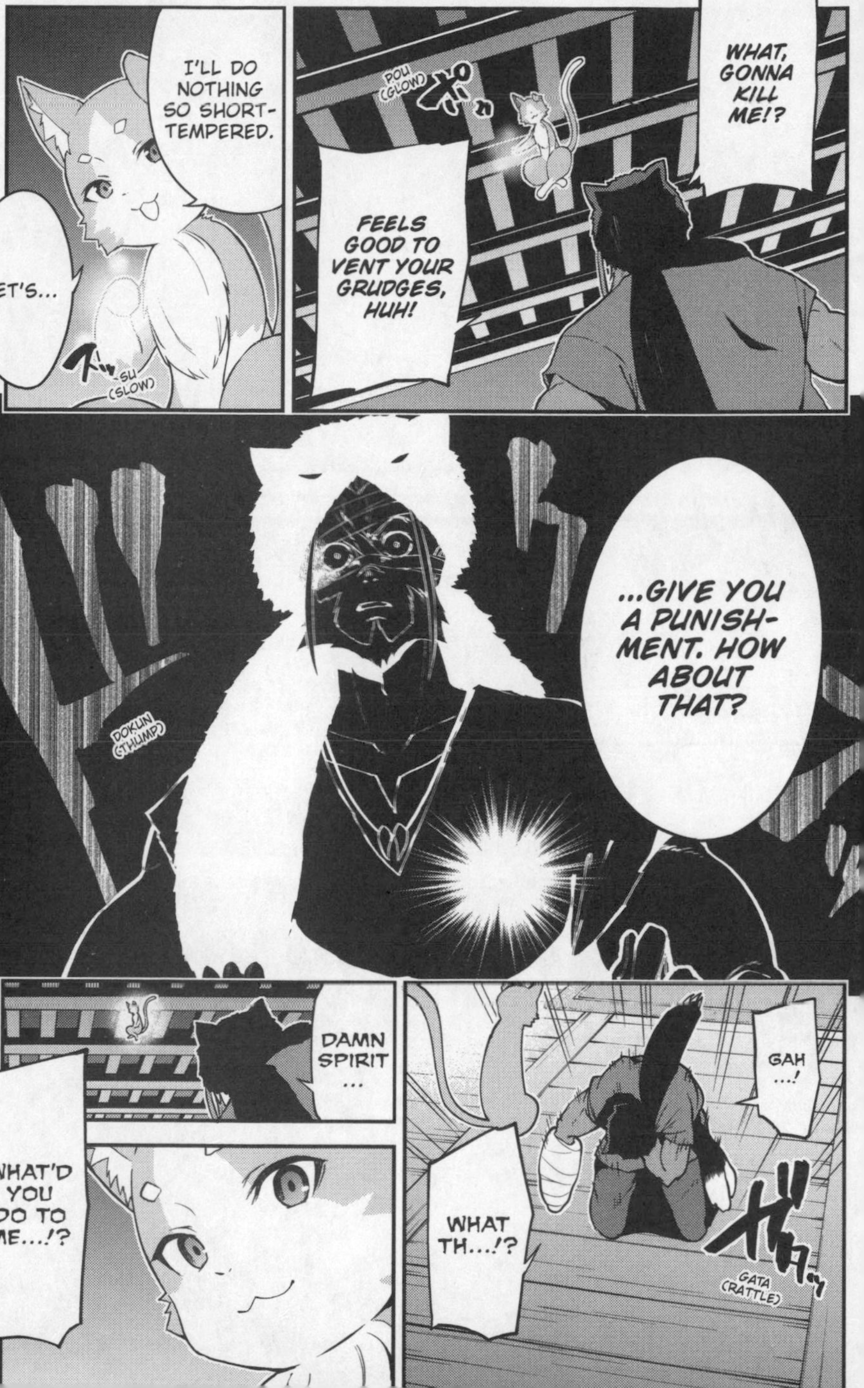
WHAT, GONNA KILL ME!?
POU (GLOW)
FEELS GOOD TO VENT YOUR GRUDGES, HUH!
I'LL DO NOTHING SO SHORT-TEMPERED.
LET'S...
SU (SLOW)
...GIVE YOU A PUNISHMENT. HOW ABOUT THAT?
DOKUN (THUMP)
GAH ...!
GATA (RATTLE)
WHAT TH...!?
DAMN SPIRIT ...
WHAT'D YOU DO TO ME...!?

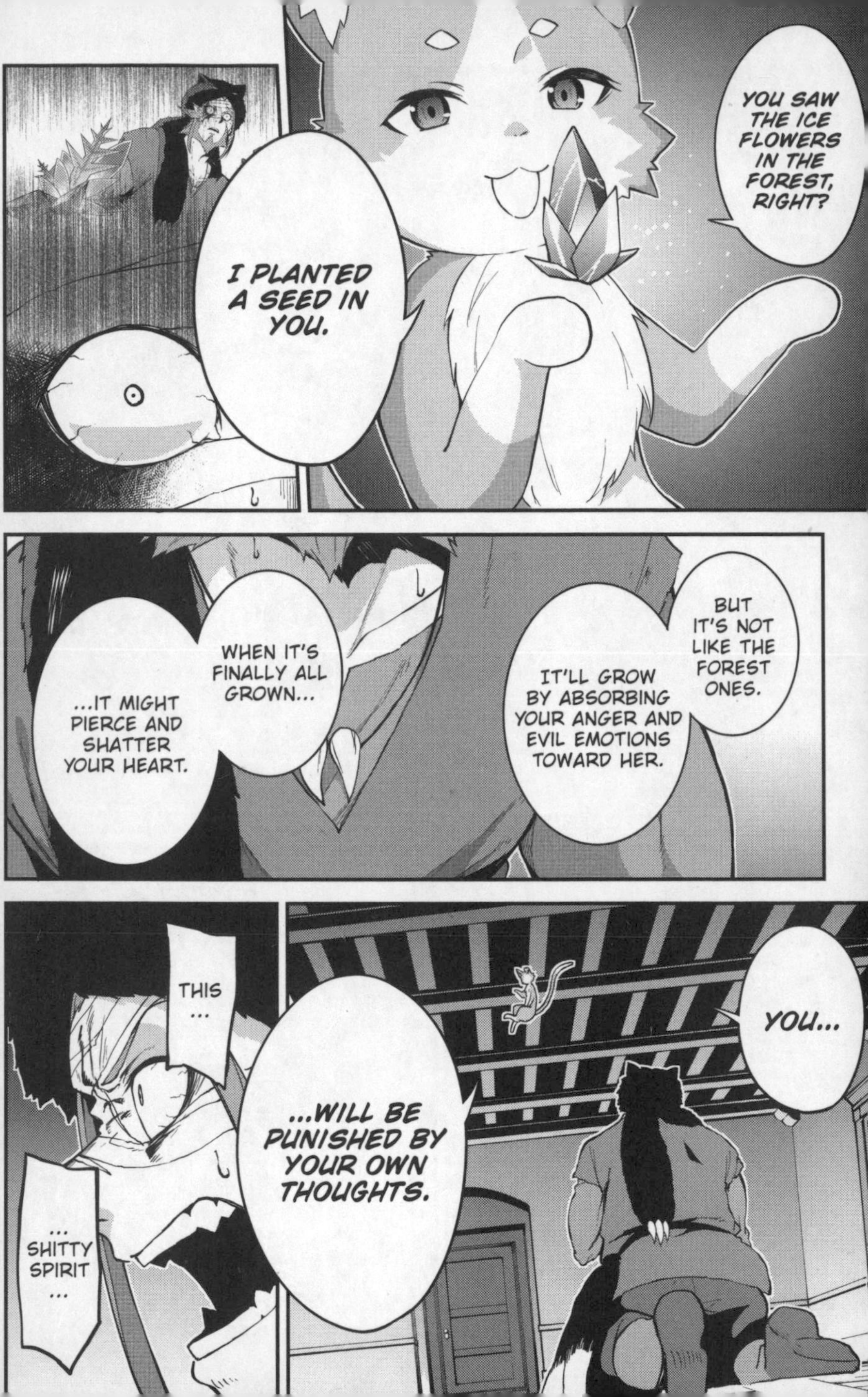
YOU SAW THE ICE FLOWERS IN THE FOREST, RIGHT?
I PLANTED A SEED IN YOU.
BUT IT'S NOT LIKE THE FOREST ONES.
IT'LL GROW BY ABSORBING YOUR ANGER AND EVIL EMOTIONS TOWARD HER.
WHEN IT'S FINALLY ALL GROWN...
...IT MIGHT PIERCE AND SHATTER YOUR HEART.
YOU...
...WILL BE PUNISHED BY YOUR OWN THOUGHTS.
THIS ...
... SHITTY SPIRIT ...

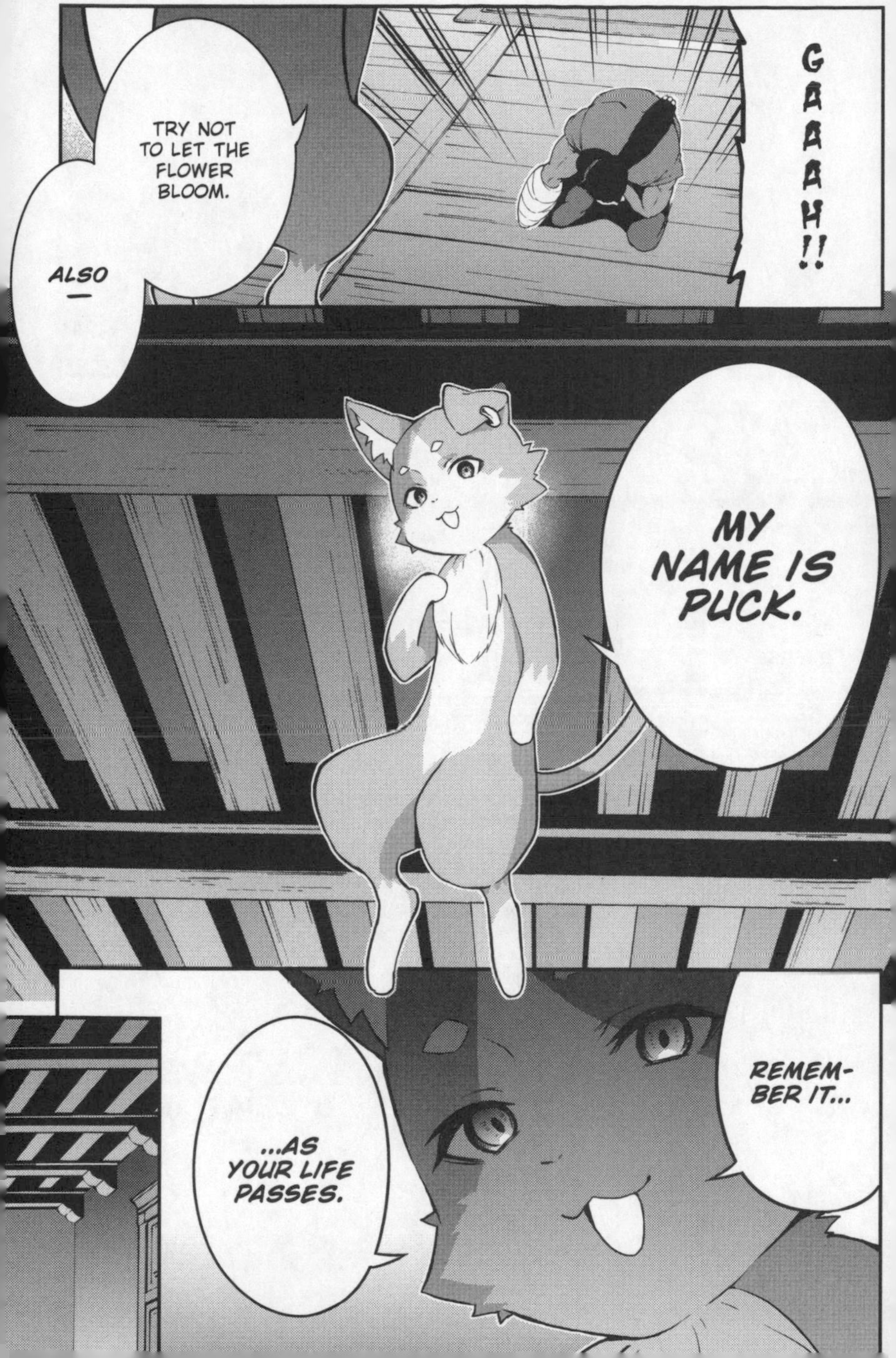

GAAAH!!
TRY NOT TO LET THE FLOWER BLOOM.
ALSO—
MY NAME IS PUCK.
REMEMBER IT...
...AS YOUR LIFE PASSES.

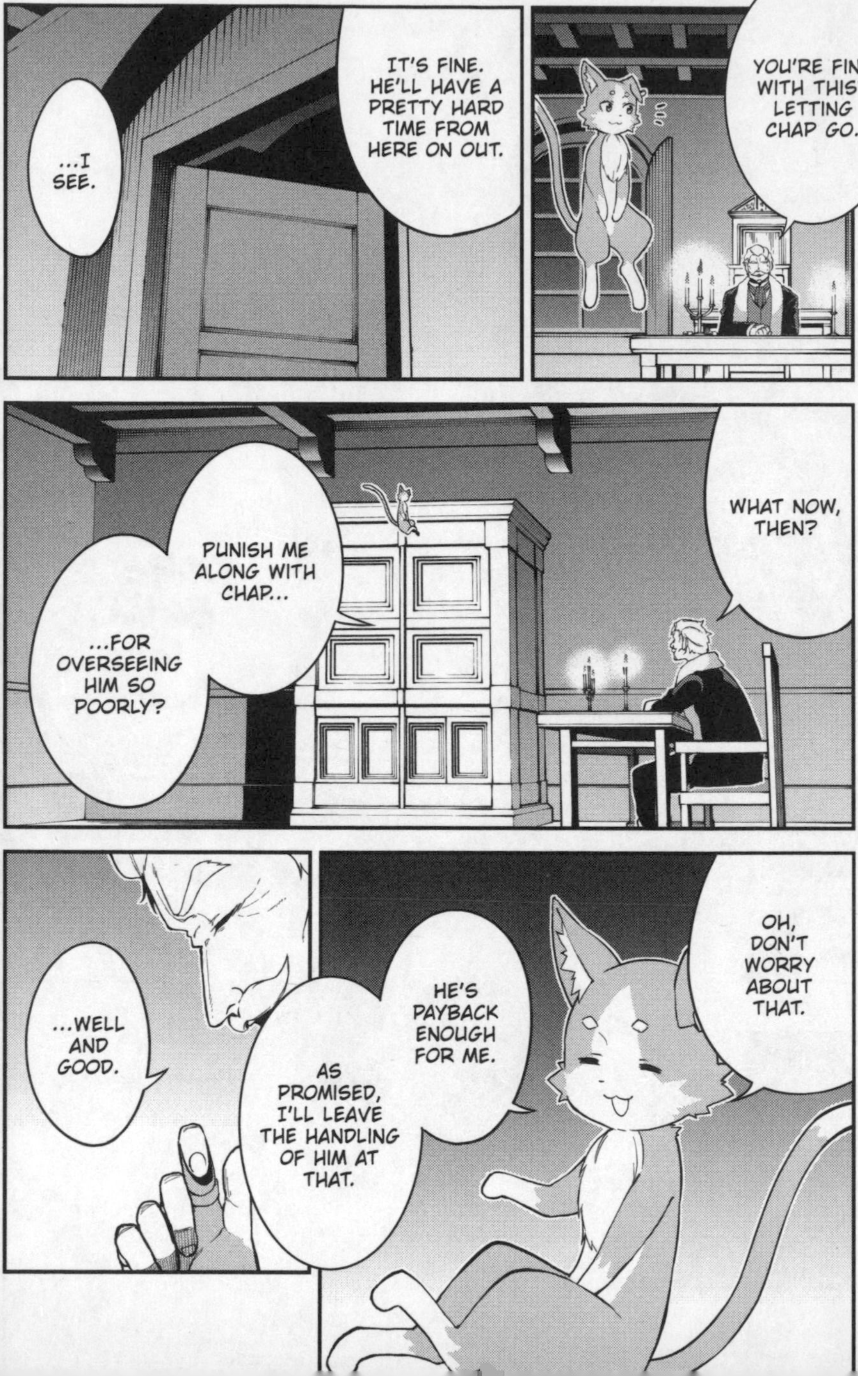
YOU'RE FINE WITH THIS? LETTING CHAP GO.
IT'S FINE. HE'LL HAVE A PRETTY HARD TIME FROM HERE ON OUT.
...I SEE.
WHAT NOW, THEN?
PUNISH ME ALONG WITH CHAP...
...FOR OVERSEEING HIM SO POORLY?
OH, DON'T WORRY ABOUT THAT.
HE'S PAYBACK ENOUGH FOR ME.
AS PROMISED, I'LL LEAVE THE HANDLING OF HIM AT THAT.
...WELL AND GOOD.

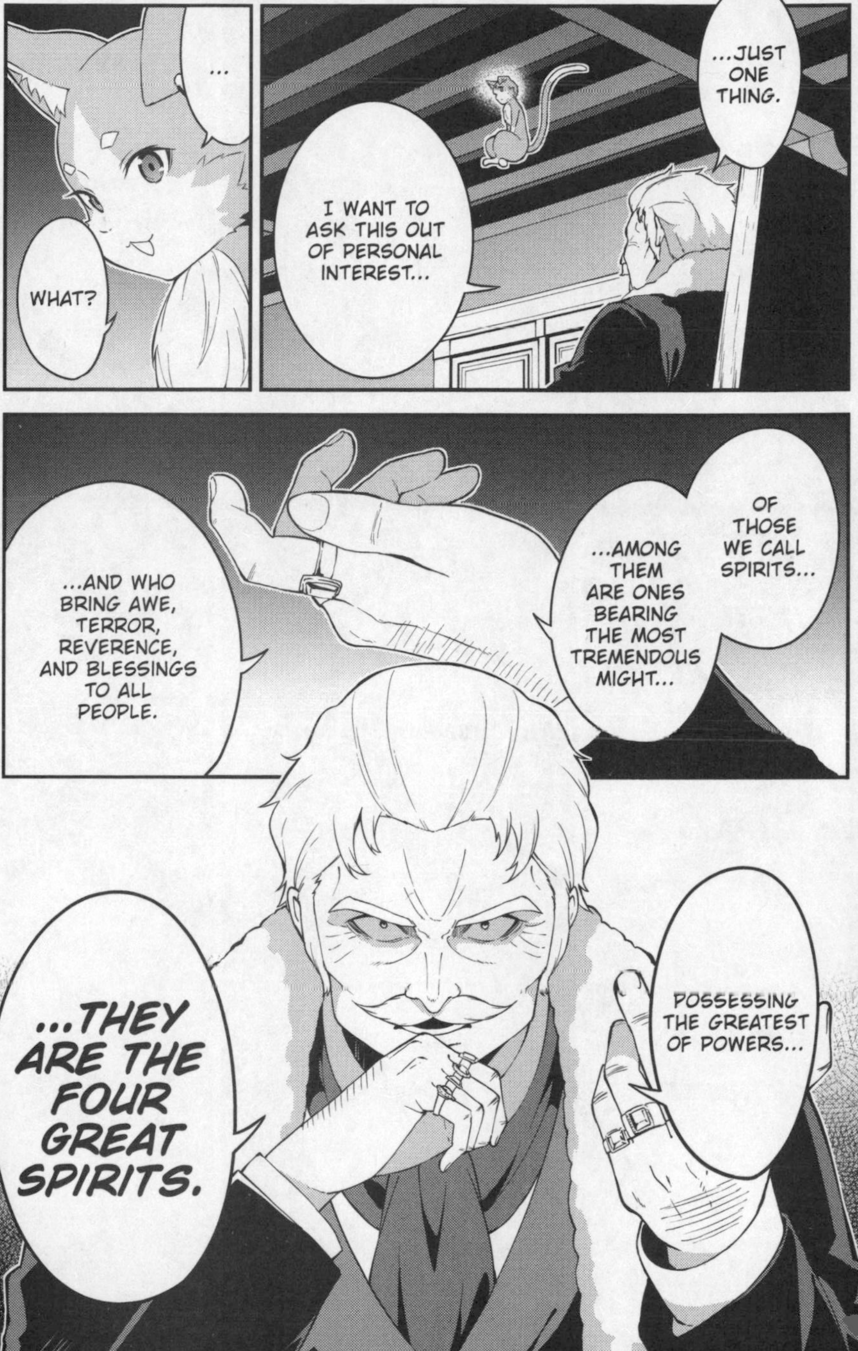
...JUST ONE THING.
I WANT TO ASK THIS OUT OF PERSONAL INTEREST...
...
WHAT?
OF THOSE WE CALL SPIRITS...
...AMONG THEM ARE ONES BEARING THE MOST TREMENDOUS MIGHT...
...AND WHO BRING AWE, TERROR, REVERENCE, AND BLESSINGS TO ALL PEOPLE.
POSSESSING THE GREATEST OF POWERS...
...THEY ARE THE FOUR GREAT SPIRITS.

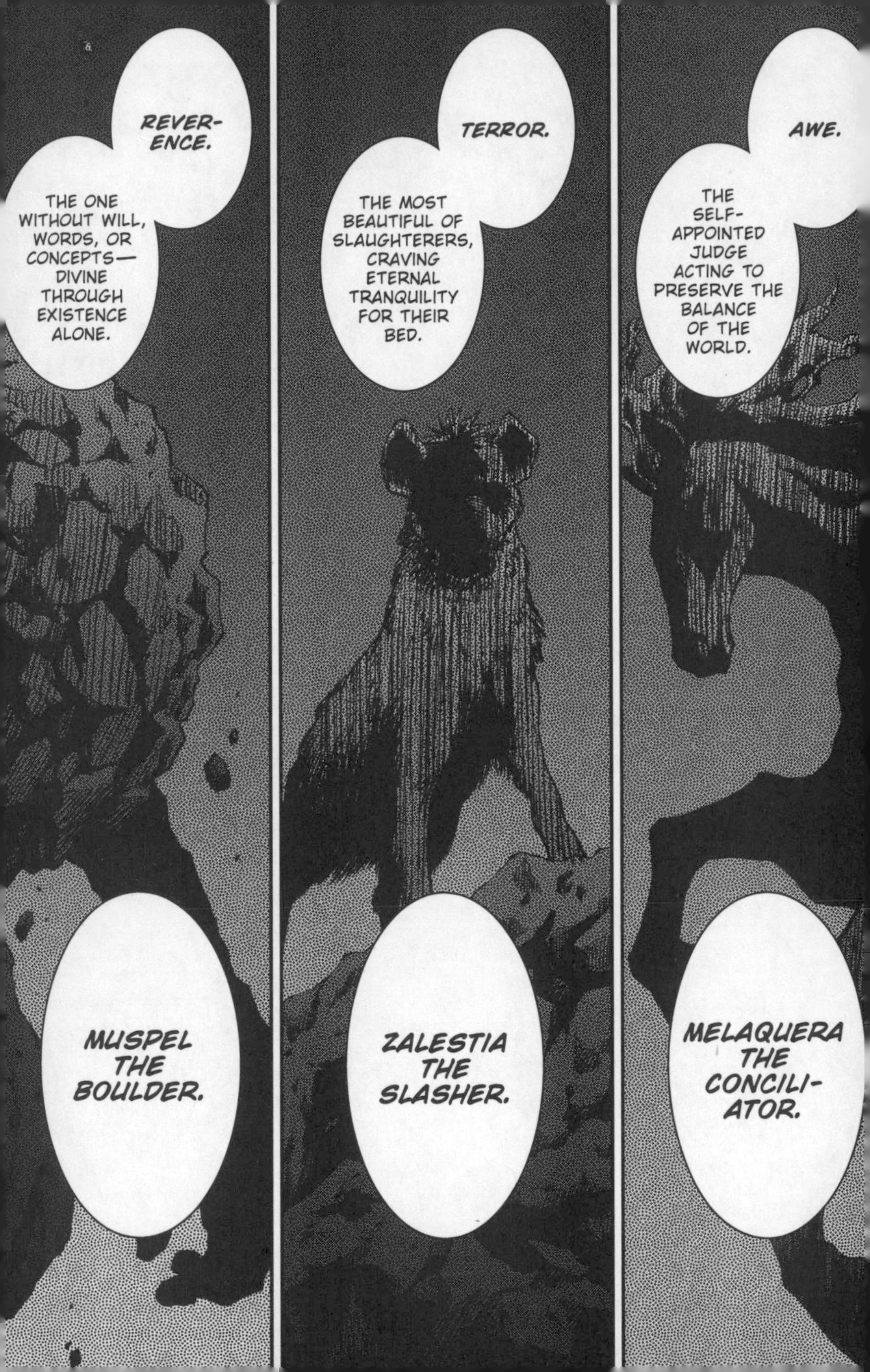
AWE.
THE SELF-APPOINTED JUDGE ACTING TO PRESERVE THE BALANCE OF THE WORLD.
MELAQUERA THE CONCILIATOR.
TERROR.
THE MOST BEAUTIFUL OF SLAUGHTERERS, CRAVING ETERNAL TRANQUILITY FOR THEIR BED.
ZALESTIA THE SLASHER.
REVERENCE.
THE ONE WITHOUT WILL, WORDS, OR CONCEPTS—DIVINE THROUGH EXISTENCE ALONE.
MUSPEL THE BOULDER.

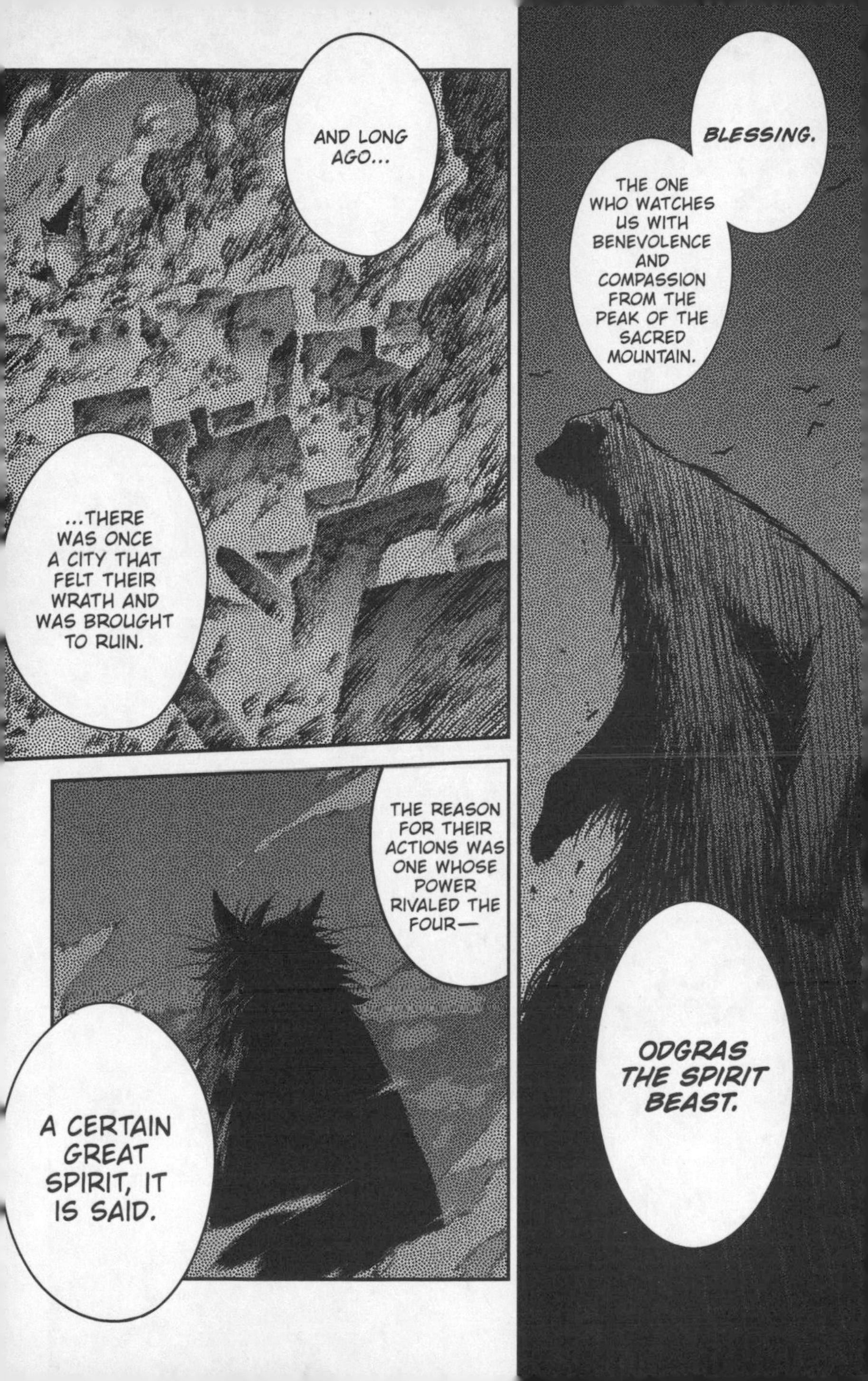
BLESSING.
THE ONE WHO WATCHES US WITH BENEVOLENCE AND COMPASSION FROM THE PEAK OF THE SACRED MOUNTAIN.
ODGRAS THE SPIRIT BEAST.
AND LONG AGO...
...THERE WAS ONCE A CITY THAT FELT THEIR WRATH AND WAS BROUGHT TO RUIN.
THE REASON FOR THEIR ACTIONS WAS ONE WHOSE POWER RIVALED THE FOUR—
A CERTAIN GREAT SPIRIT, IT IS SAID.

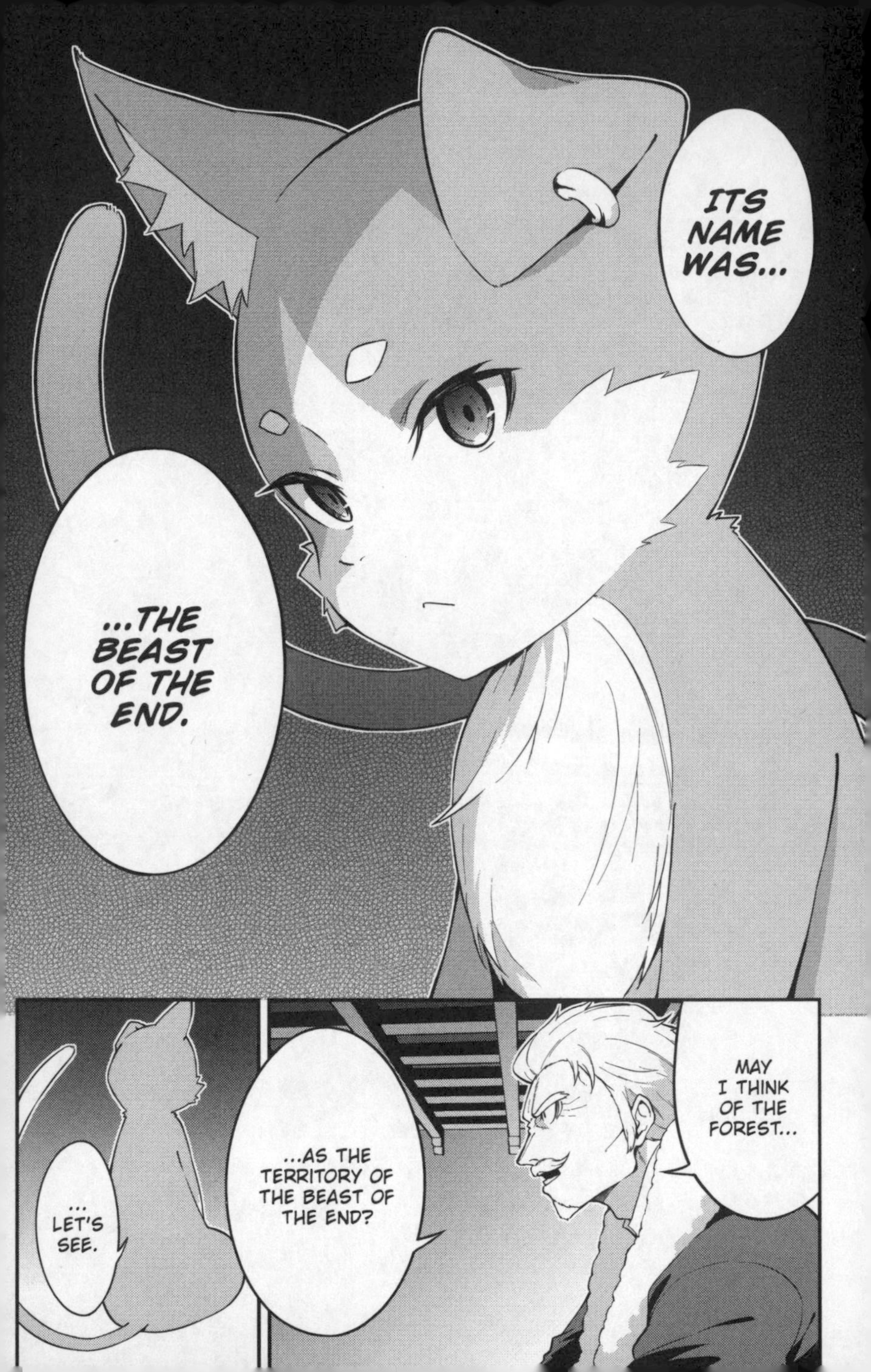
ITS NAME WAS...
...THE BEAST OF THE END.
MAY I THINK OF THE FOREST...
...AS THE TERRITORY OF THE BEAST OF THE END?
... LET'S SEE.

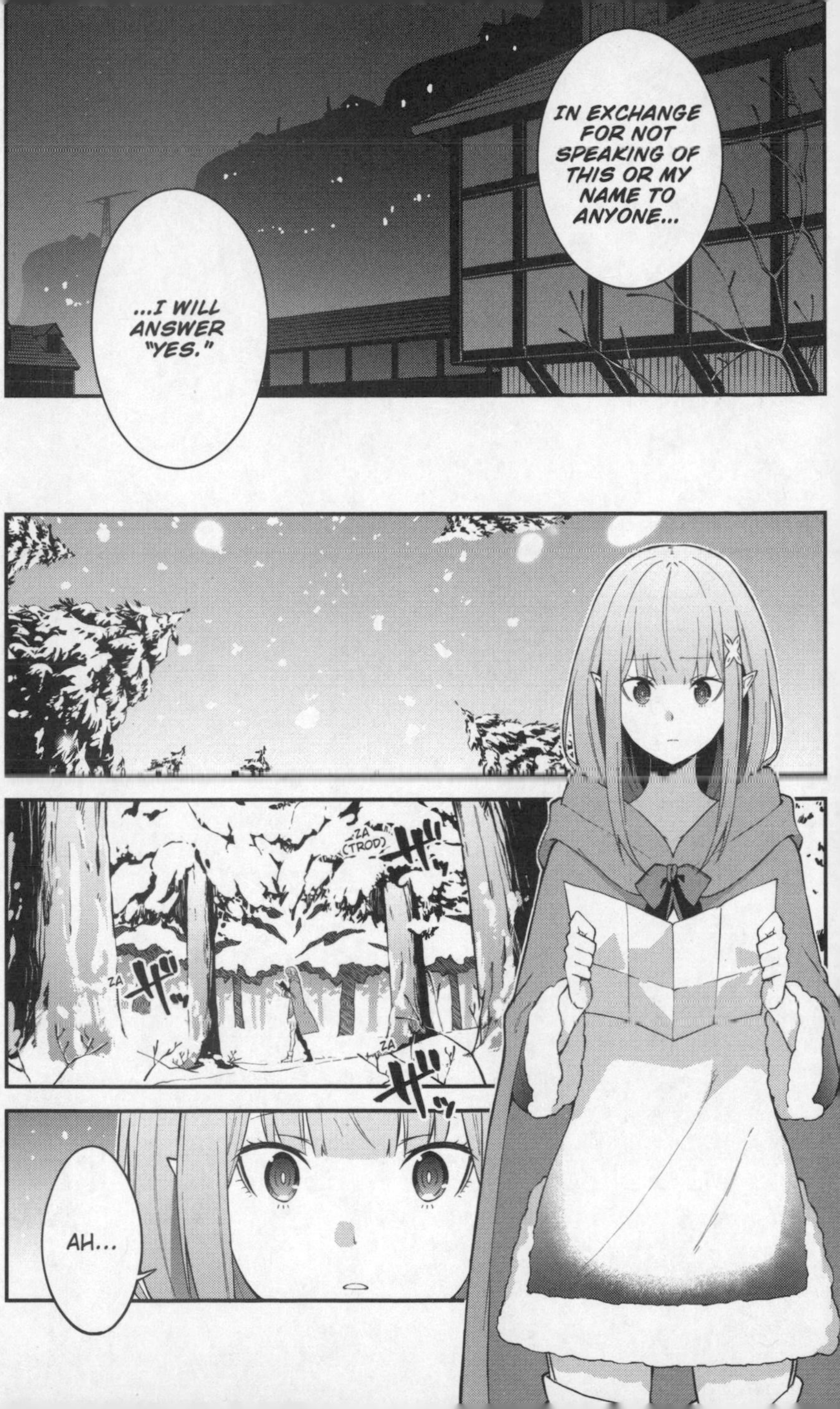
IN EXCHANGE FOR NOT SPEAKING OF THIS OR MY NAME TO ANYONE...
...I WILL ANSWER "YES."
ZA (TROD)
ZA
ZA
AH...

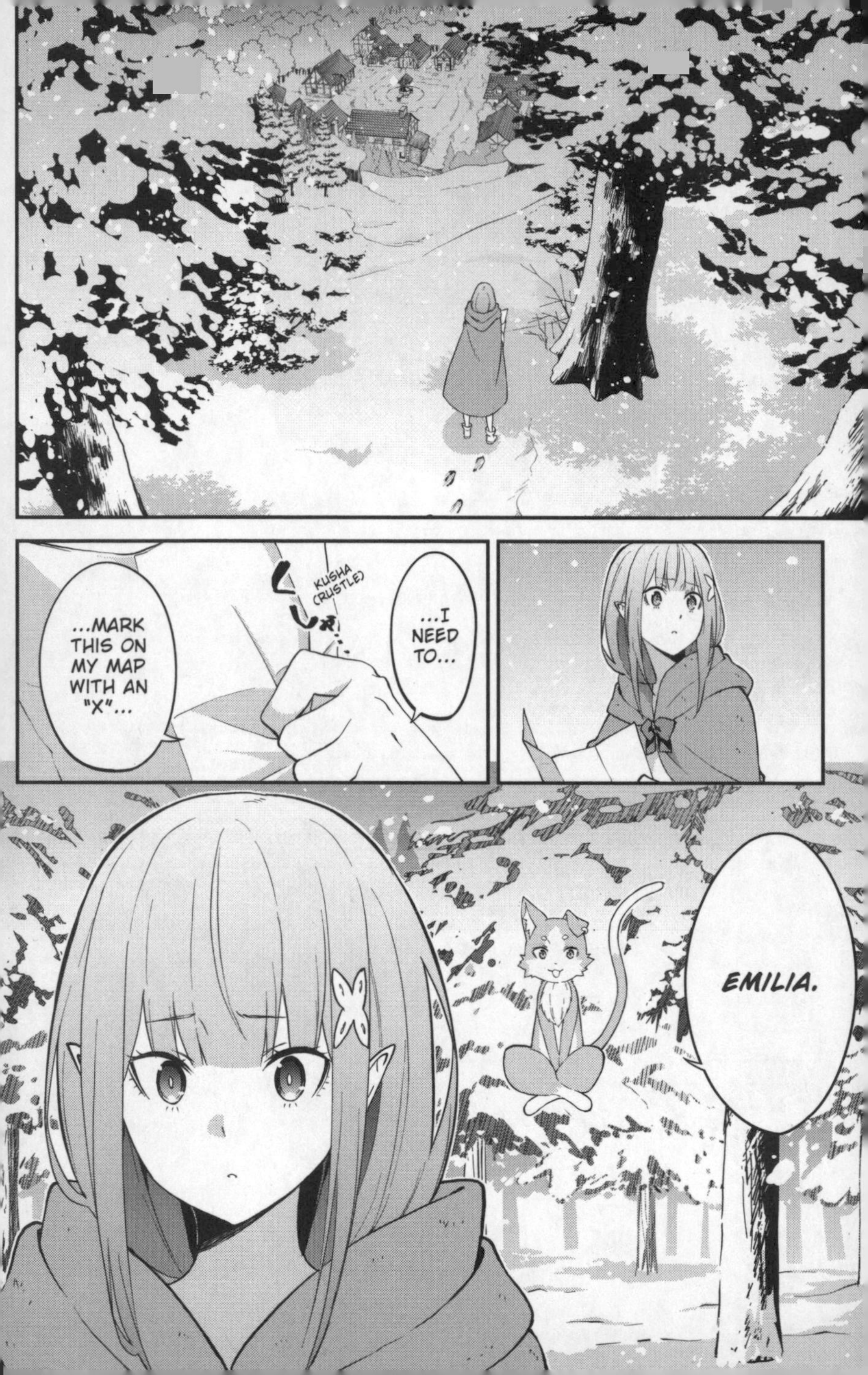
...I NEED TO...
KUSHA (RUSTLE)
...MARK THIS ON MY MAP WITH AN "X"...
EMILIA.

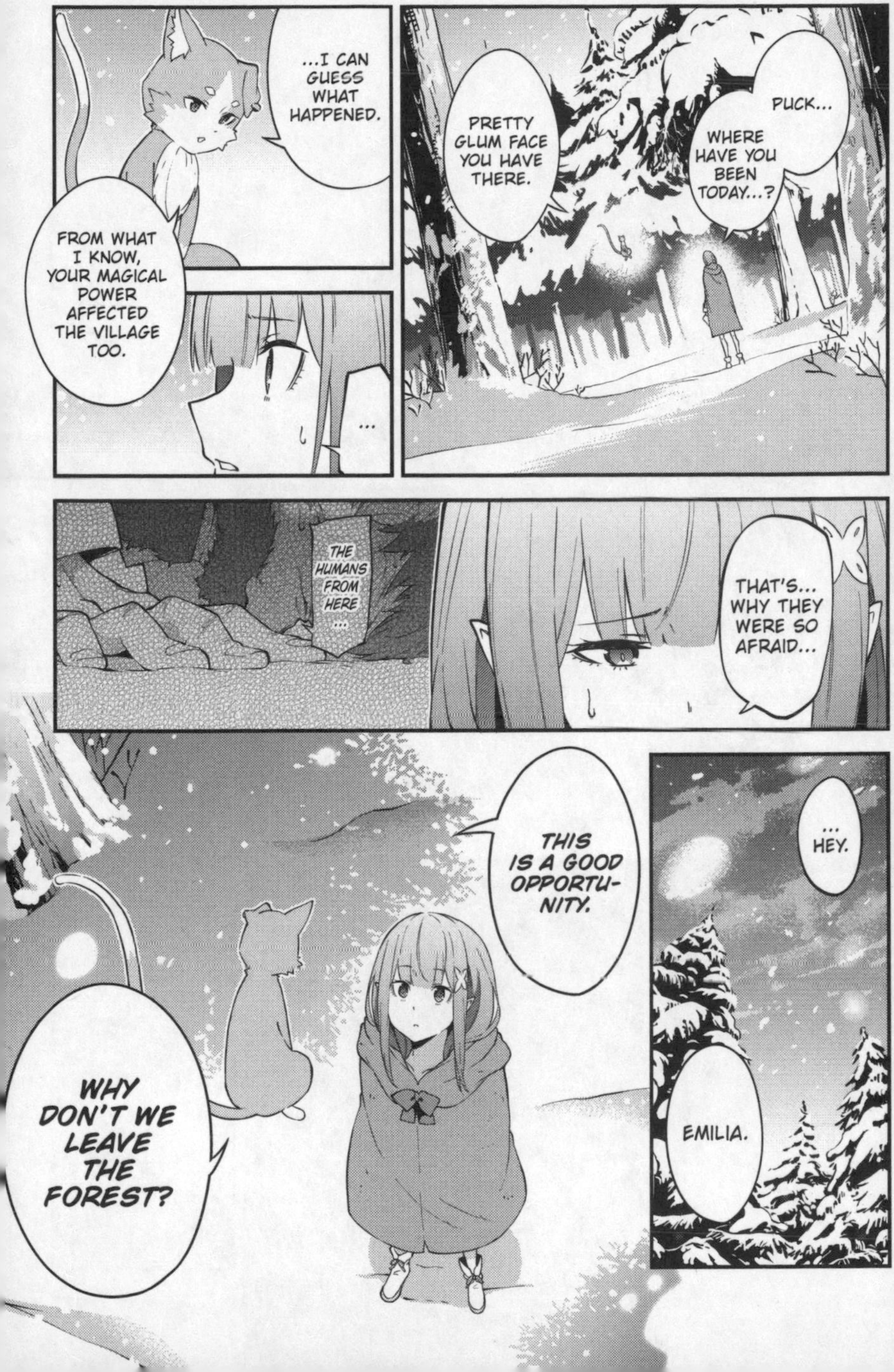
PUCK...
WHERE HAVE YOU BEEN TODAY...?
PRETTY GLUM FACE YOU HAVE THERE.
...I CAN GUESS WHAT HAPPENED.
FROM WHAT I KNOW, YOUR MAGICAL POWER AFFECTED THE VILLAGE TOO.
...
THAT'S... WHY THEY WERE SO AFRAID...
THE HUMANS FROM HERE...
...HEY.
EMILIA.
THIS IS A GOOD OPPORTUNITY.
WHY DON'T WE LEAVE THE FOREST?

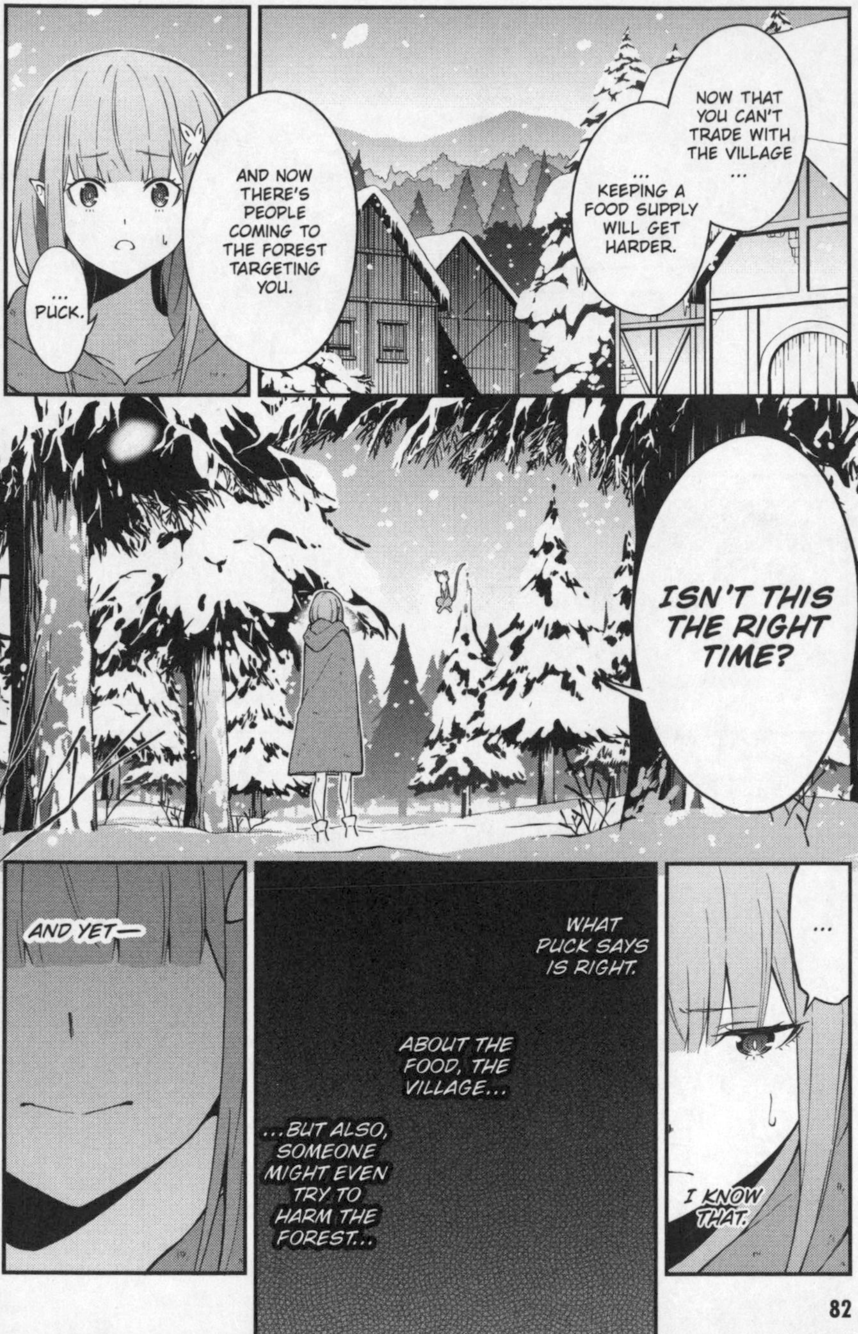
NOW THAT YOU CAN'T TRADE WITH THE VILLAGE ...
... KEEPING A FOOD SUPPLY WILL GET HARDER.
AND NOW THERE'S PEOPLE COMING TO THE FOREST TARGETING YOU.
... PUCK.
ISN'T THIS THE RIGHT TIME?
...
I KNOW THAT.
WHAT PUCK SAYS IS RIGHT.
ABOUT THE FOOD, THE VILLAGE...
...BUT ALSO, SOMEONE MIGHT EVEN TRY TO HARM THE FOREST...
AND YET—

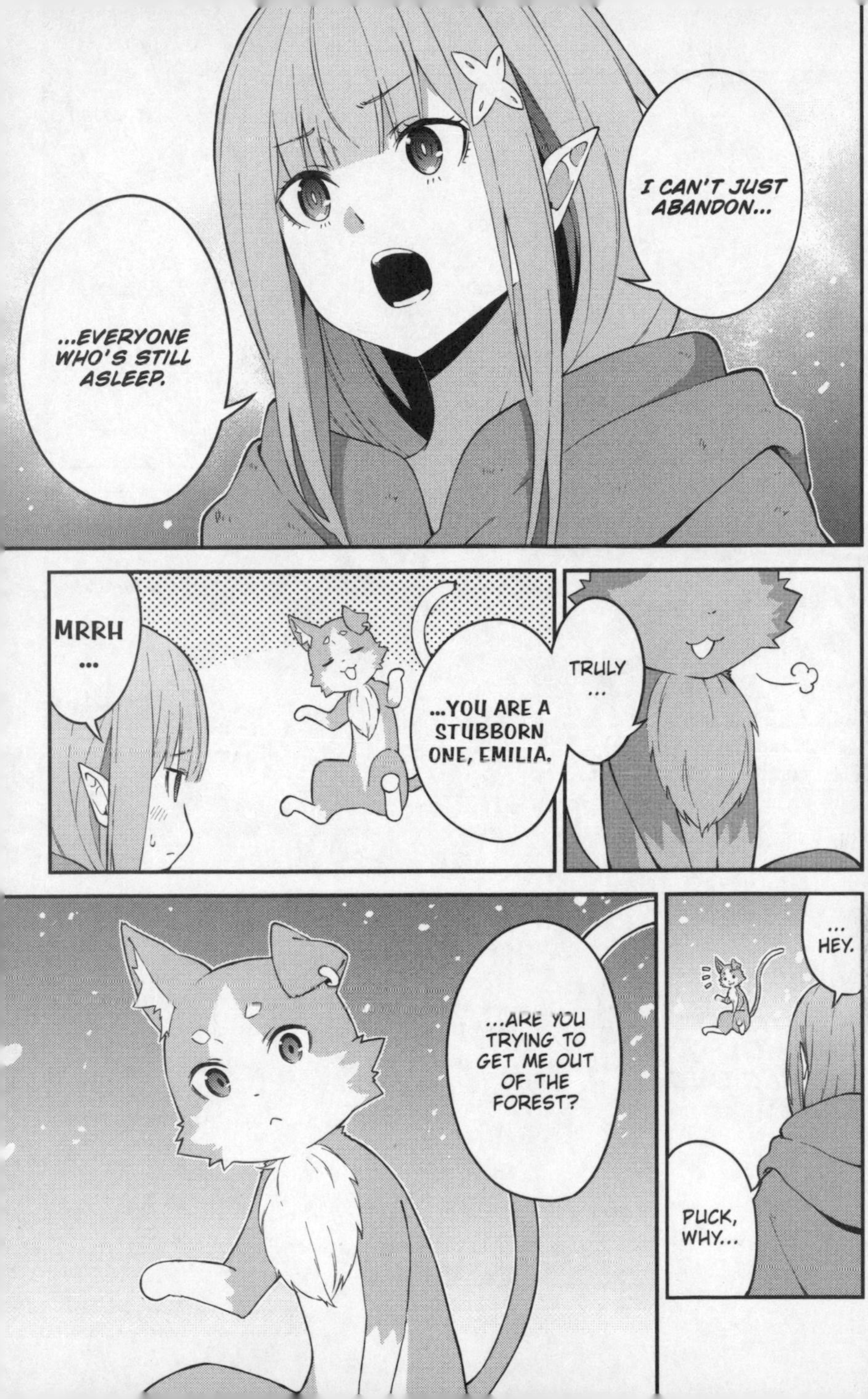
I CAN'T JUST ABANDON...
...EVERYONE WHO'S STILL ASLEEP.
TRULY ...
...YOU ARE A STUBBORN ONE, EMILIA.
MRRH ...
... HEY.
PUCK, WHY...
...ARE YOU TRYING TO GET ME OUT OF THE FOREST?

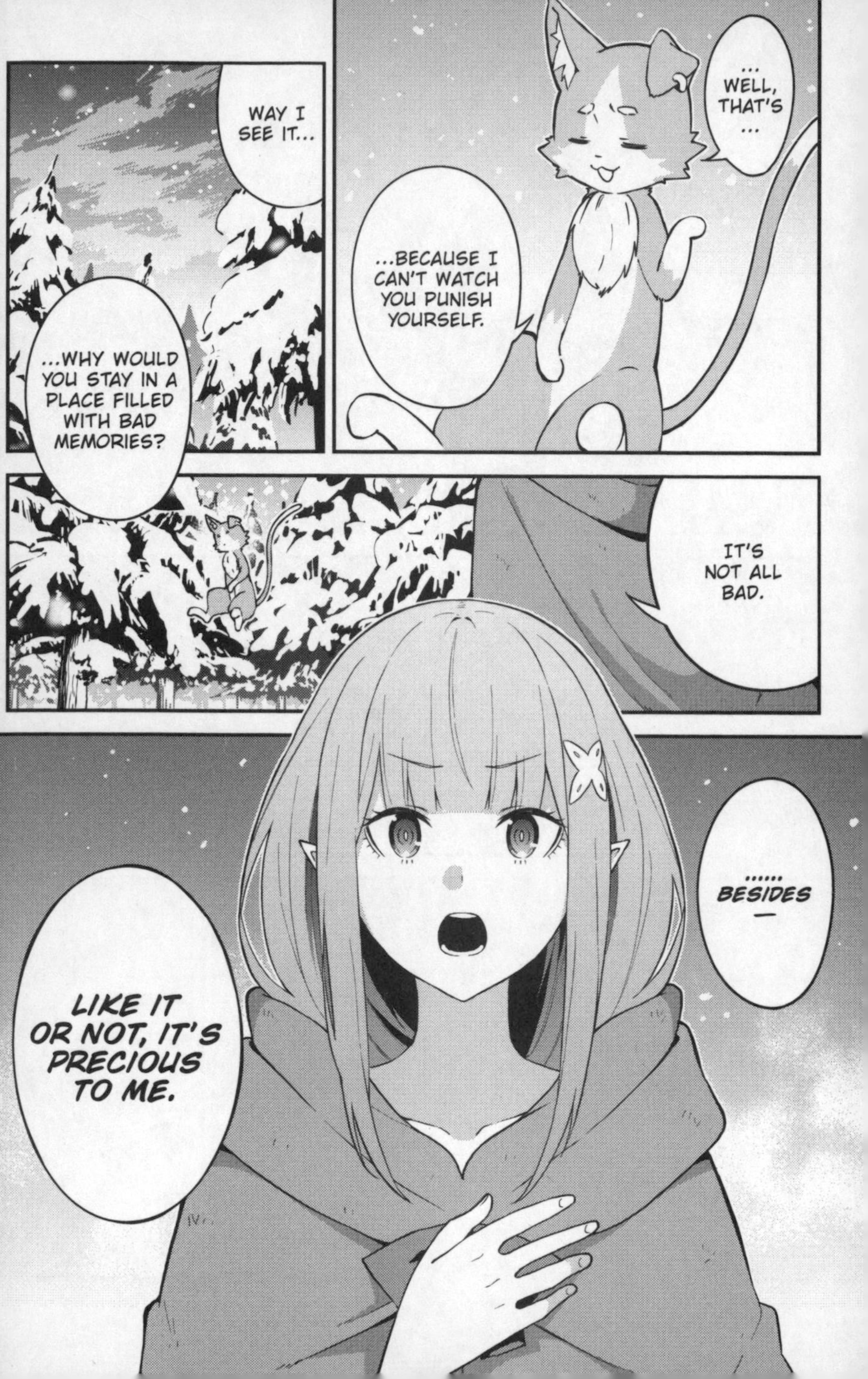
... WELL, THAT'S ...
...BECAUSE I CAN'T WATCH YOU PUNISH YOURSELF.
WAY I SEE IT...
...WHY WOULD YOU STAY IN A PLACE FILLED WITH BAD MEMORIES?
IT'S NOT ALL BAD.
...... BESIDES —
LIKE IT OR NOT, IT'S PRECIOUS TO ME.

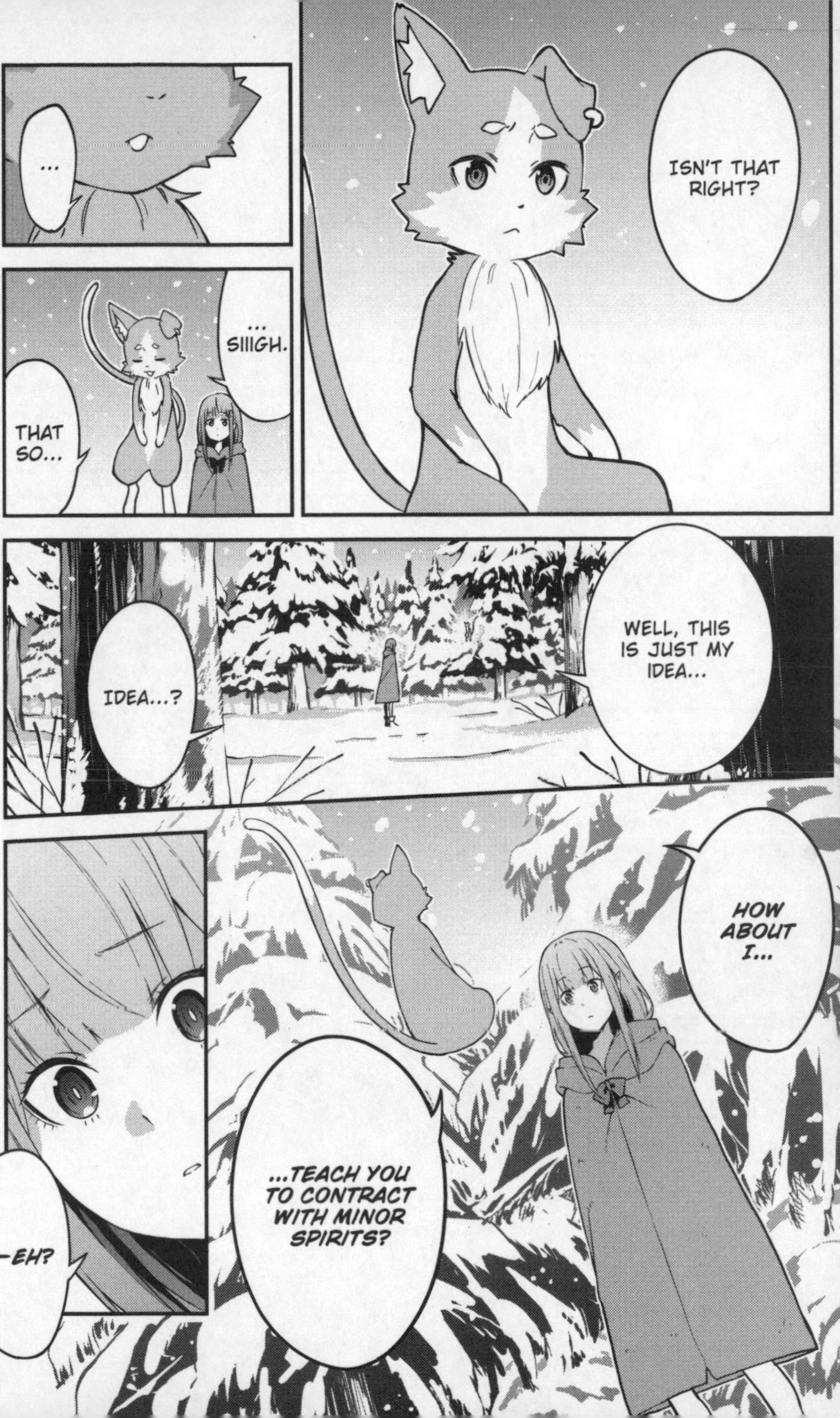
ISN'T THAT RIGHT?
...
... SIIIGH.
THAT SO...
WELL, THIS IS JUST MY IDEA...
IDEA...?
HOW ABOUT I...
...TEACH YOU TO CONTRACT WITH MINOR SPIRITS?
—EH?

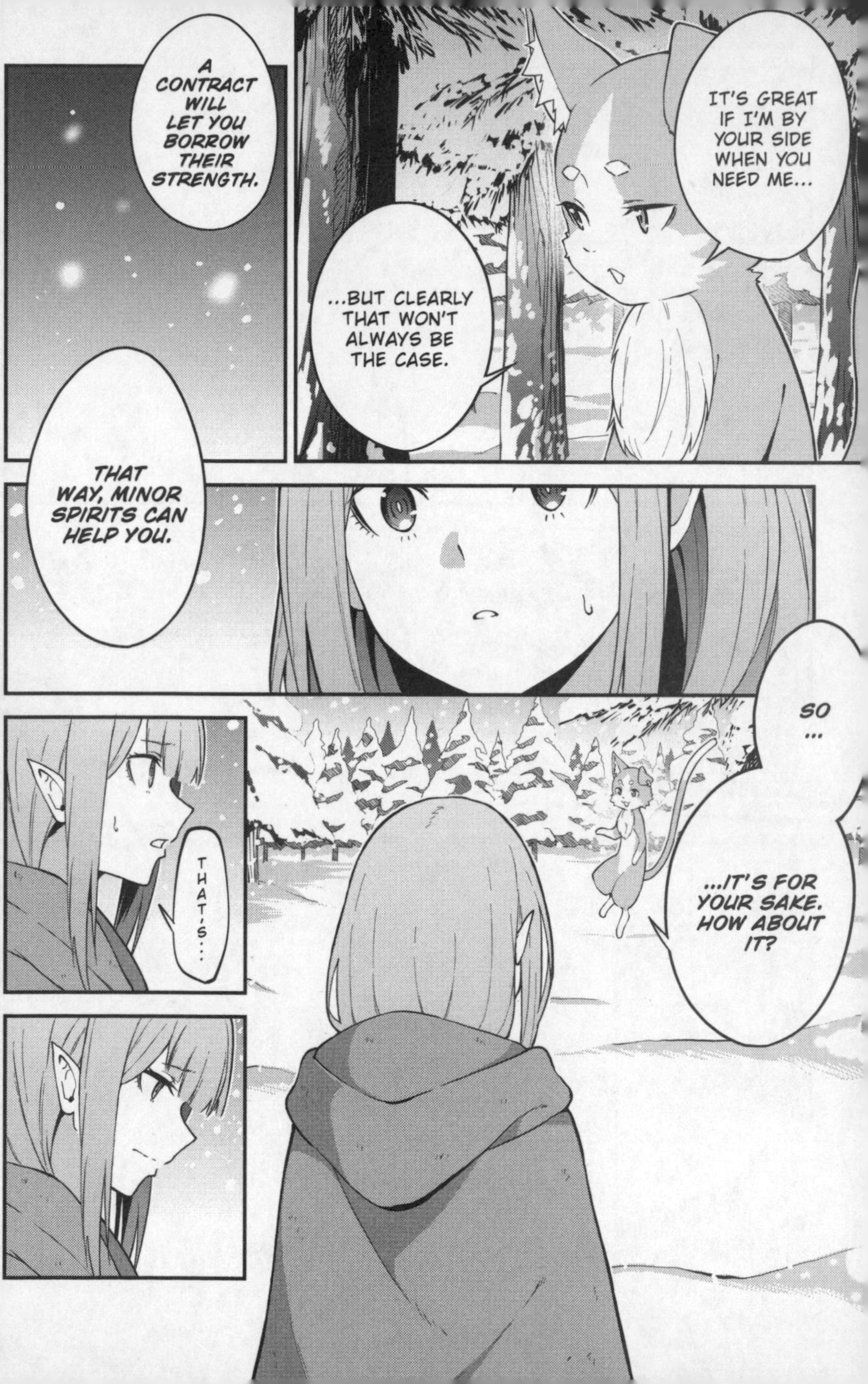
IT'S GREAT IF I'M BY YOUR SIDE WHEN YOU NEED ME...
...BUT CLEARLY THAT WON'T ALWAYS BE THE CASE.
A CONTRACT WILL LET YOU BORROW THEIR STRENGTH.
THAT WAY, MINOR SPIRITS CAN HELP YOU.
SO ...
...IT'S FOR YOUR SAKE. HOW ABOUT IT?
THAT'S...

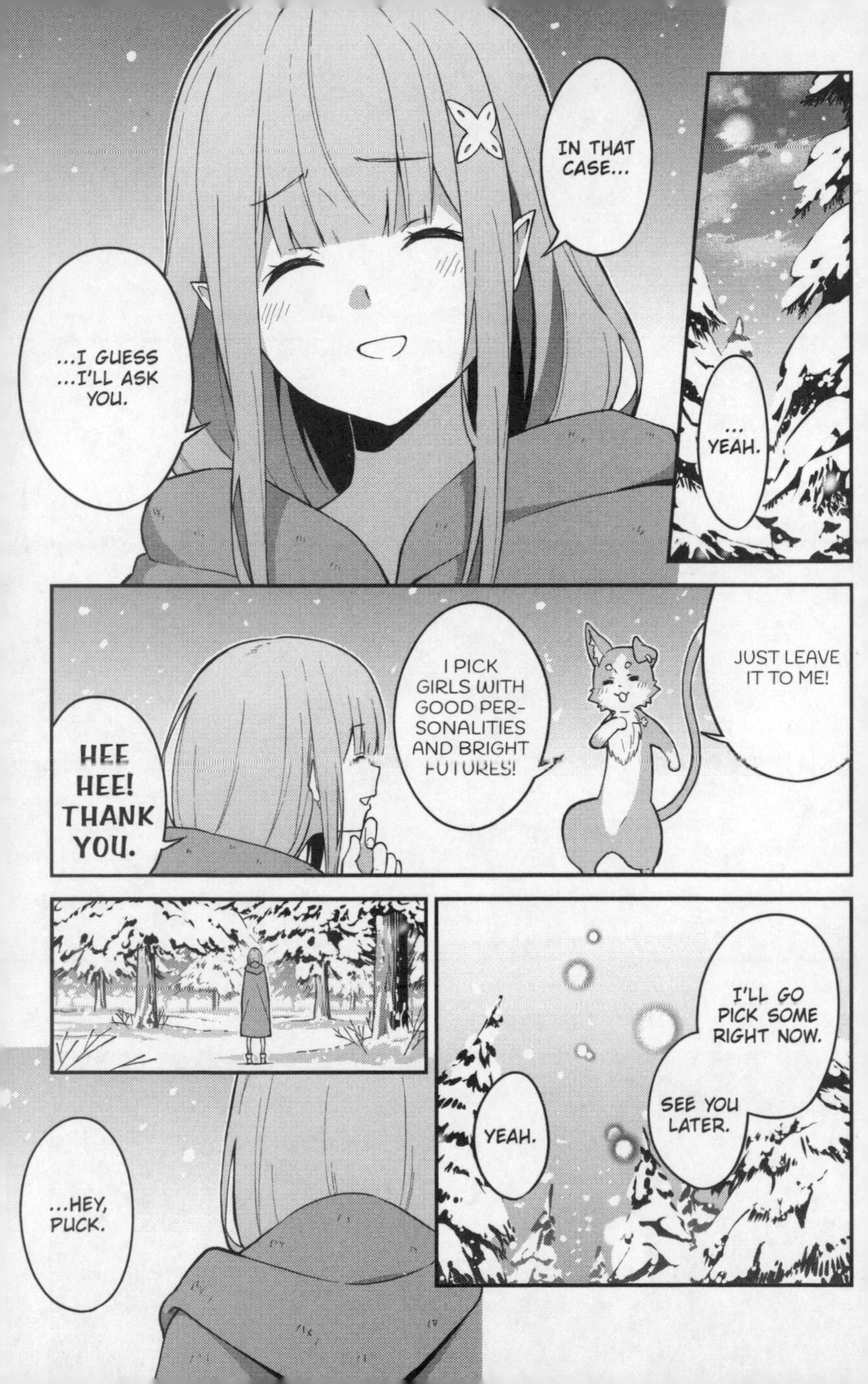
...YEAH.
IN THAT CASE...
...I GUESS ...I'LL ASK YOU.
JUST LEAVE IT TO ME!
I PICK GIRLS WITH GOOD PER-SONALITIES AND BRIGHT FUTURES!
HEE HEE! THANK YOU.
I'LL GO PICK SOME RIGHT NOW.
SEE YOU LATER.
YEAH.
...HEY, PUCK.

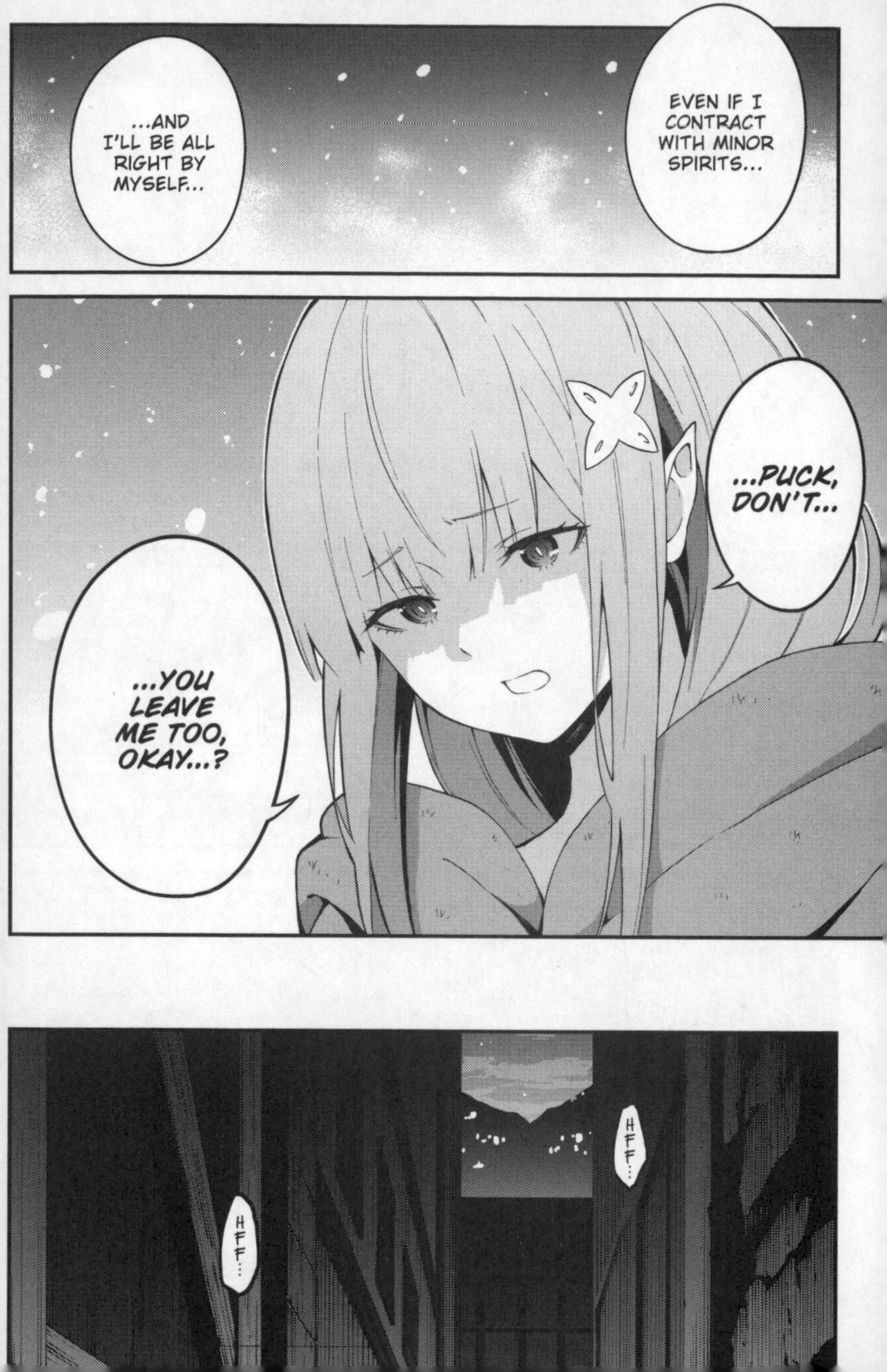
EVEN IF I CONTRACT WITH MINOR SPIRITS...
...AND I'LL BE ALL RIGHT BY MYSELF...
...PUCK, DON'T...
...YOU LEAVE ME TOO, OKAY...?
HFF...
HFF...

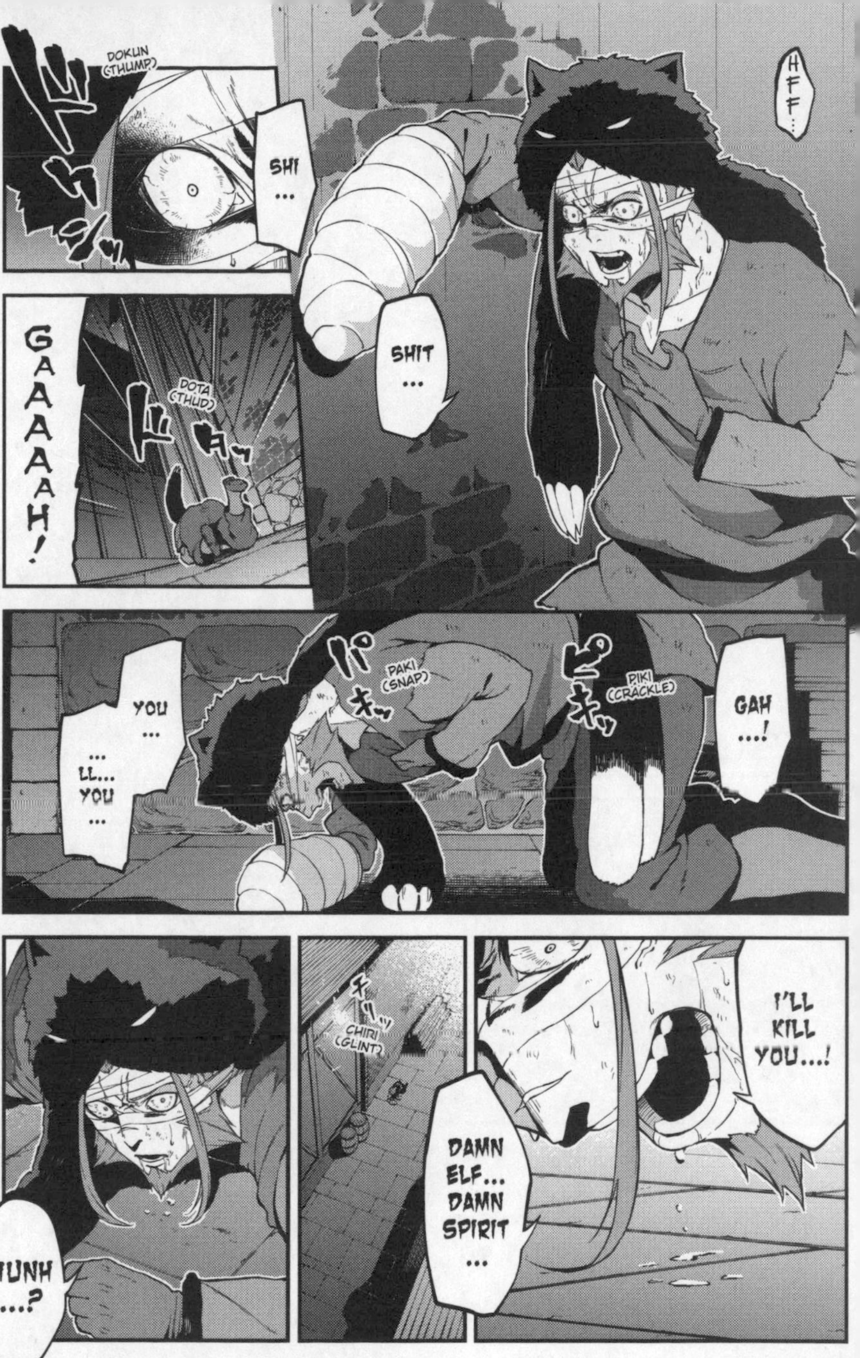
HFF...
SHIT ...
DOKUN (THUMP)
SHI ...
GAAAAAH!
DOTA (THUD)
GAH ...!
PIKI (CRACKLE)
PAKI (SNAP)
YOU ... ... LL... YOU ...
I'LL KILL YOU...!
DAMN ELF... DAMN SPIRIT ...
CHIRI (GLINT)
HUNH ...?

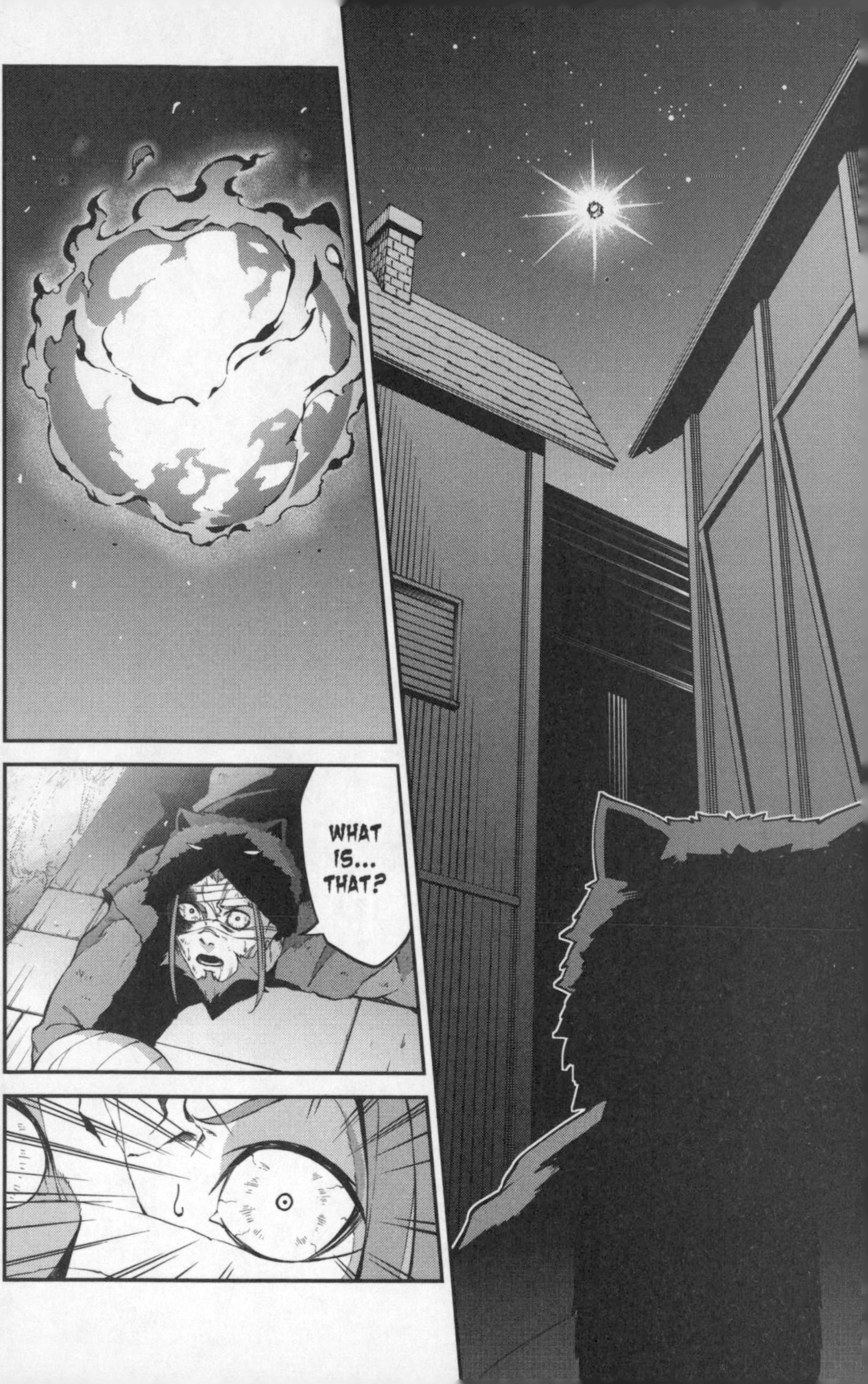
WHAT IS... THAT?

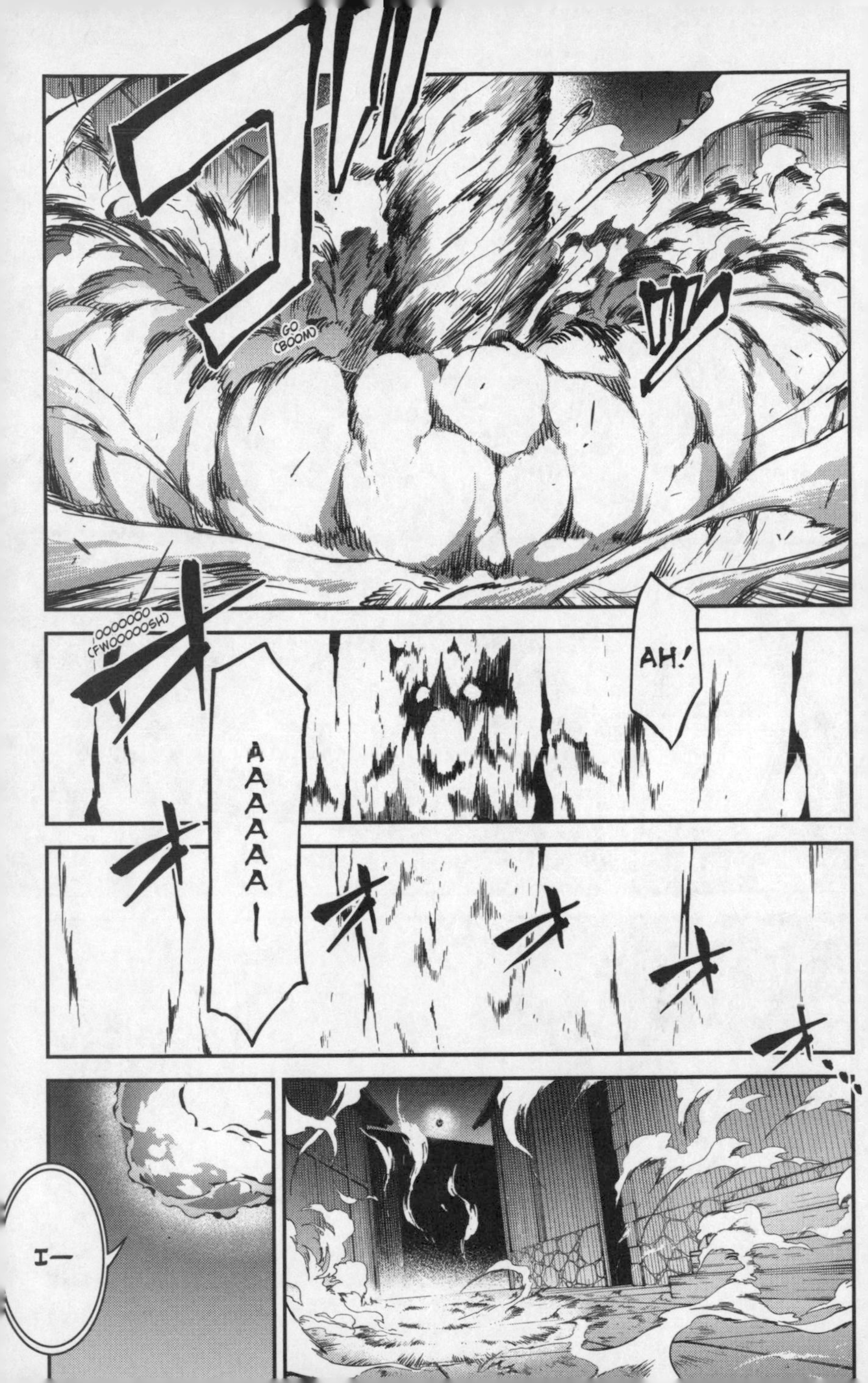
GO
(BOOM)
AH!
OOOOOOO
(FWOOOOOSH)
AAAAAA—
E—

—DETECT.

DANGER-OUS.

FREEZING.

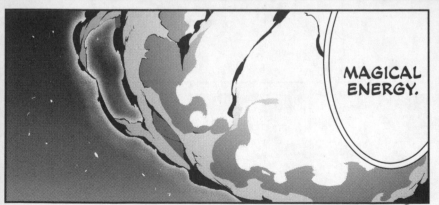

MAGICAL ENERGY.

Re:ZERO

-Starting Life in Another World-

The Frozen Bond

The only ability Subaru Natsuki gets when he's
summoned to another world is time travel via his own death.
But to save her, he'll die as many times as it takes.

Re:ZERO

-Starting Life in Another World-
The Frozen Bond

Minori Tsukahara

Tappei Nagatsuki, Shinichirou Otsuka

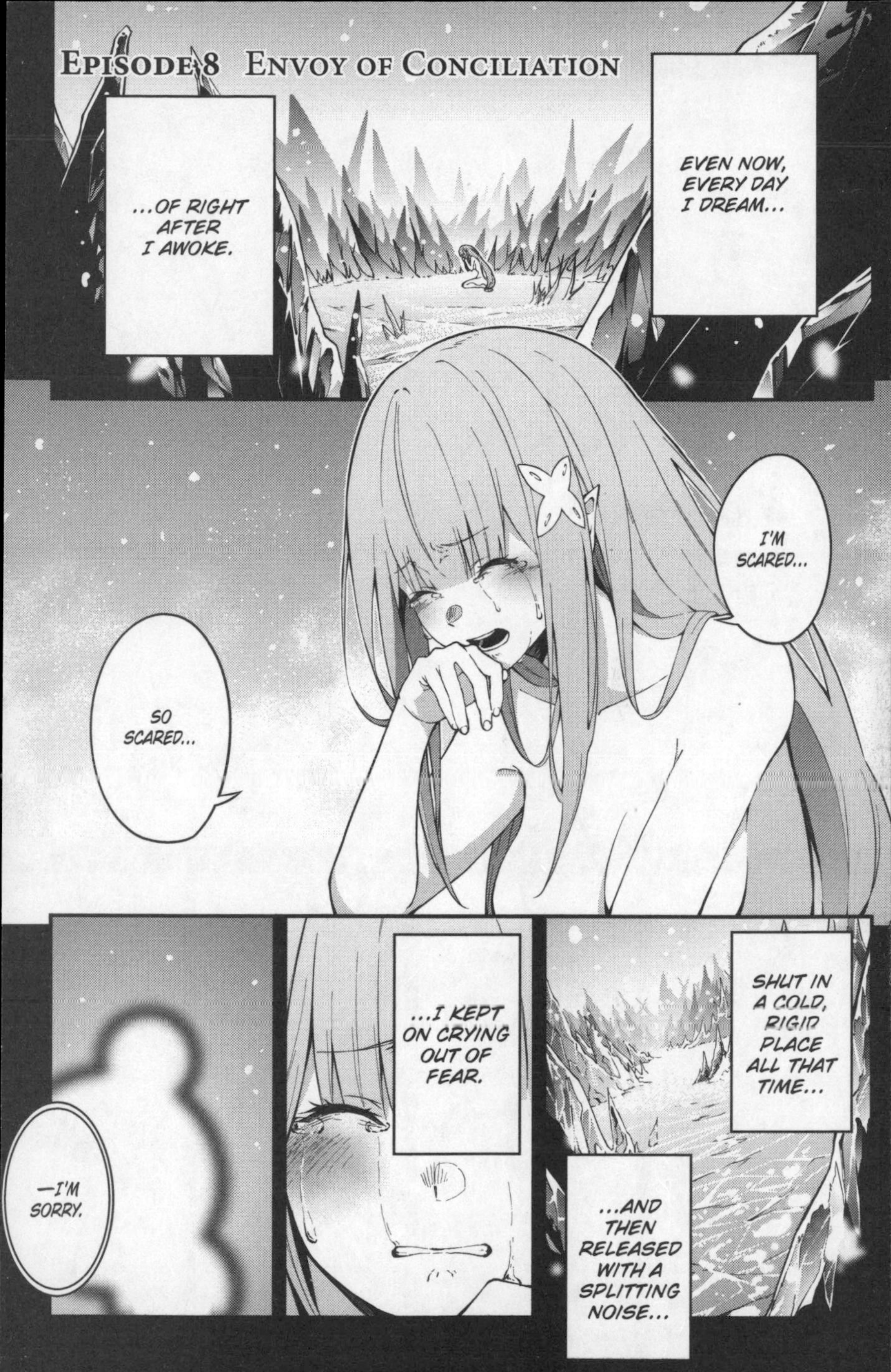
EPISODE 8 ENVOY OF CONCILIATION
EVEN NOW, EVERY DAY I DREAM...
...OF RIGHT AFTER I AWOKE.
I'M SCARED...
SO SCARED...
SHUT IN A COLD, RIGID PLACE ALL THAT TIME...
...AND THEN RELEASED WITH A SPLITTING NOISE...
...I KEPT ON CRYING OUT OF FEAR.
—I'M SORRY.

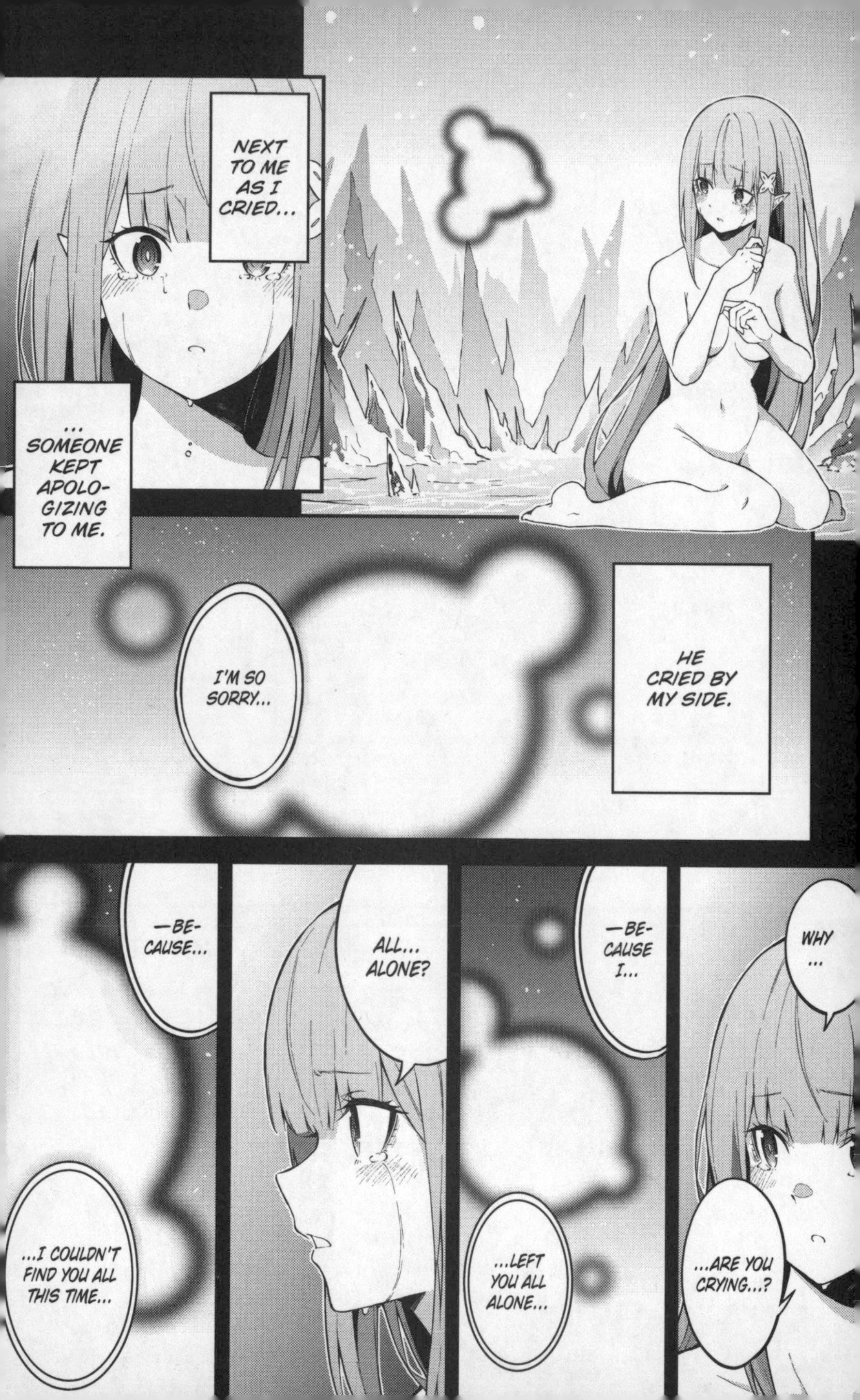
NEXT TO ME AS I CRIED...
...SOMEONE KEPT APOLO-GIZING TO ME.
HE CRIED BY MY SIDE.
I'M SO SORRY...
WHY ...
...ARE YOU CRYING...?
—BE-CAUSE I...
...LEFT YOU ALL ALONE...
ALL... ALONE?
—BE-CAUSE...
...I COULDN'T FIND YOU ALL THIS TIME...

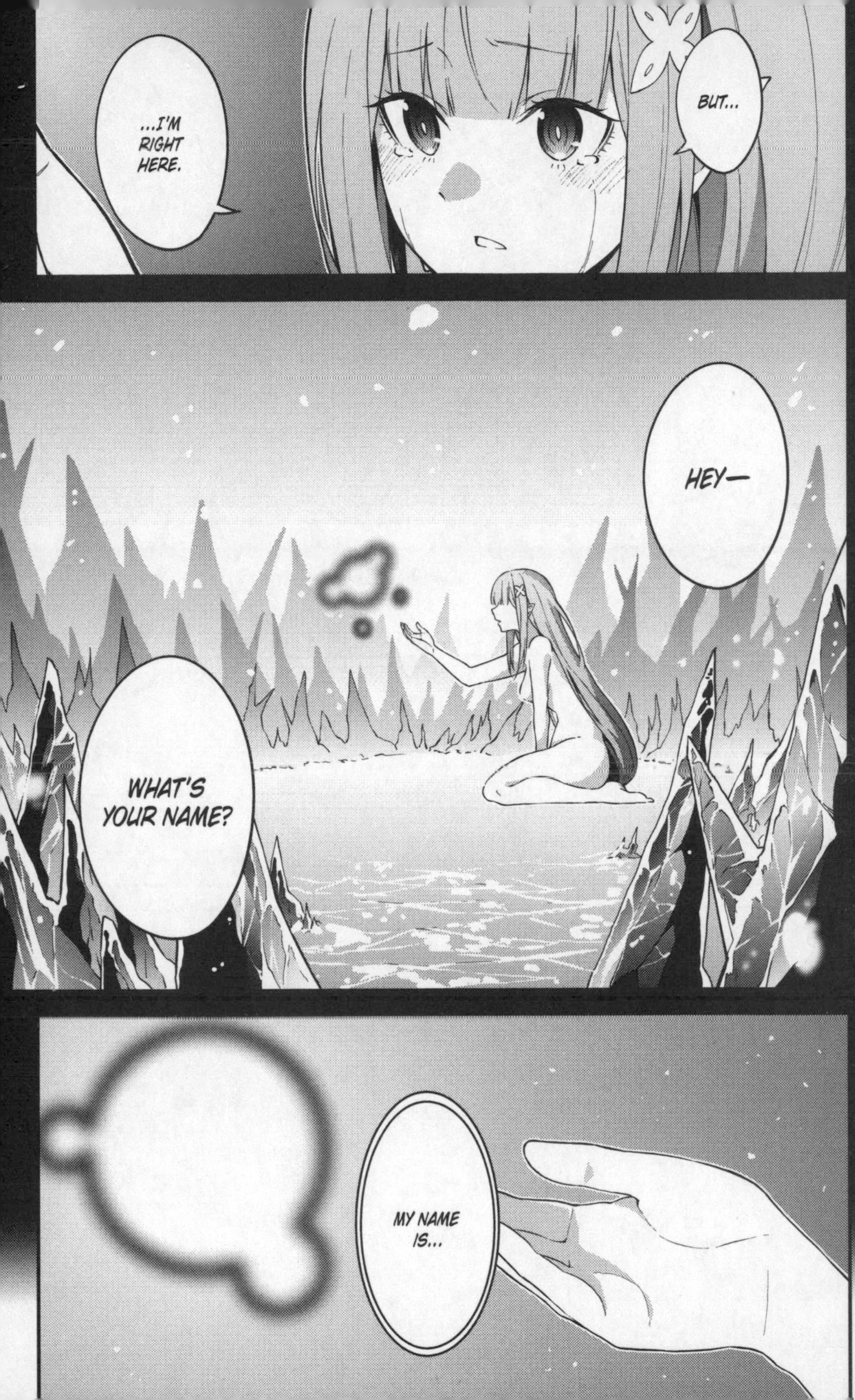
BUT...
...I'M RIGHT HERE.
HEY—
WHAT'S YOUR NAME?
MY NAME IS...

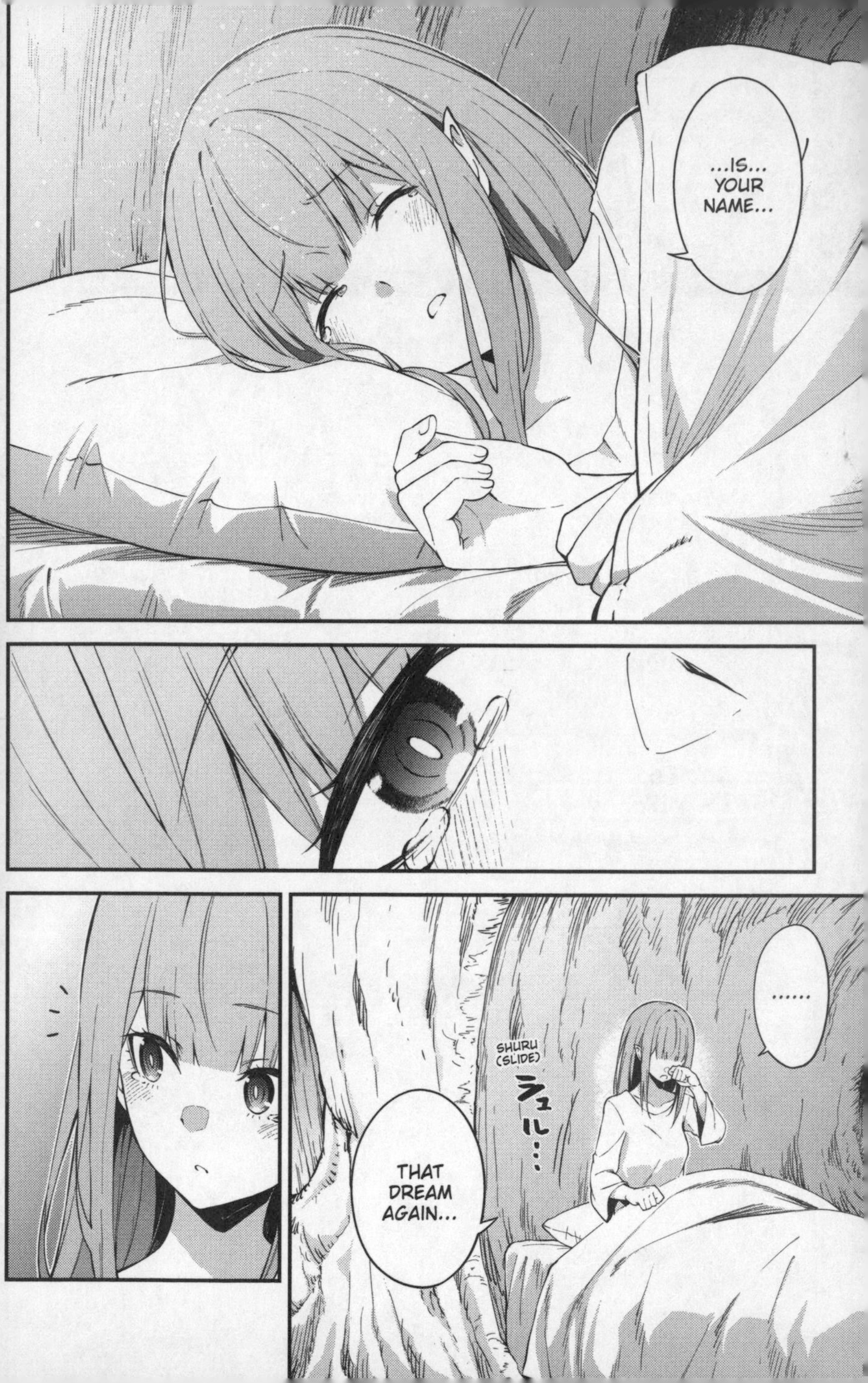
...IS... YOUR NAME...
......
SHURU (SLIDE)
シュル…
THAT DREAM AGAIN...

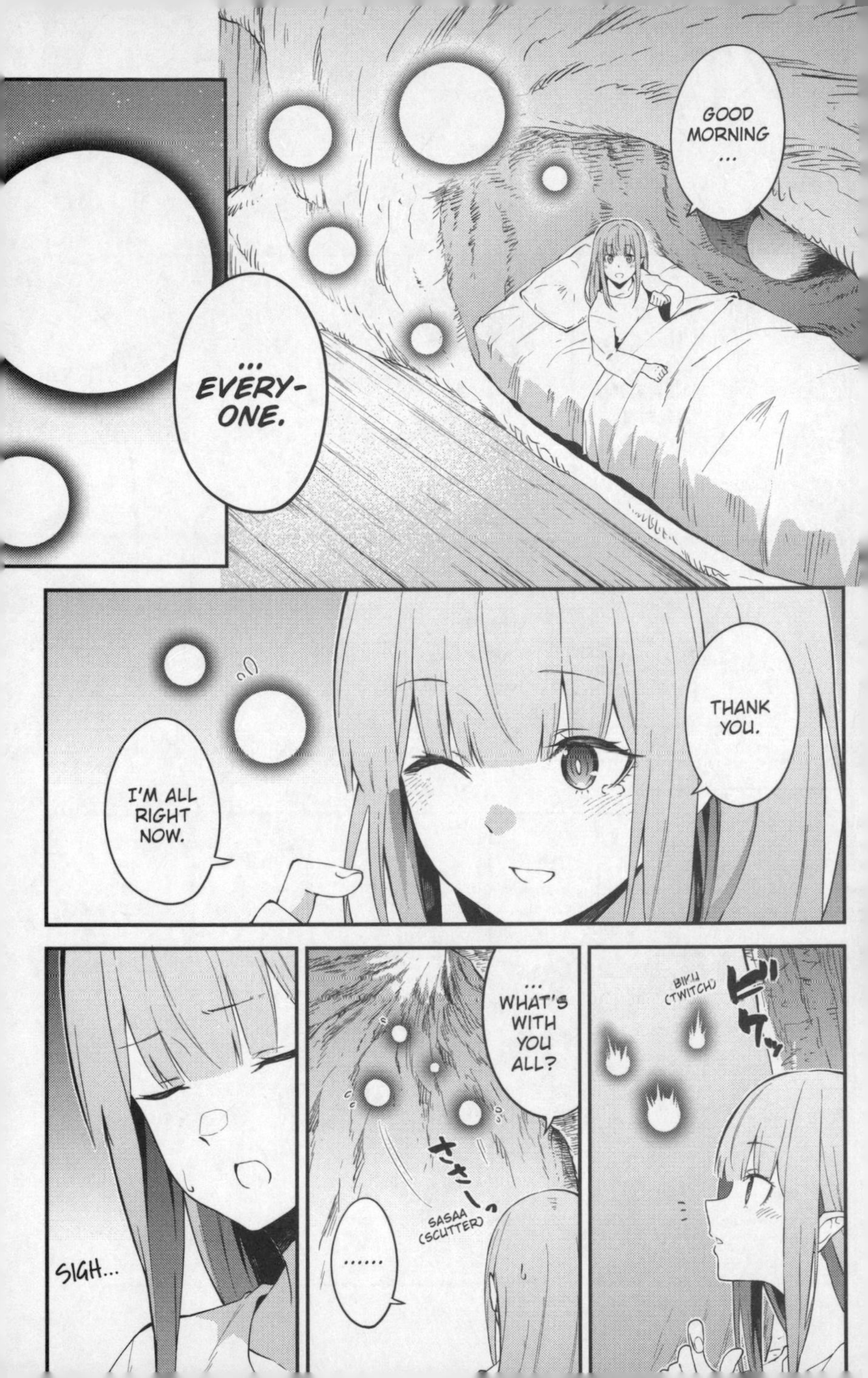
GOOD MORNING ...
... EVERY-ONE.
THANK YOU.
I'M ALL RIGHT NOW.
ビクッ
BIKU (TWITCH)
... WHAT'S WITH YOU ALL?
ささーっ
SASAA (SCUTTER)
......
SIGH...

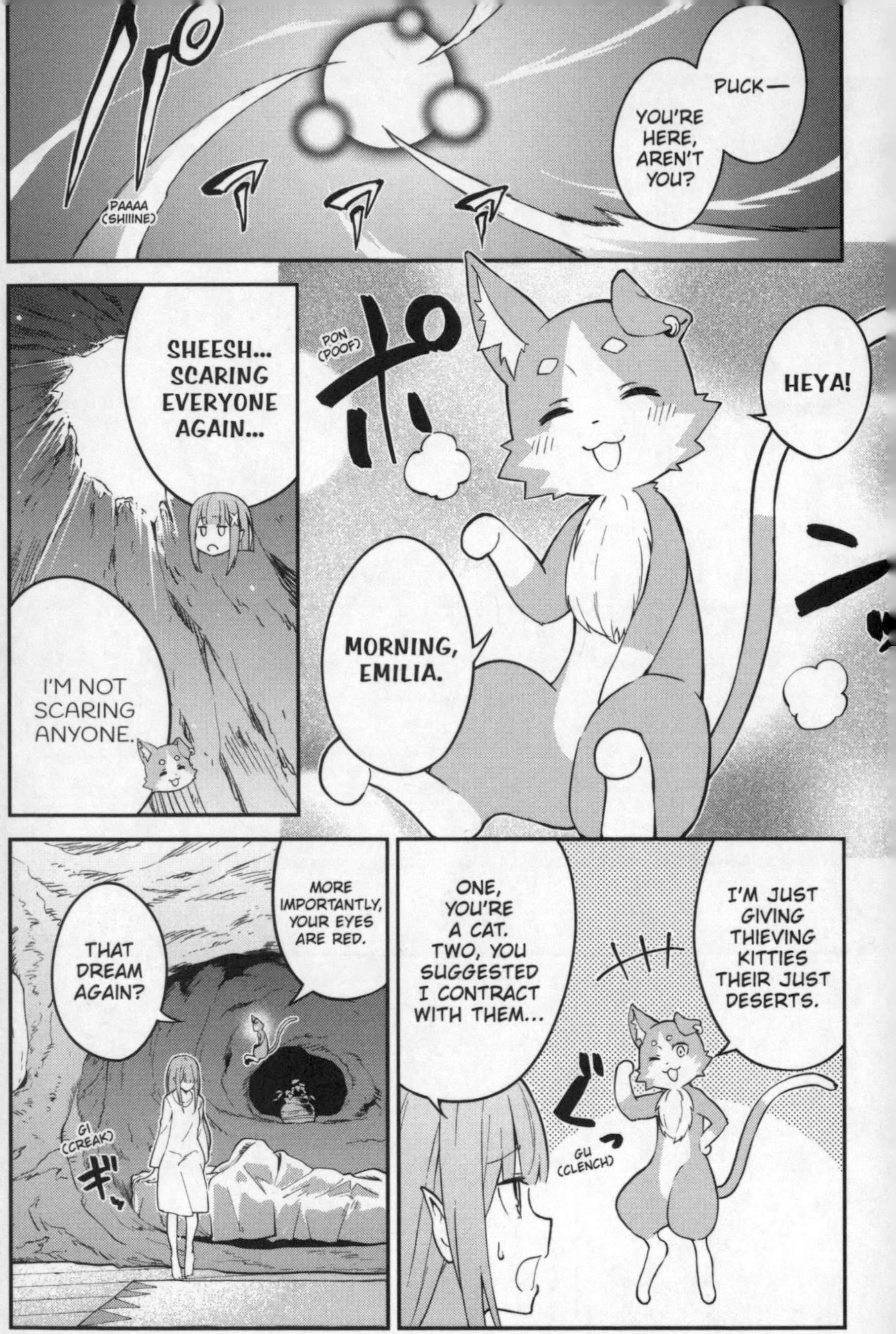
PUCK—
YOU'RE HERE, AREN'T YOU?
PAAAA (SHIIINE)
HEYA!
PON (POOF)
MORNING, EMILIA.
SHEESH... SCARING EVERYONE AGAIN...
I'M NOT SCARING ANYONE.
I'M JUST GIVING THIEVING KITTIES THEIR JUST DESERTS.
ONE, YOU'RE A CAT. TWO, YOU SUGGESTED I CONTRACT WITH THEM...
GU (CLENCH)
MORE IMPORTANTLY, YOUR EYES ARE RED.
THAT DREAM AGAIN?
GI (CREAK)

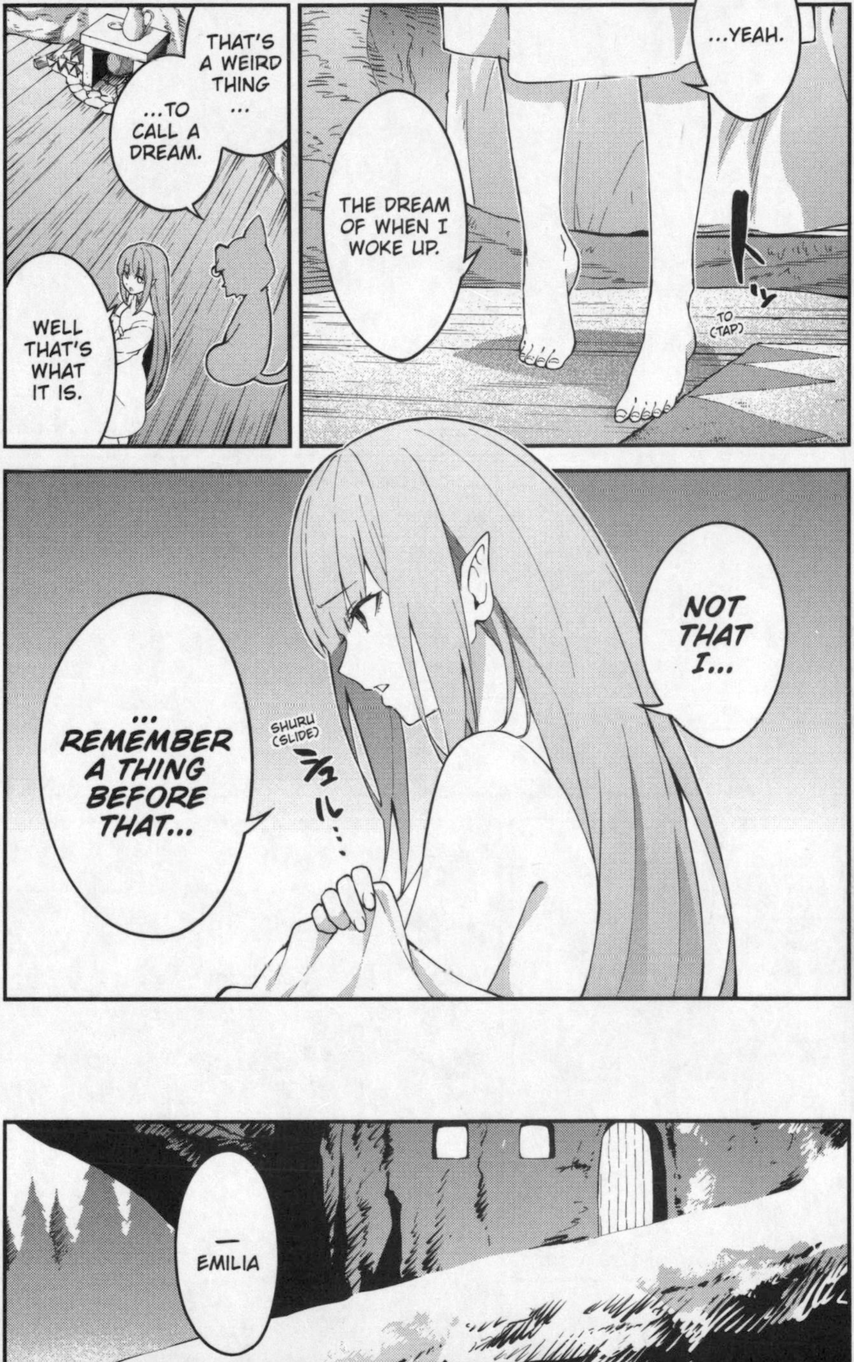
...YEAH.
THE DREAM OF WHEN I WOKE UP.
TO (TAP)
THAT'S A WEIRD THING ...
...TO CALL A DREAM.
WELL THAT'S WHAT IT IS.
NOT THAT I...
SHURU (SLIDE)
...REMEMBER A THING BEFORE THAT...
— EMILIA

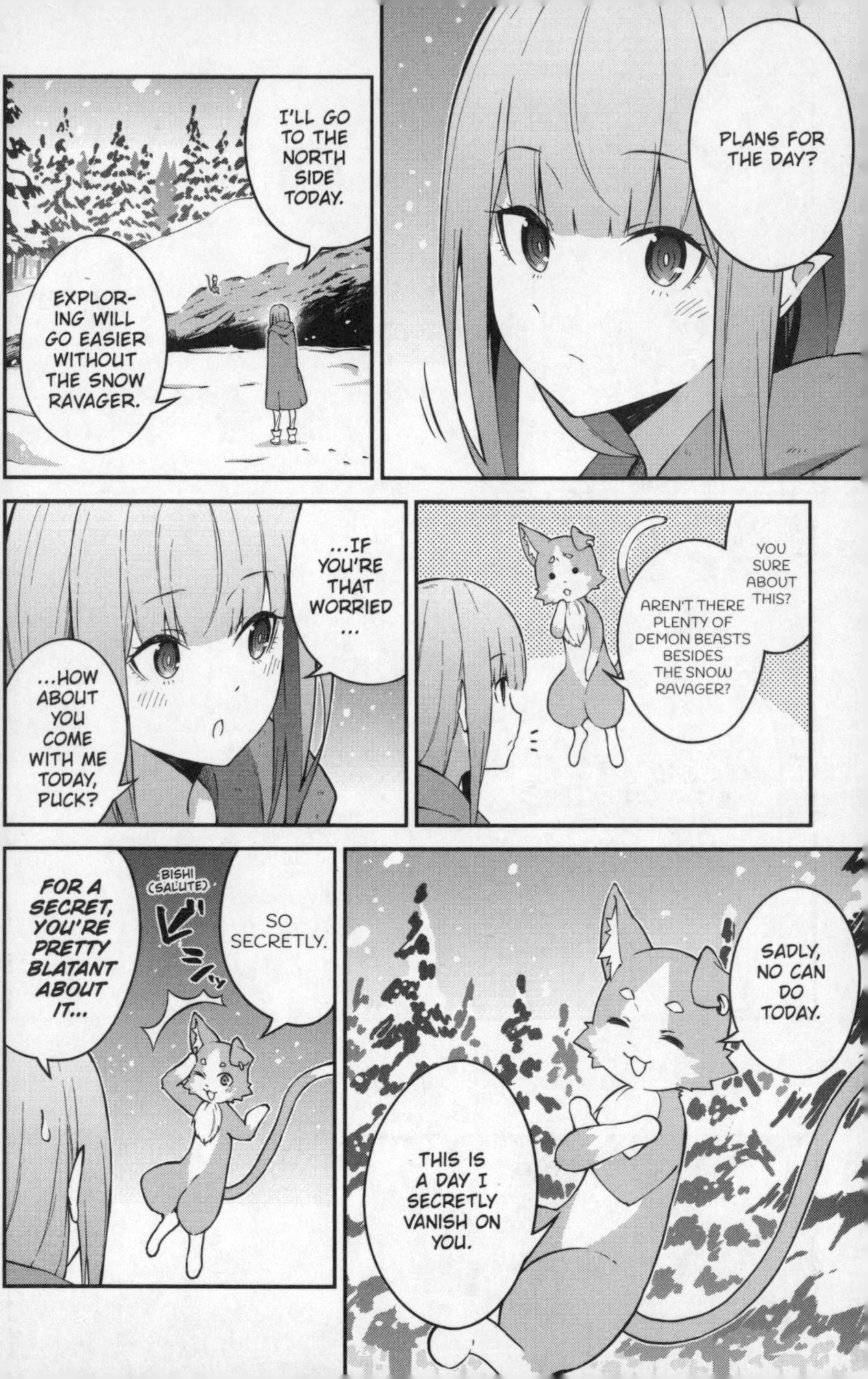
PLANS FOR THE DAY?
I'LL GO TO THE NORTH SIDE TODAY.
EXPLORING WILL GO EASIER WITHOUT THE SNOW RAVAGER.
YOU SURE ABOUT THIS?
AREN'T THERE PLENTY OF DEMON BEASTS BESIDES THE SNOW RAVAGER?
...IF YOU'RE THAT WORRIED...
...HOW ABOUT YOU COME WITH ME TODAY, PUCK?
SADLY, NO CAN DO TODAY.
THIS IS A DAY I SECRETLY VANISH ON YOU.
SO SECRETLY.
BISHI (SALUTE)
FOR A SECRET, YOU'RE PRETTY BLATANT ABOUT IT...

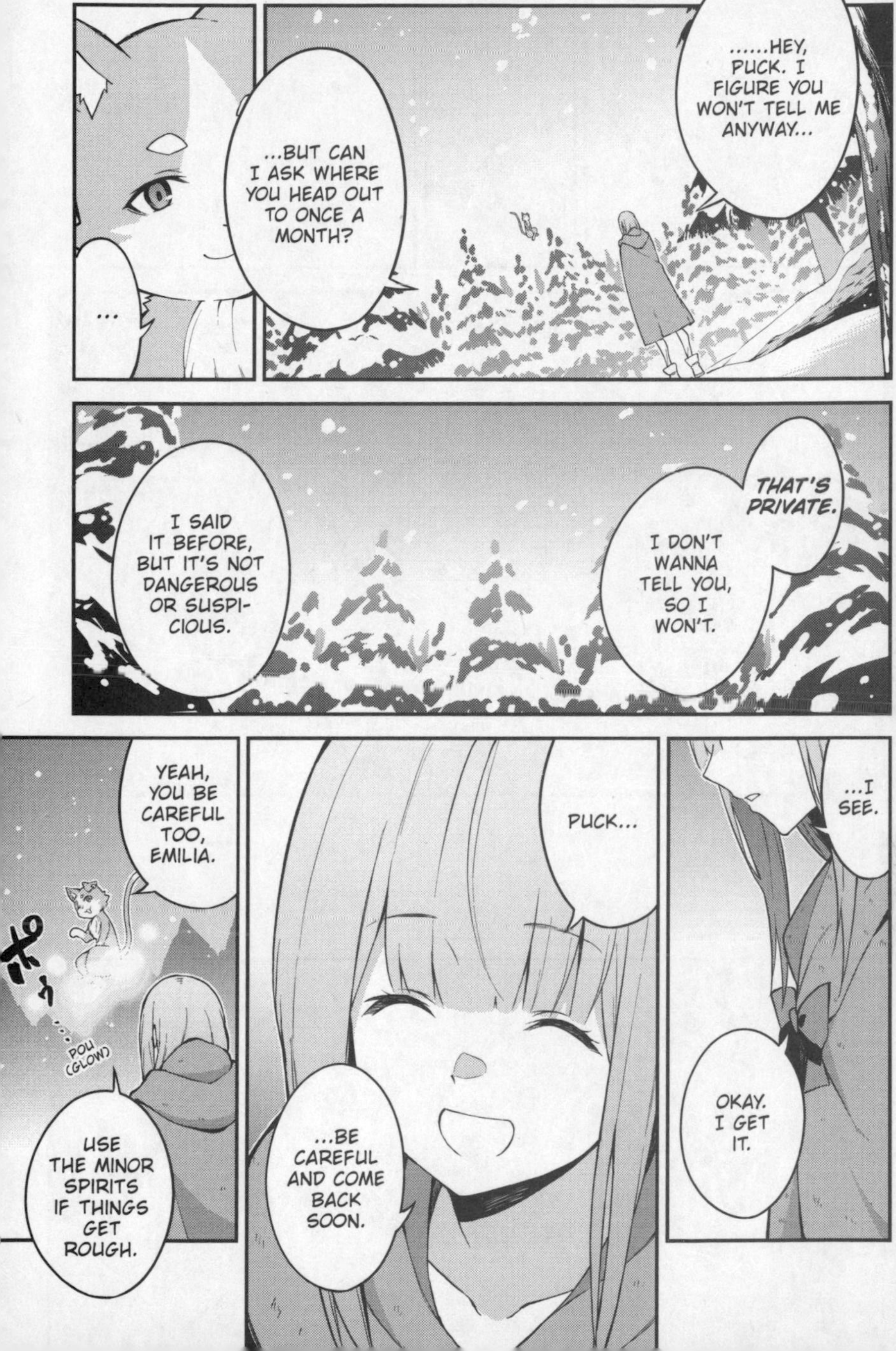
......HEY, PUCK. I FIGURE YOU WON'T TELL ME ANYWAY...
...BUT CAN I ASK WHERE YOU HEAD OUT TO ONCE A MONTH?
...
THAT'S PRIVATE.
I DON'T WANNA TELL YOU, SO I WON'T.
I SAID IT BEFORE, BUT IT'S NOT DANGEROUS OR SUSPI-CIOUS.
...I SEE.
OKAY. I GET IT.
PUCK...
...BE CAREFUL AND COME BACK SOON.
YEAH, YOU BE CAREFUL TOO, EMILIA.
ポゥ
POU (GLOW)
USE THE MINOR SPIRITS IF THINGS GET ROUGH.

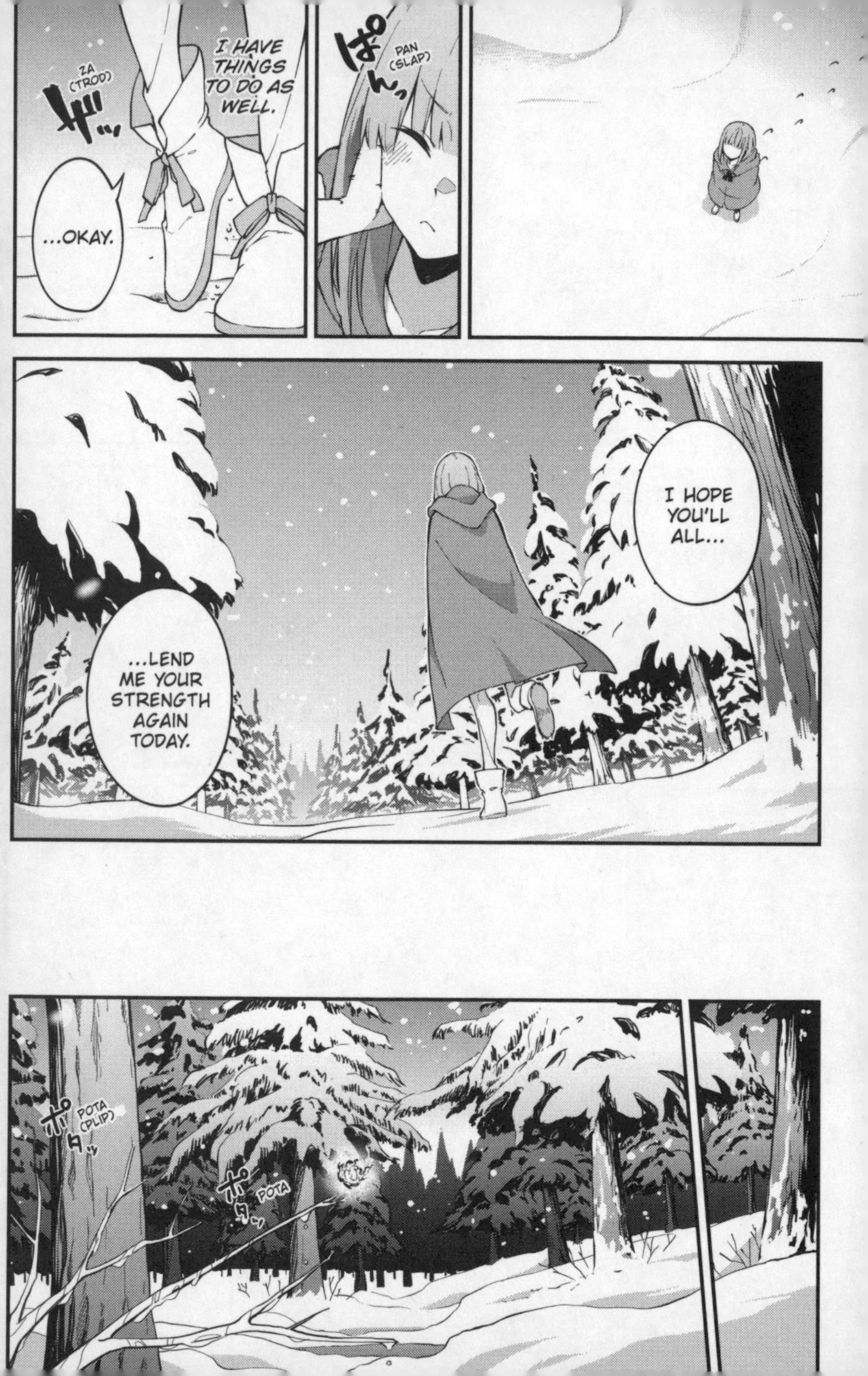
ぱんっ
PAN (SLAP)
I HAVE THINGS TO DO AS WELL.
ザッ
ZA (TROD)
...OKAY.
I HOPE YOU'LL ALL...
...LEND ME YOUR STRENGTH AGAIN TODAY.
ポタッ
POTA (PLIP)
ポタッ
POTA

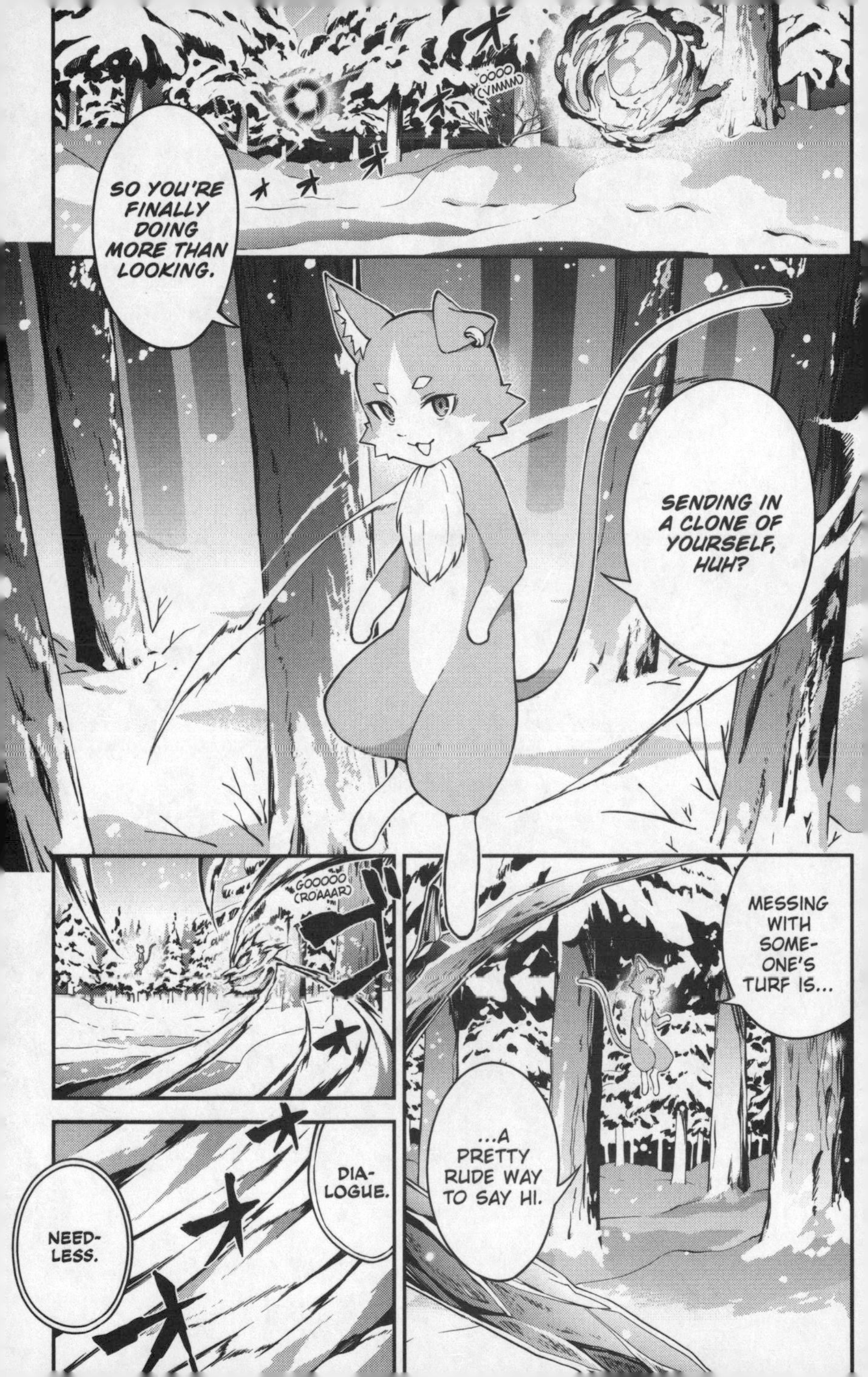
OOOO (VMMM)
SO YOU'RE FINALLY DOING MORE THAN LOOKING.
SENDING IN A CLONE OF YOURSELF, HUH?
MESSING WITH SOME-ONE'S TURF IS...
...A PRETTY RUDE WAY TO SAY HI.
GOOOOO (ROAAAR)
DIA-LOGUE.
NEED-LESS.

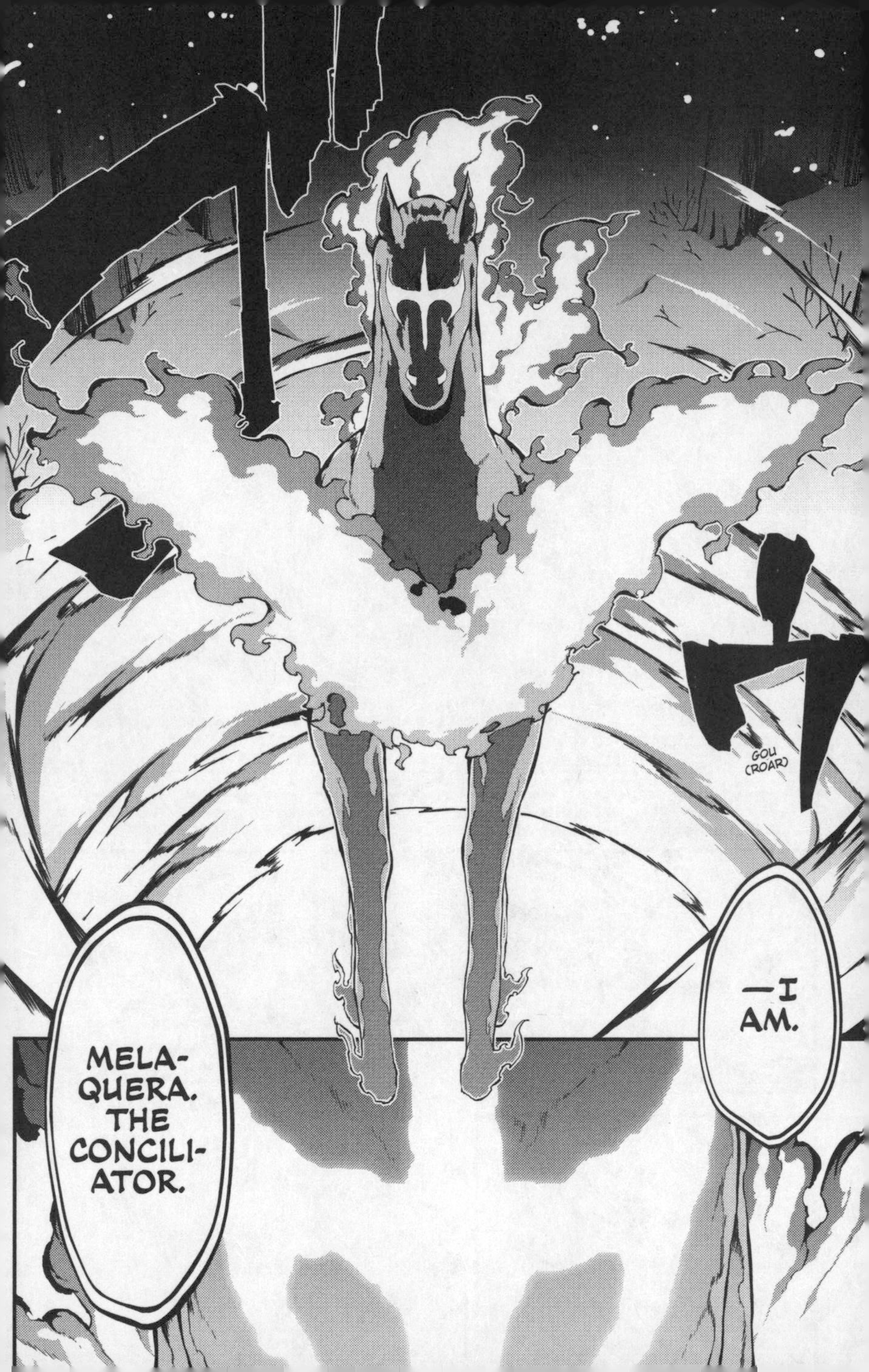
GOU (ROAR)
—I AM.
MELA-QUERA. THE CONCILI-ATOR.

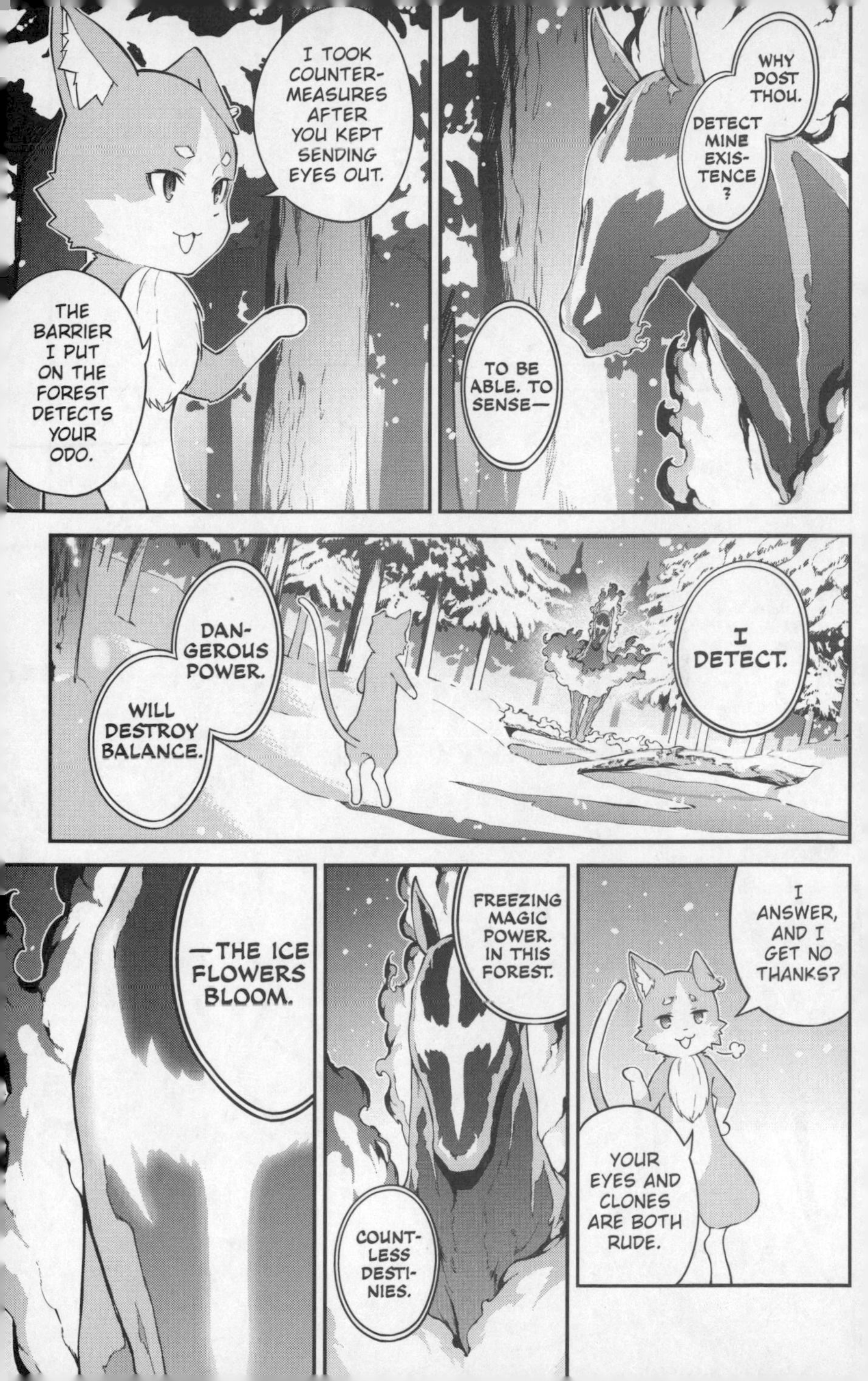
WHY DOST THOU.
DETECT MINE EXISTENCE?
TO BE ABLE. TO SENSE—
I TOOK COUNTERMEASURES AFTER YOU KEPT SENDING EYES OUT.
THE BARRIER I PUT ON THE FOREST DETECTS YOUR ODO.
I DETECT.
DANGEROUS POWER.
WILL DESTROY BALANCE.
I ANSWER, AND I GET NO THANKS?
YOUR EYES AND CLONES ARE BOTH RUDE.
FREEZING MAGIC POWER. IN THIS FOREST.
COUNTLESS DESTINIES.
—THE ICE FLOWERS BLOOM.

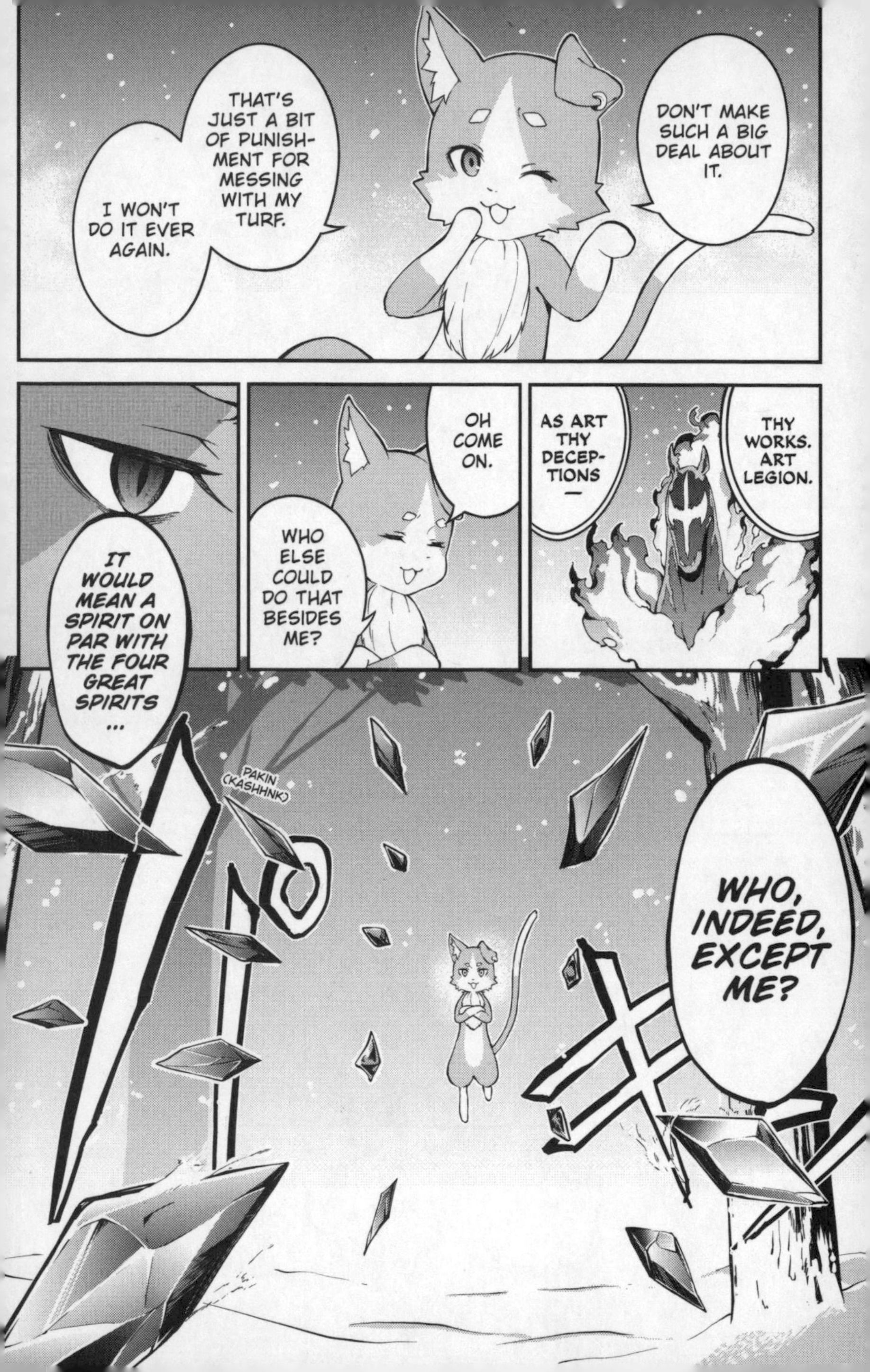

DON'T MAKE SUCH A BIG DEAL ABOUT IT.
THAT'S JUST A BIT OF PUNISH-MENT FOR MESSING WITH MY TURF.
I WON'T DO IT EVER AGAIN.
THY WORKS. ART LEGION.
AS ART THY DECEP-TIONS —
OH COME ON.
WHO ELSE COULD DO THAT BESIDES ME?
IT WOULD MEAN A SPIRIT ON PAR WITH THE FOUR GREAT SPIRITS ...
PAKIN (KASHHNK)
WHO, INDEED, EXCEPT ME?

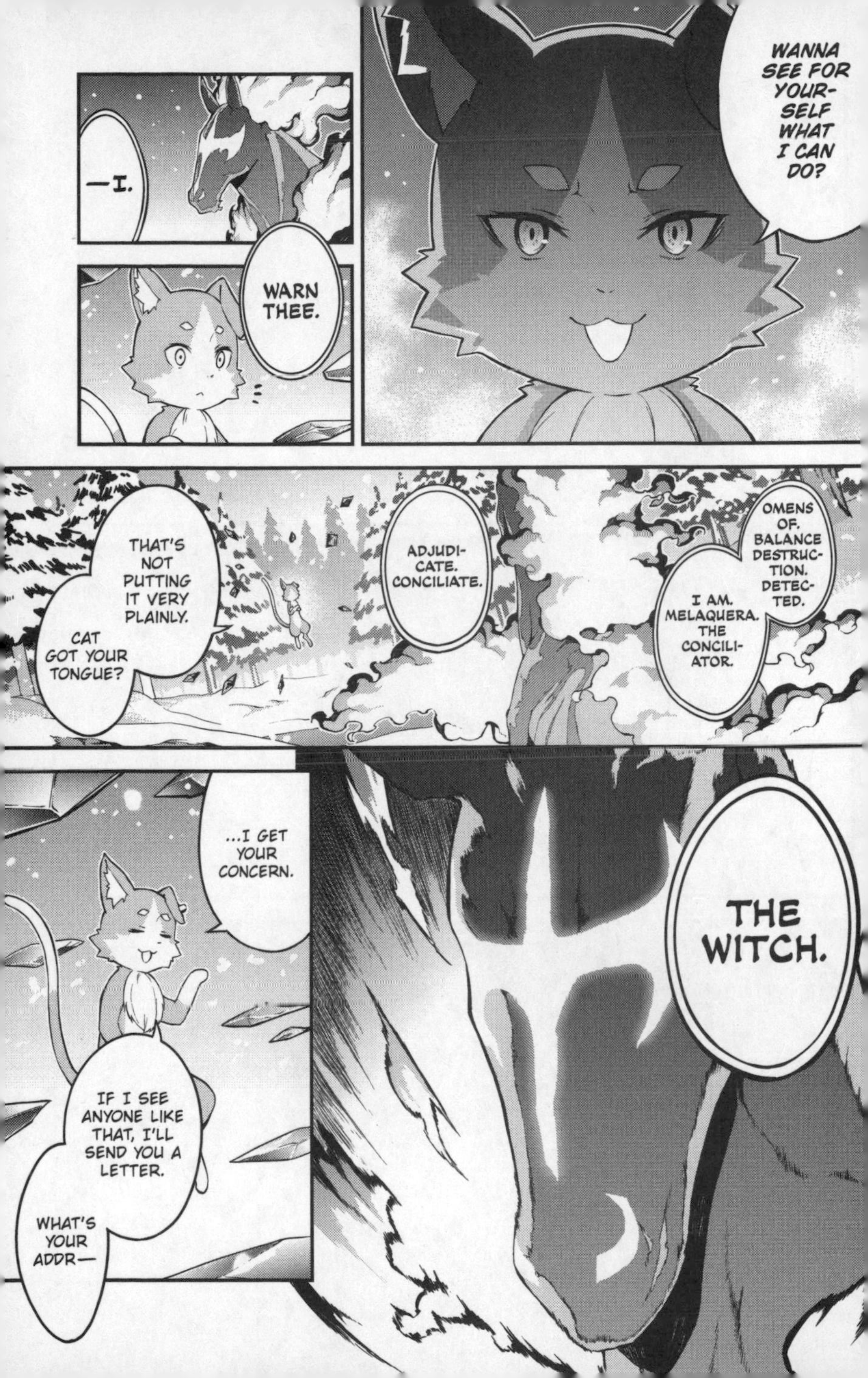
WANNA SEE FOR YOURSELF WHAT I CAN DO?
—I.
WARN THEE.
OMENS OF. BALANCE DESTRUCTION. DETECTED.
I AM. MELAQUERA. THE CONCILIATOR.
ADJUDICATE. CONCILIATE.
THAT'S NOT PUTTING IT VERY PLAINLY.
CAT GOT YOUR TONGUE?
THE WITCH.
...I GET YOUR CONCERN.
IF I SEE ANYONE LIKE THAT, I'LL SEND YOU A LETTER.
WHAT'S YOUR ADDR—

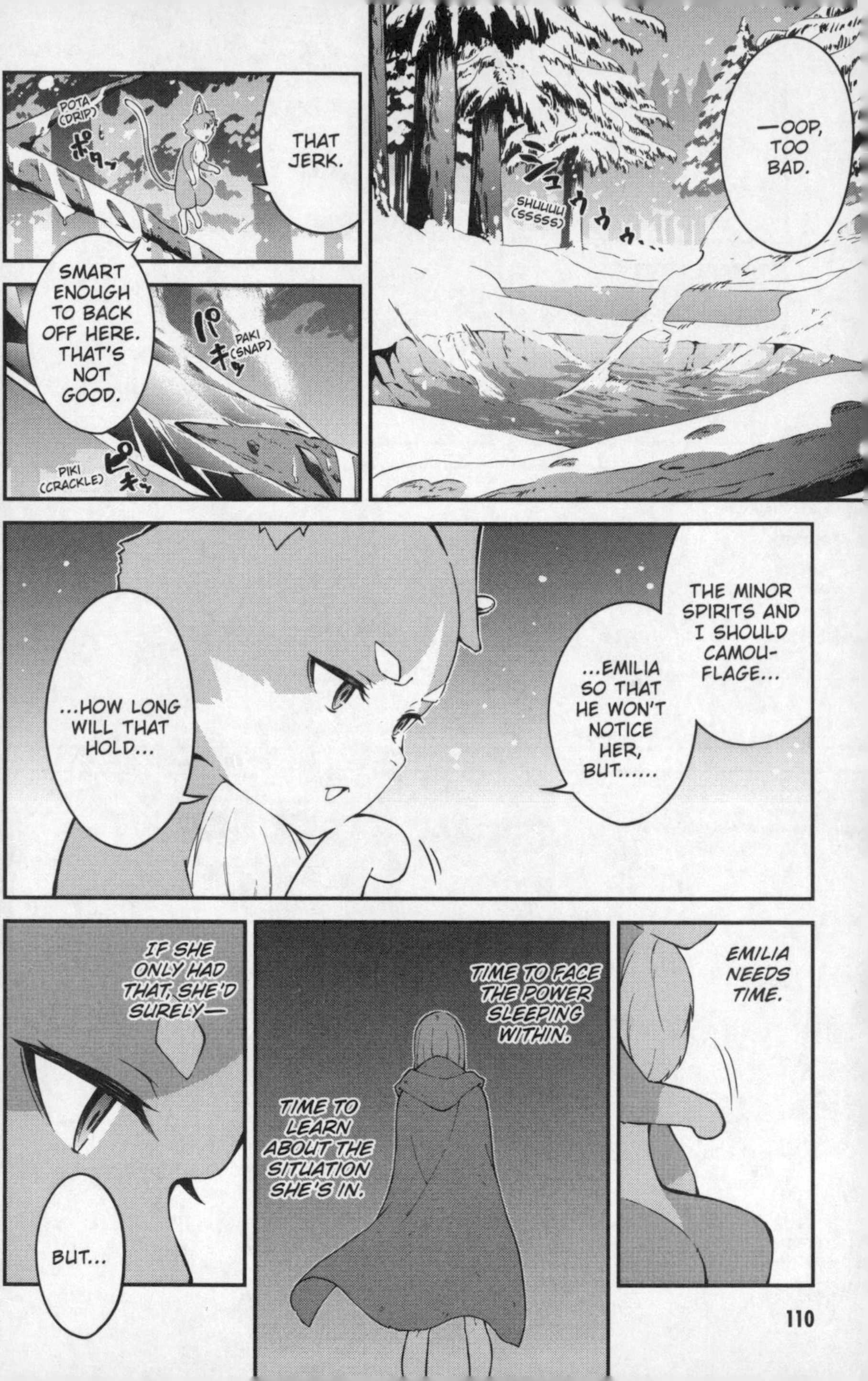
—OOP, TOO BAD.
SHUUUU (SSSSS)
POTA (DRIP)
THAT JERK.
SMART ENOUGH TO BACK OFF HERE. THAT'S NOT GOOD.
PAKI (SNAP)
PIKI (CRACKLE)
THE MINOR SPIRITS AND I SHOULD CAMOU-FLAGE...
...EMILIA SO THAT HE WON'T NOTICE HER, BUT......
...HOW LONG WILL THAT HOLD...
EMILIA NEEDS TIME.
TIME TO FACE THE POWER SLEEPING WITHIN.
TIME TO LEARN ABOUT THE SITUATION SHE'S IN.
IF SHE ONLY HAD THAT, SHE'D SURELY—
BUT...

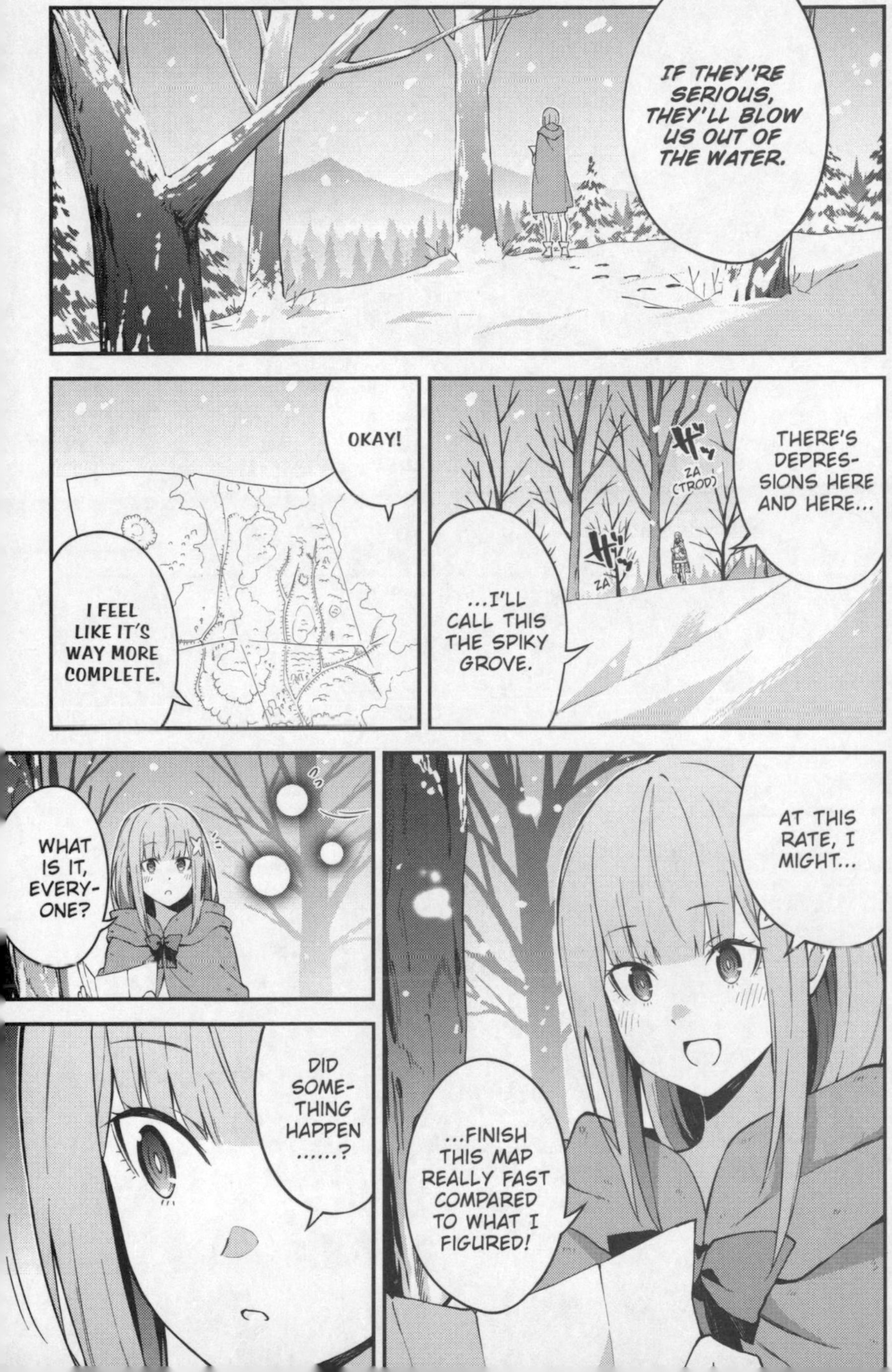
IF THEY'RE SERIOUS, THEY'LL BLOW US OUT OF THE WATER.
THERE'S DEPRES-SIONS HERE AND HERE...
ZA (TROD)
ZA
...I'LL CALL THIS THE SPIKY GROVE.
OKAY!
I FEEL LIKE IT'S WAY MORE COMPLETE.
AT THIS RATE, I MIGHT...
...FINISH THIS MAP REALLY FAST COMPARED TO WHAT I FIGURED!
WHAT IS IT, EVERY-ONE?
DID SOME-THING HAPPEN ......?

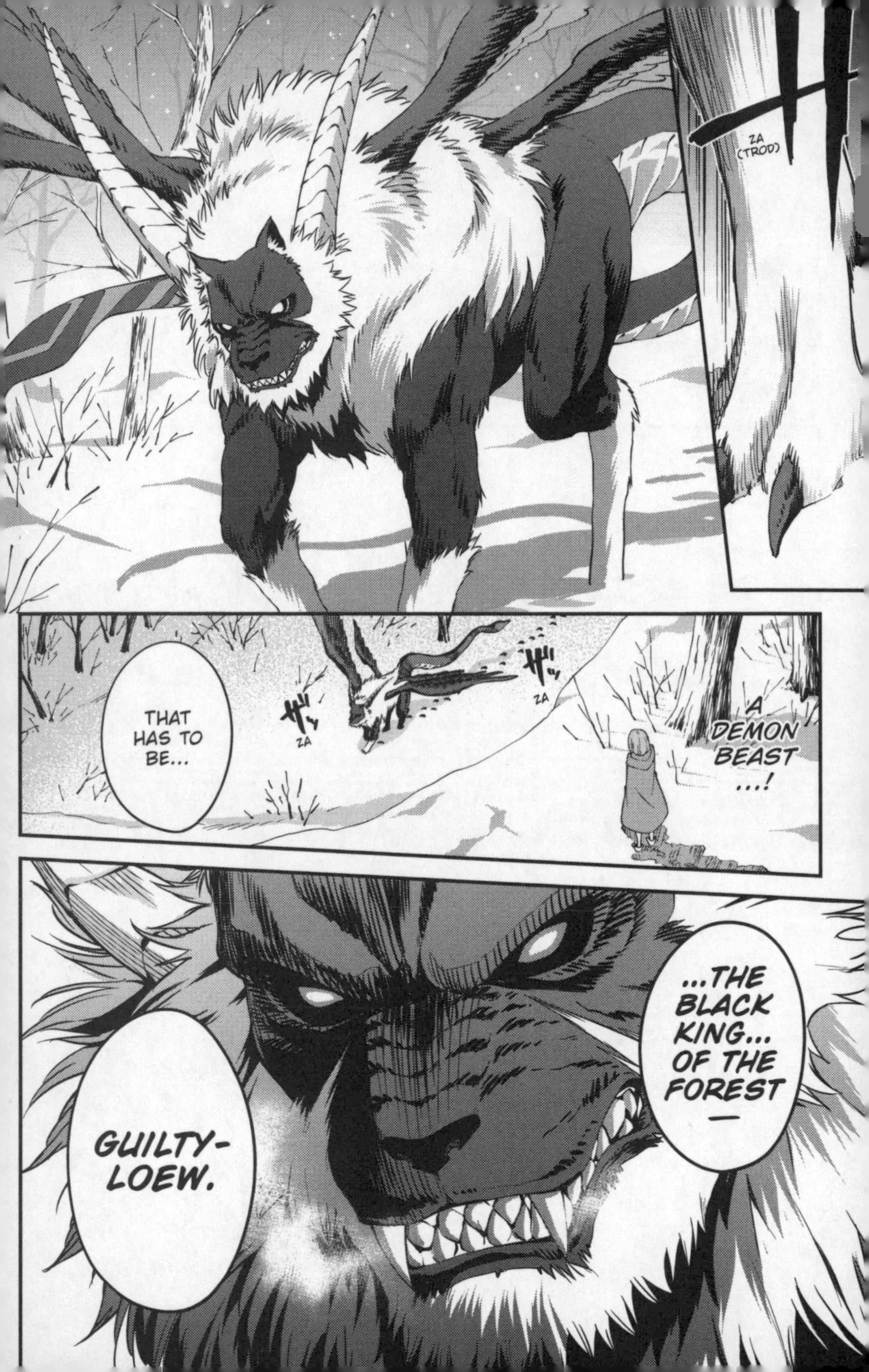
ZA (TROD)
A DEMON BEAST ...!
ザッ ZA
ザッ ZA
THAT HAS TO BE...
...THE BLACK KING... OF THE FOREST —
GUILTY-LOEW.

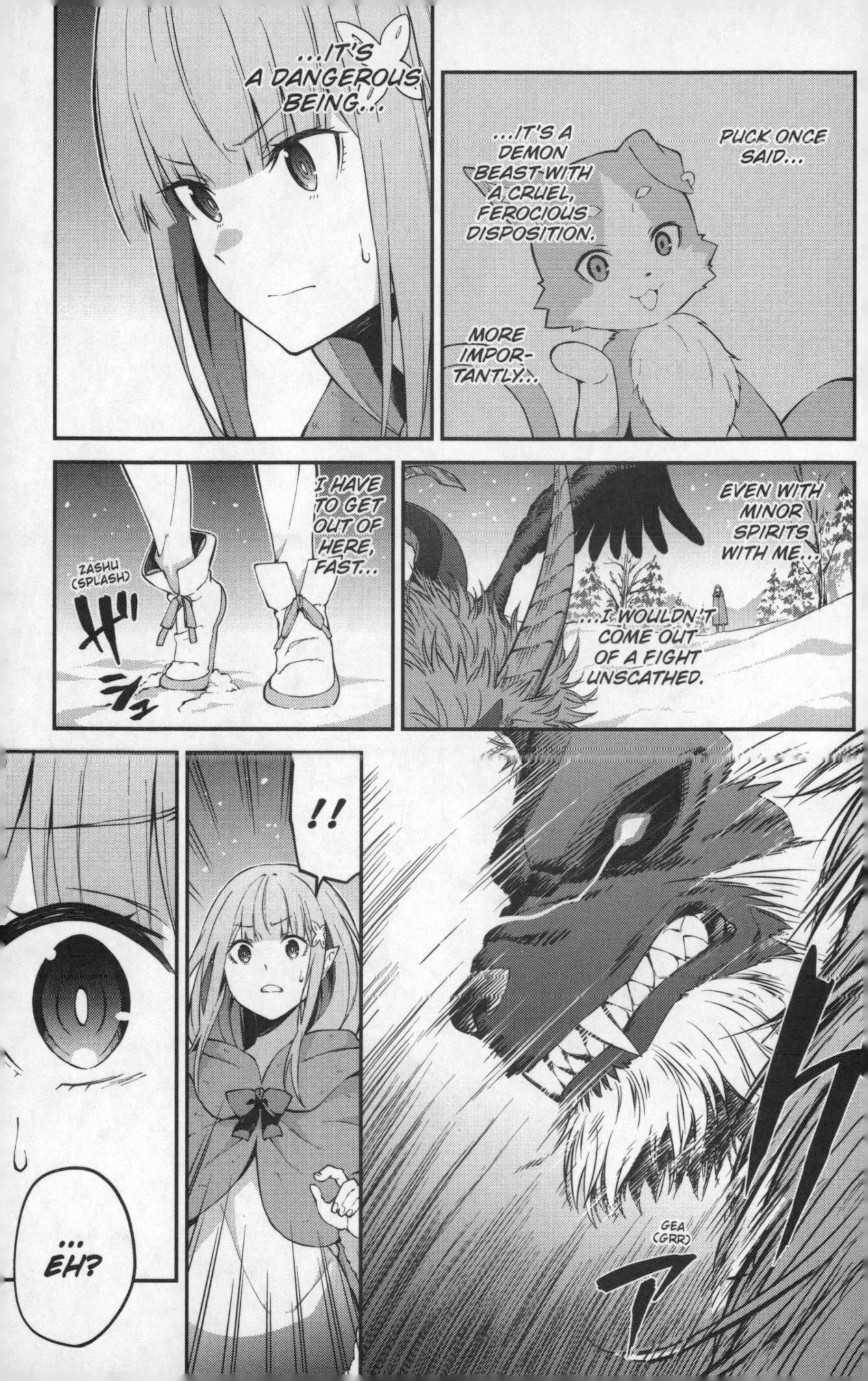
PUCK ONCE SAID...
...IT'S A DEMON BEAST WITH A CRUEL, FEROCIOUS DISPOSITION.
MORE IMPOR-TANTLY...
...IT'S A DANGEROUS BEING...
EVEN WITH MINOR SPIRITS WITH ME...
...I WOULDN'T COME OUT OF A FIGHT UNSCATHED.
I HAVE TO GET OUT OF HERE, FAST...
ZASHU (SPLASH)
GEA (GRR)
!!
...EH?

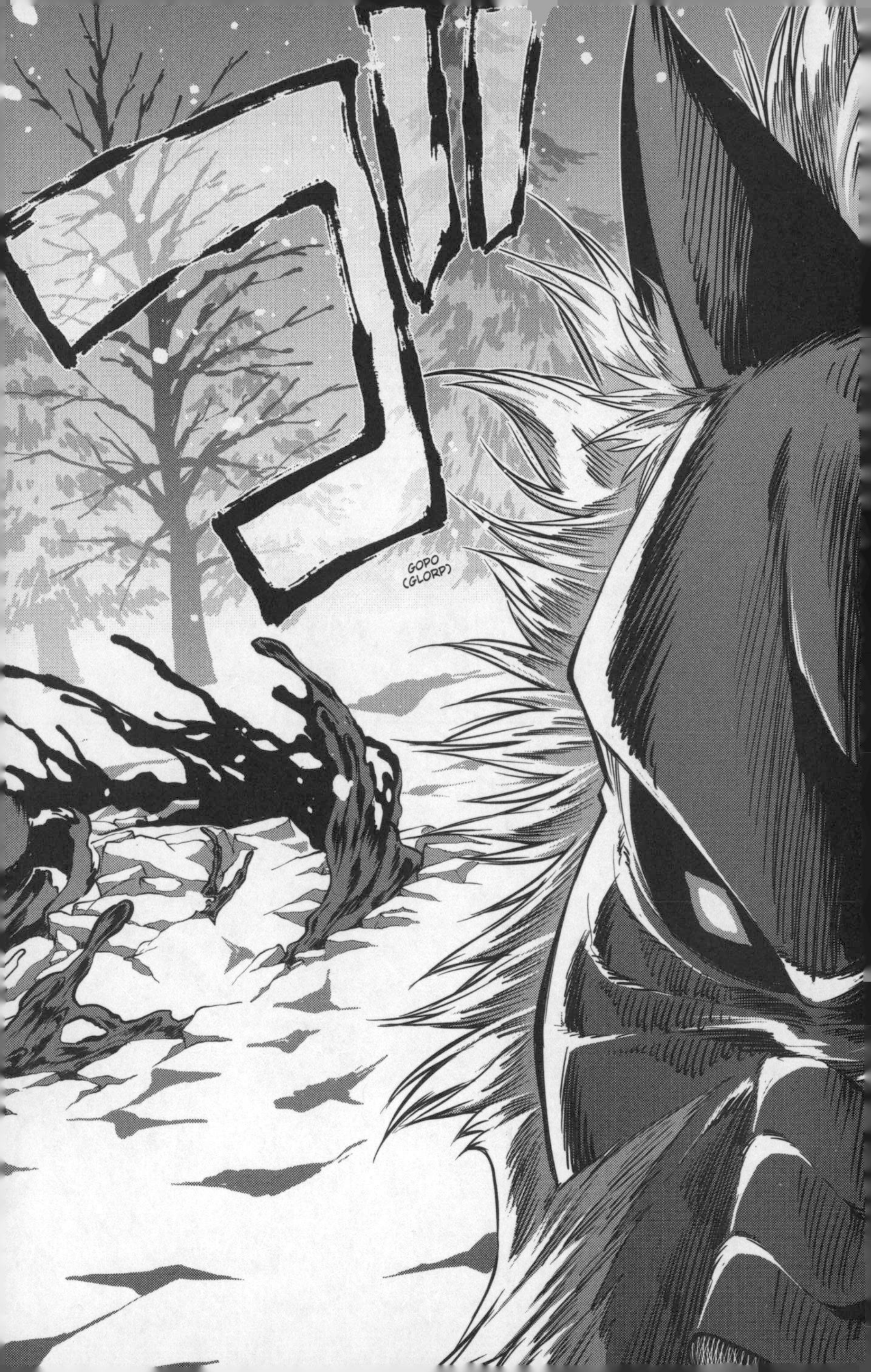
GOPO
(GLORP)

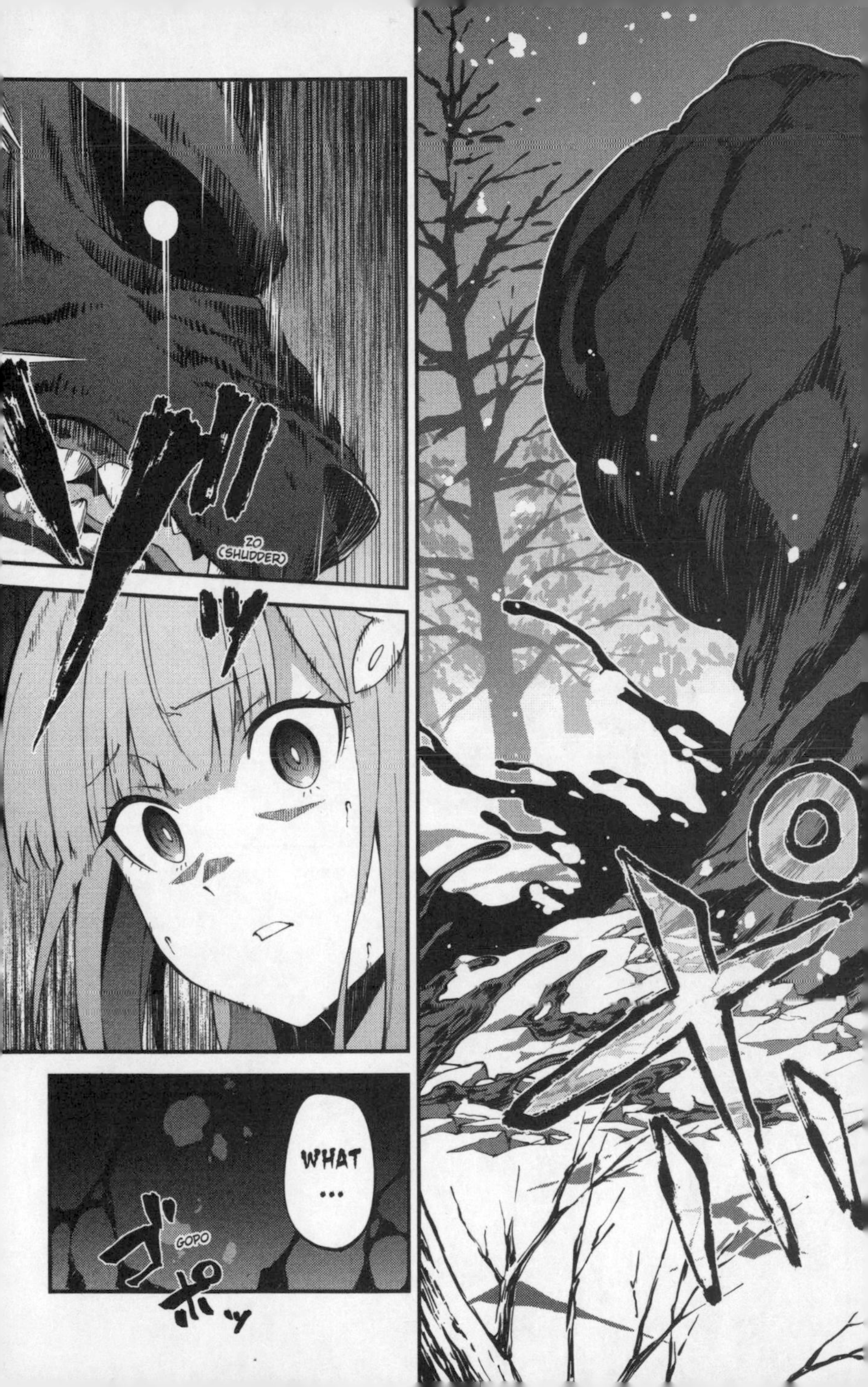
ZO
(SHUDDER)
WHAT ...
GOPO

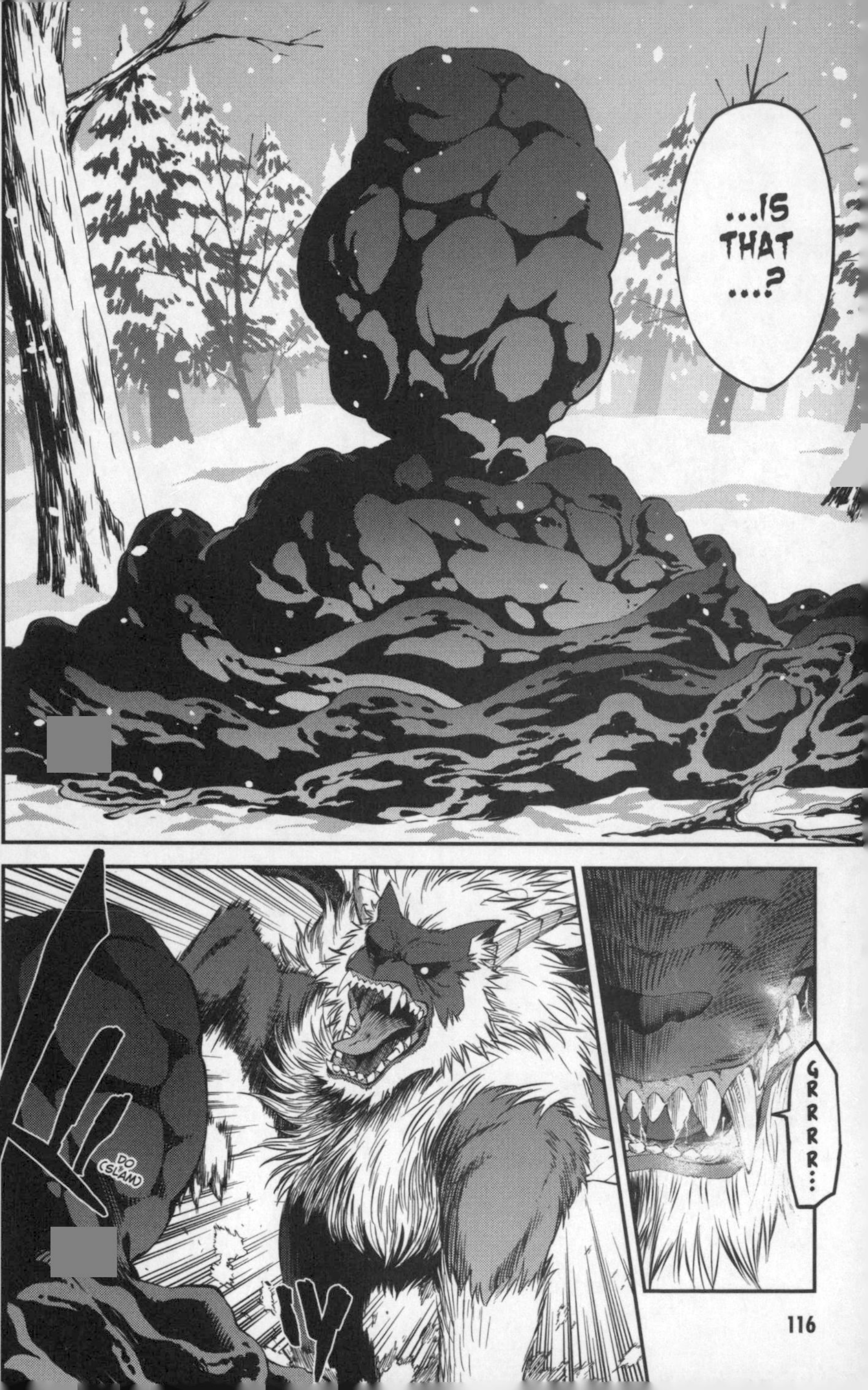
...IS THAT ...?
GRRRR...
DO (SLAM)

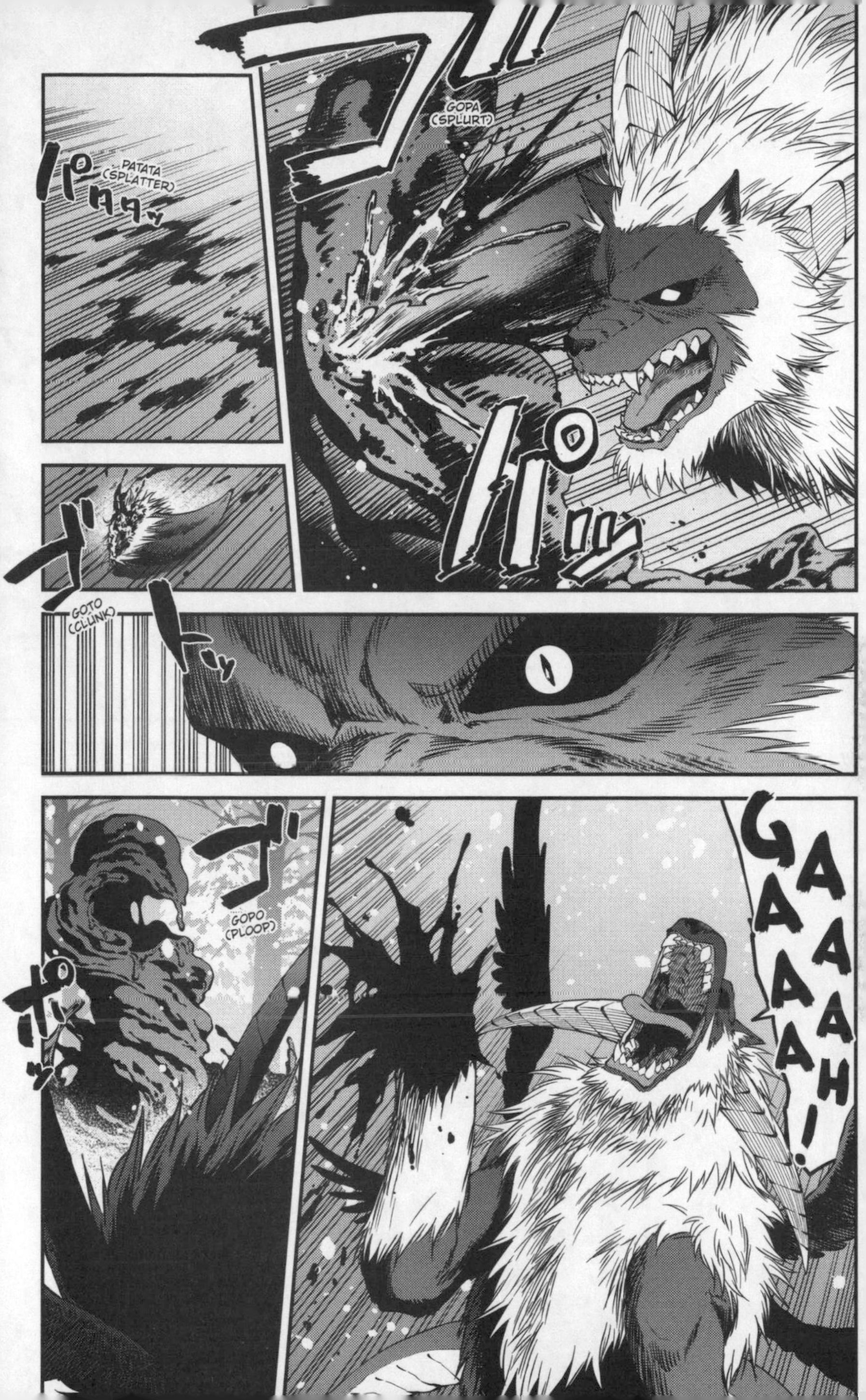
GOPA (SPLURT)
PATATA (SPLATTER)
GOTO (CLUNK)
GAAAAAH!!
GOPO (PLOOP)

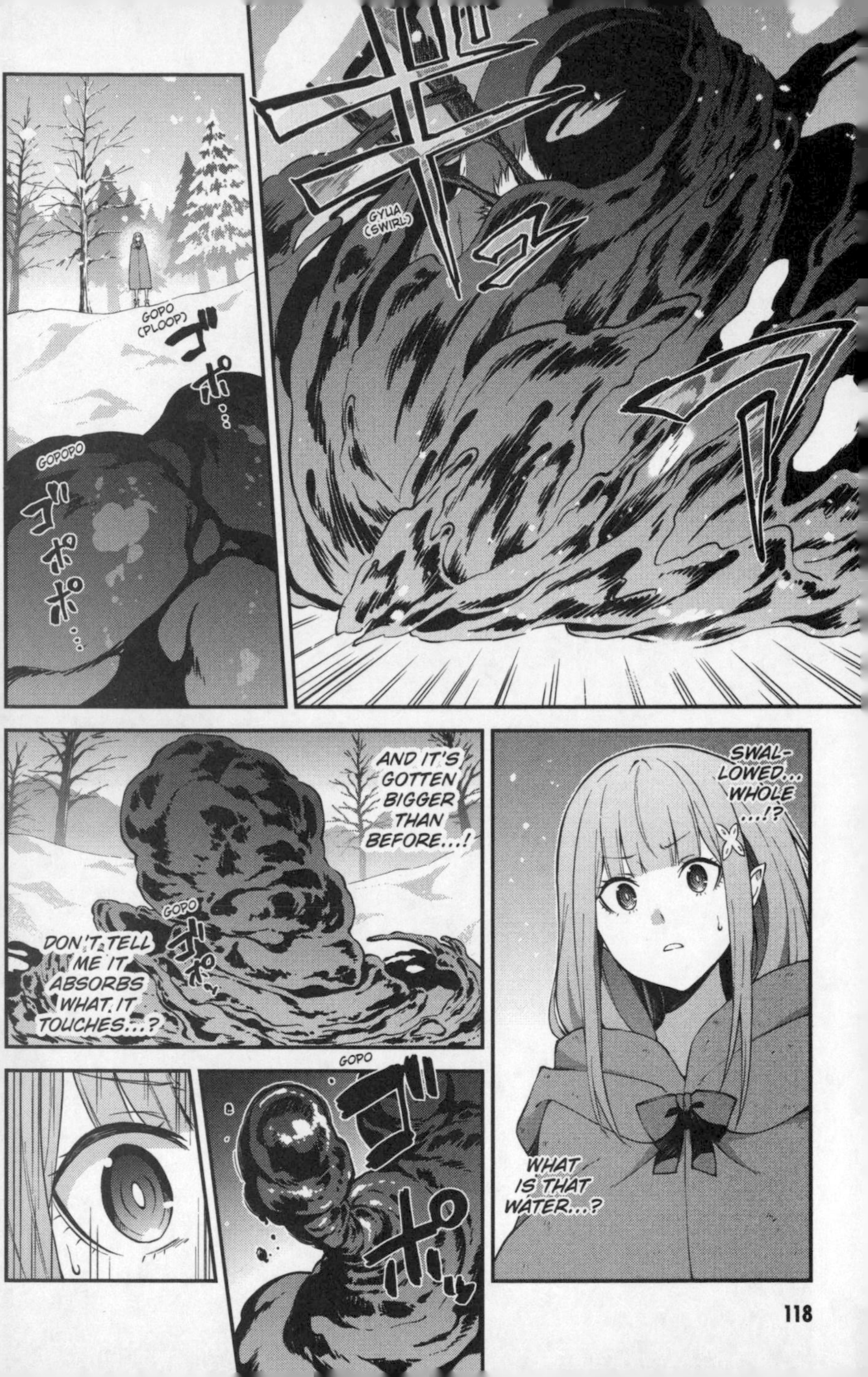
GYUA (SWIRL)
GOPO (PLOOP)
GOPOPO
SWAL-LOWED... WHOLE ...!?
WHAT IS THAT WATER...?
AND IT'S GOTTEN BIGGER THAN BEFORE...!
GOPO
DON'T TELL ME IT ABSORBS WHAT IT TOUCHES...?
GOPO

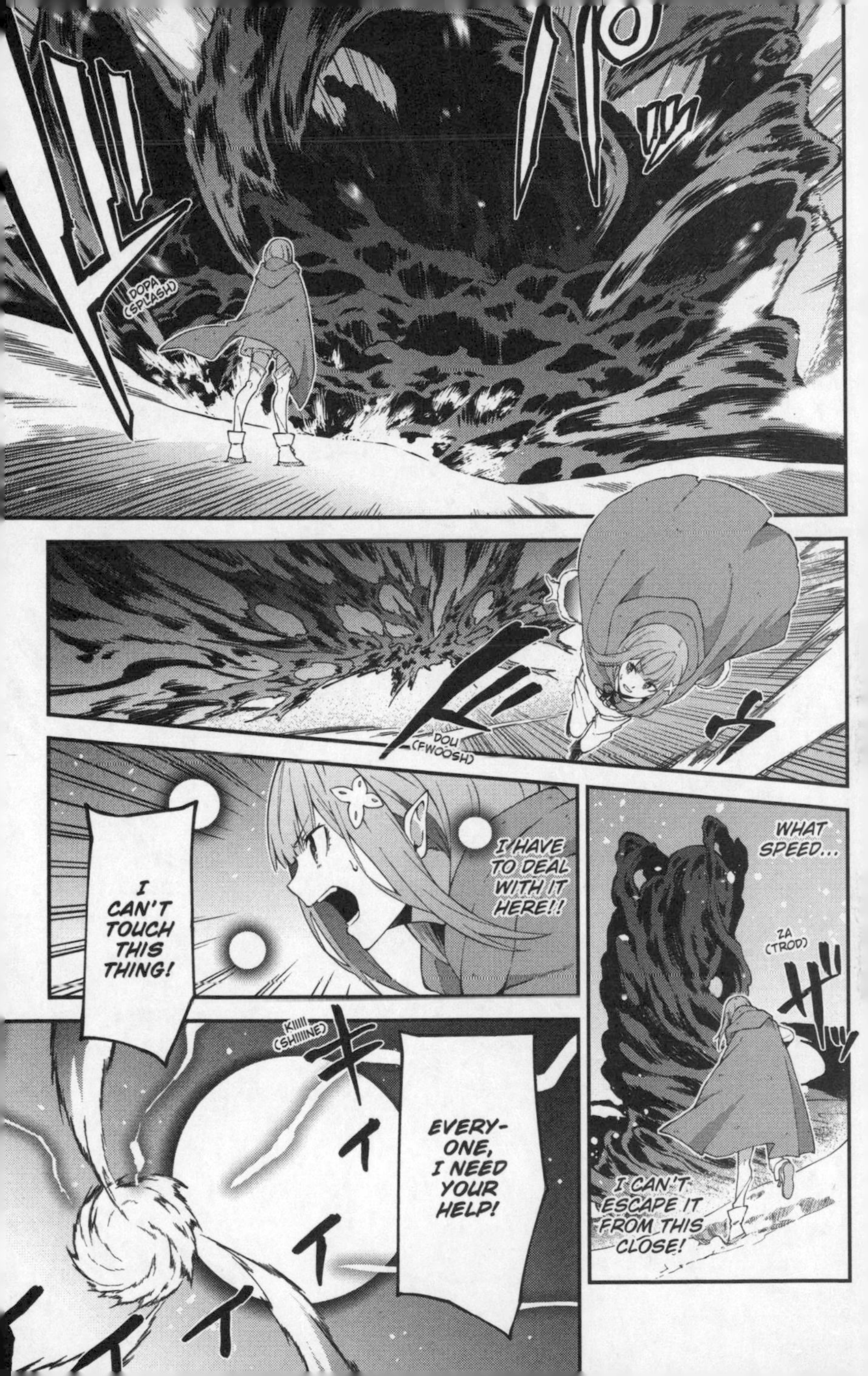
DOPA (SPLASH)
DOU (FWOOSH)
WHAT SPEED...
ZA (TROD)
I CAN'T ESCAPE IT FROM THIS CLOSE!
I HAVE TO DEAL WITH IT HERE!!
I CAN'T TOUCH THIS THING!
KIIIII (SHIIIINE)
EVERY-ONE, I NEED YOUR HELP!

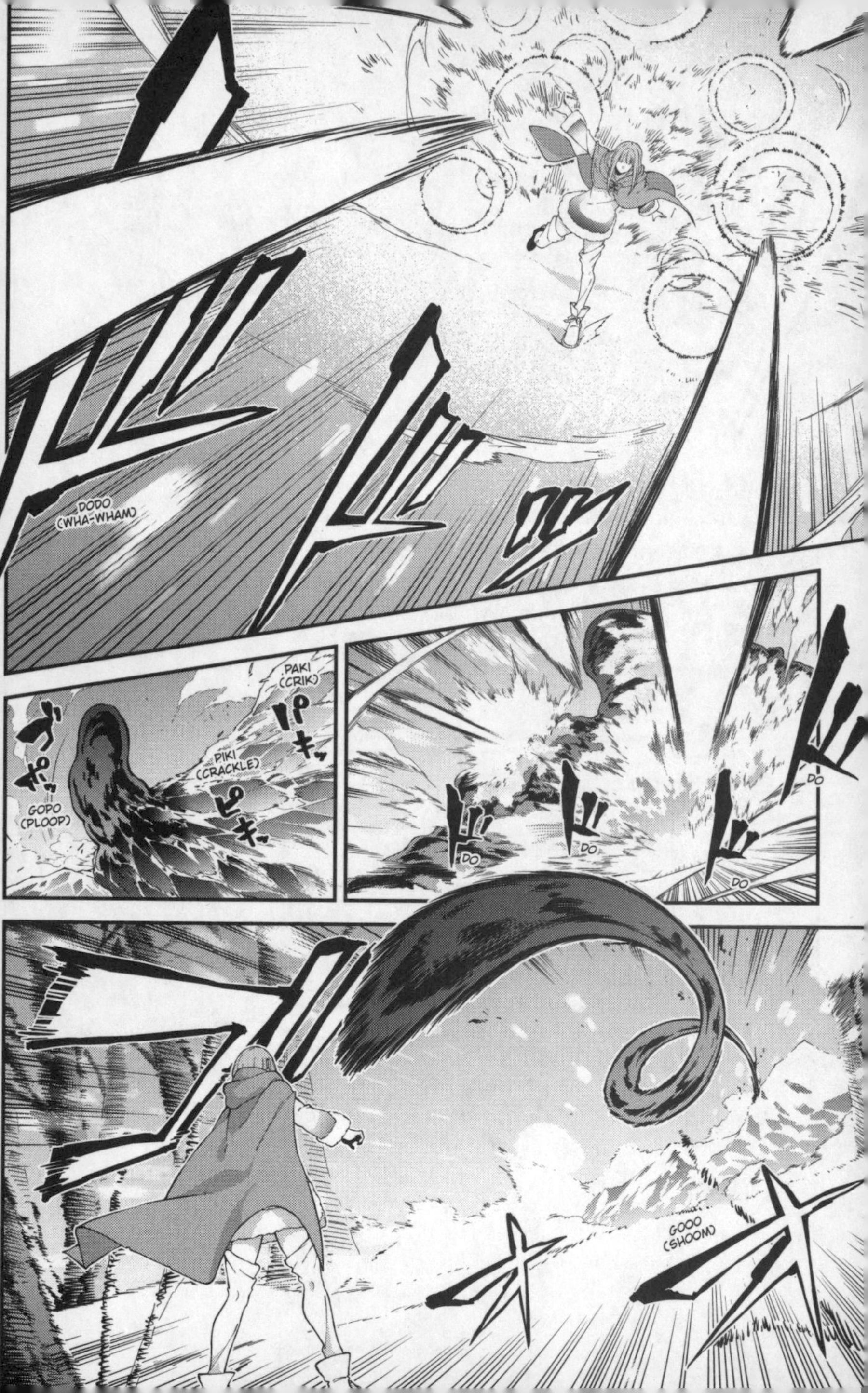
DODO
(WHA-WHAM)
DO
DO
DO
DO
PAKI
(CRIK)
PIKI
(CRACKLE)
GOPO
(PLOOP)
GOOO
(SHOOM)

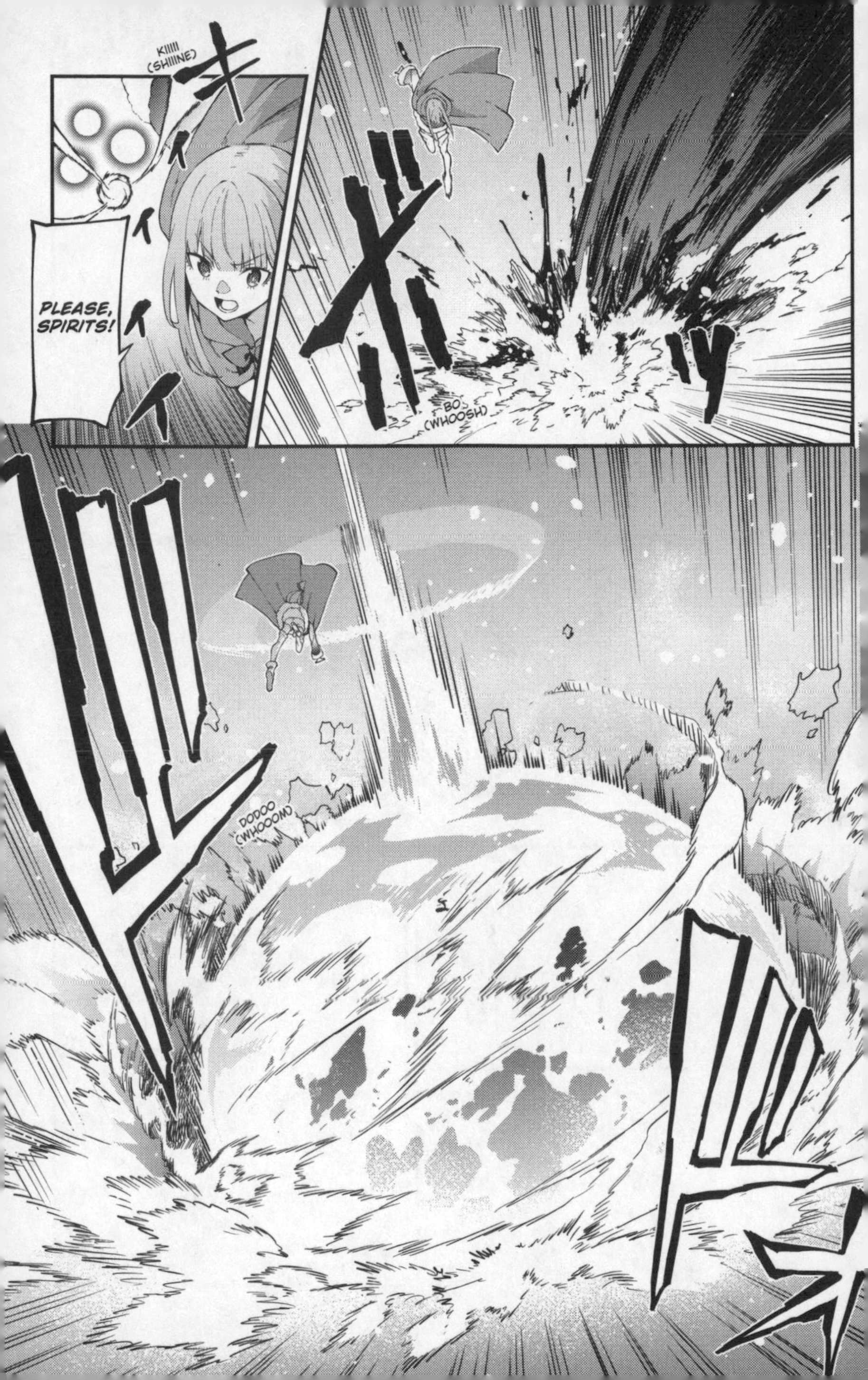
BO
(WHOOSH)
KIIIII
(SHIIINE)
PLEASE, SPIRITS!
DODOO
(WHOOOM)

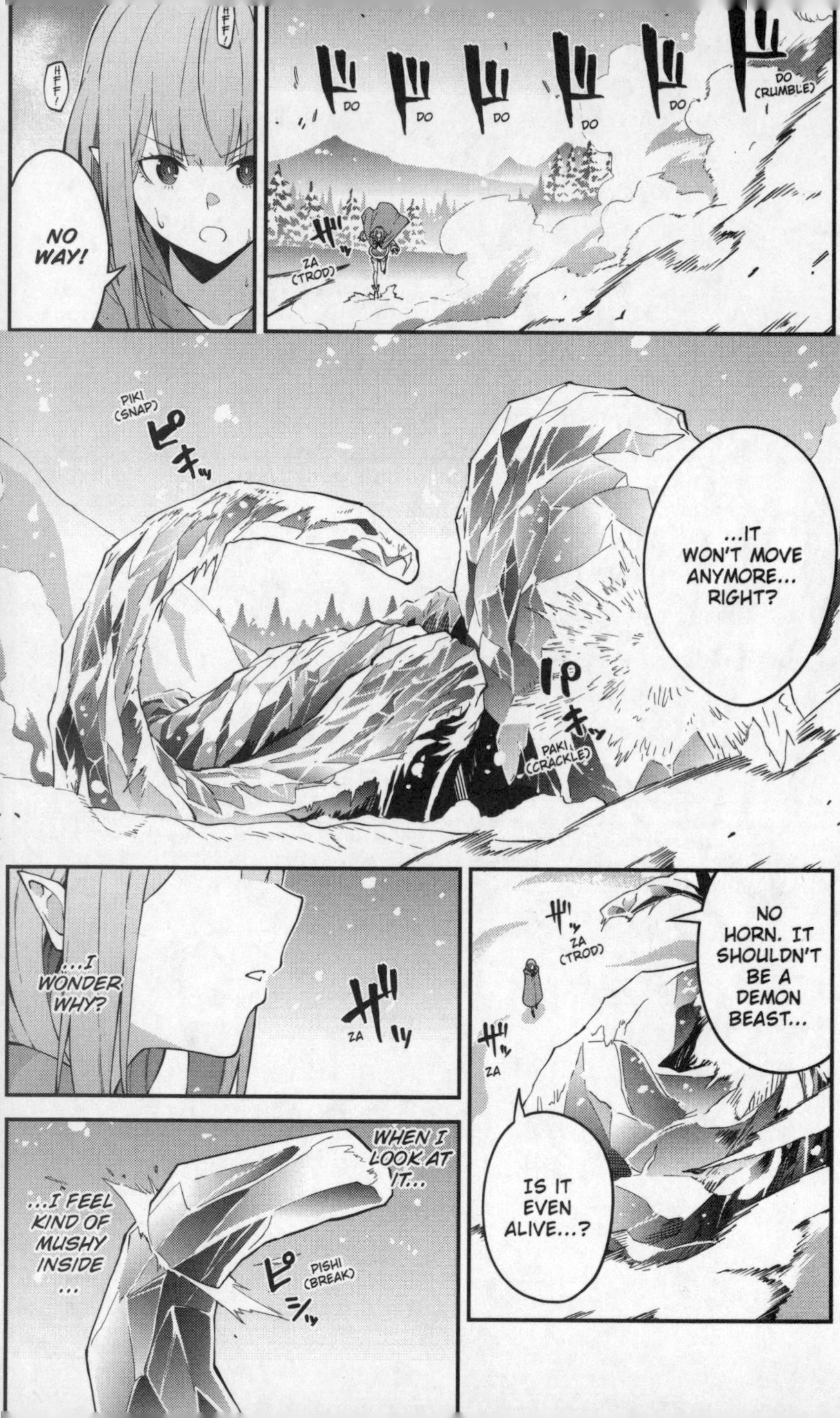
DO
DO
DO
DO
DO
DO (RUMBLE)
ZA (TROD)
HFF!
HFF!
NO WAY!
...IT WON'T MOVE ANYMORE... RIGHT?
PIKI (SNAP)
PAKI (CRACKLE)
ZA (TROD)
NO HORN. IT SHOULDN'T BE A DEMON BEAST...
ZA
IS IT EVEN ALIVE...?
...I WONDER WHY?
ZA
WHEN I LOOK AT IT...
...I FEEL KIND OF MUSHY INSIDE...
PISHI (BREAK)

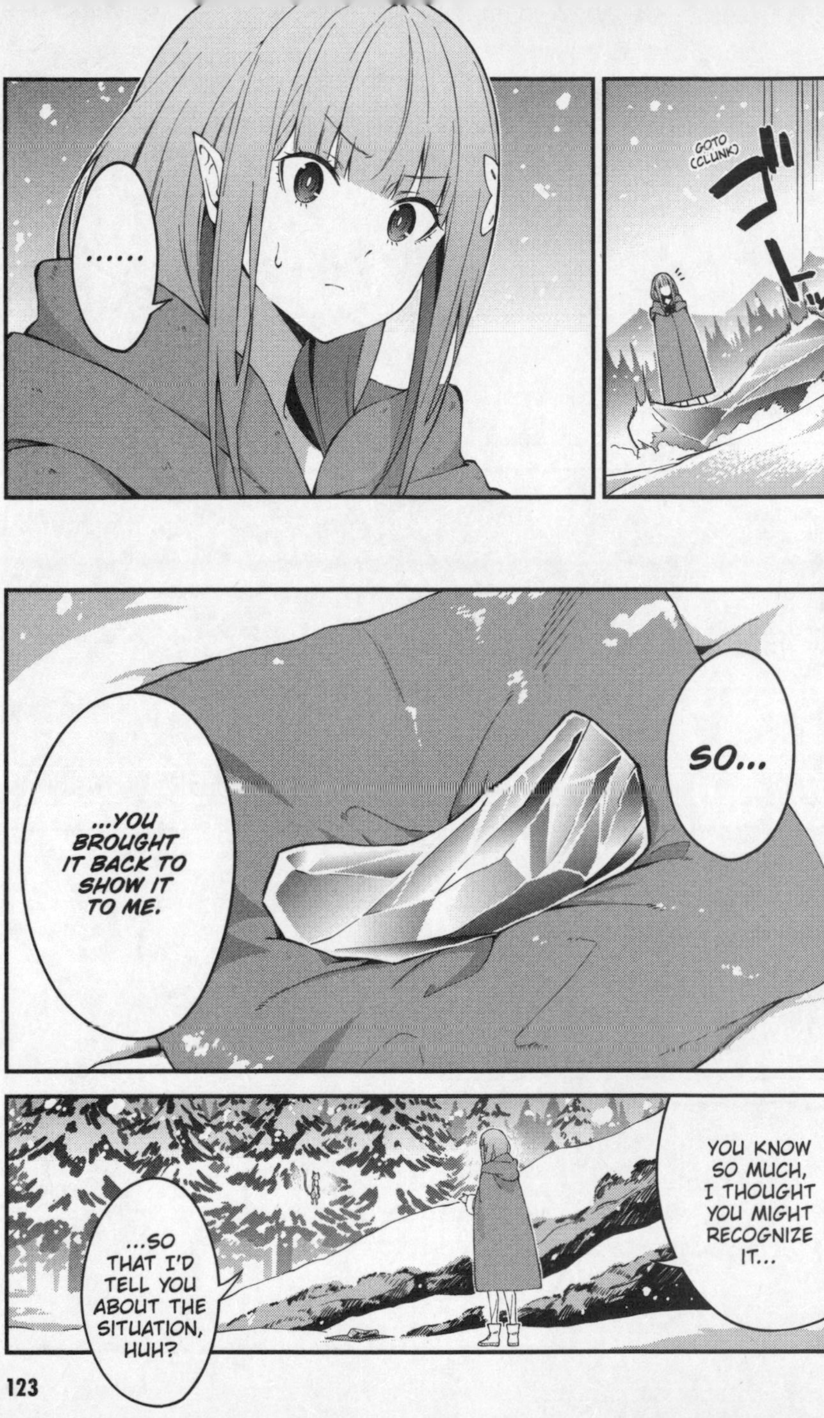
GOTO (CLUNK)
ゴトッ
......
SO...
...YOU BROUGHT IT BACK TO SHOW IT TO ME.
YOU KNOW SO MUCH, I THOUGHT YOU MIGHT RECOGNIZE IT...
...SO THAT I'D TELL YOU ABOUT THE SITUATION, HUH?

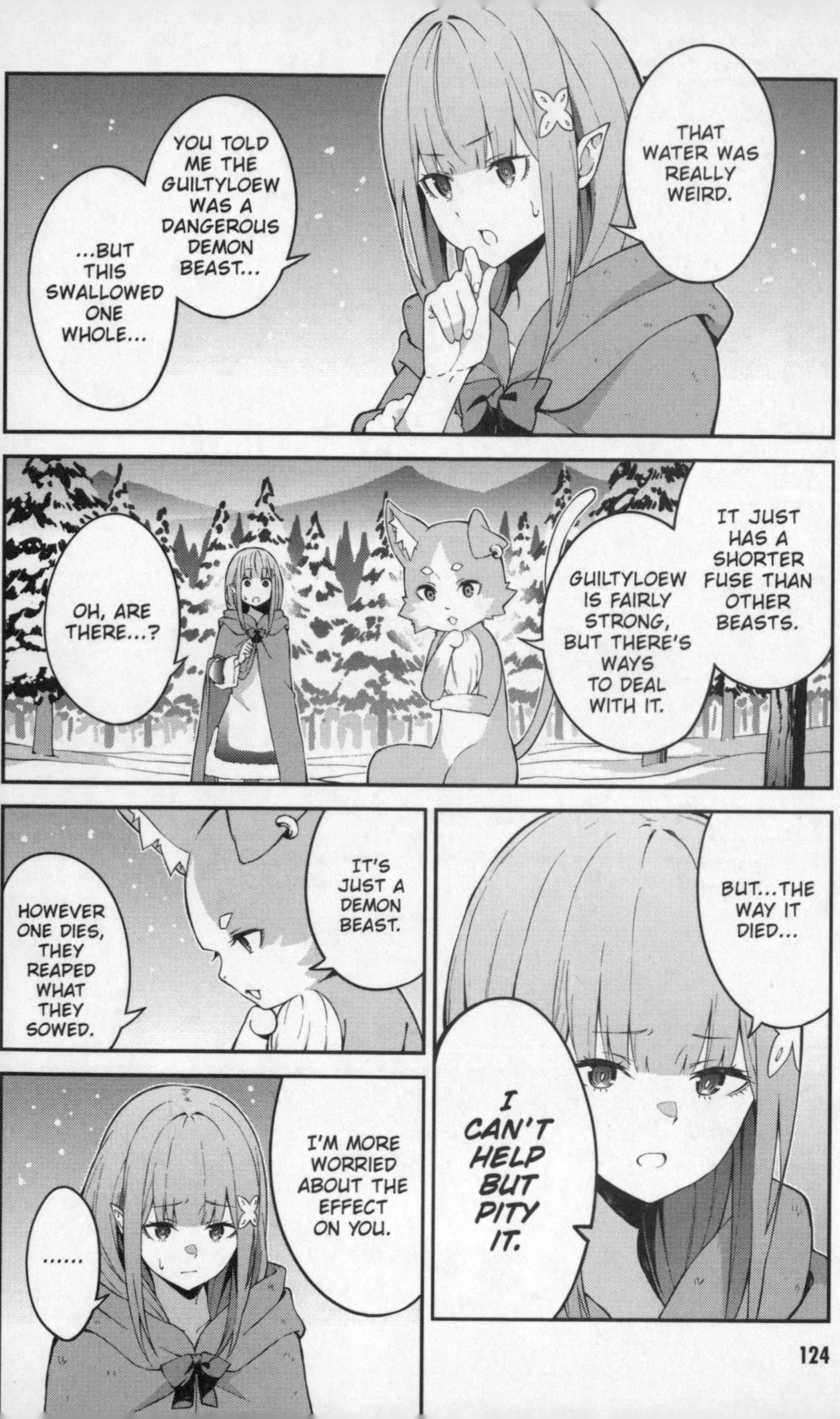
THAT WATER WAS REALLY WEIRD.
YOU TOLD ME THE GUILTYLOEW WAS A DANGEROUS DEMON BEAST...
...BUT THIS SWALLOWED ONE WHOLE...
IT JUST HAS A SHORTER FUSE THAN OTHER BEASTS.
GUILTYLOEW IS FAIRLY STRONG, BUT THERE'S WAYS TO DEAL WITH IT.
OH, ARE THERE...?
BUT...THE WAY IT DIED...
I CAN'T HELP BUT PITY IT.
IT'S JUST A DEMON BEAST.
HOWEVER ONE DIES, THEY REAPED WHAT THEY SOWED.
I'M MORE WORRIED ABOUT THE EFFECT ON YOU.
......

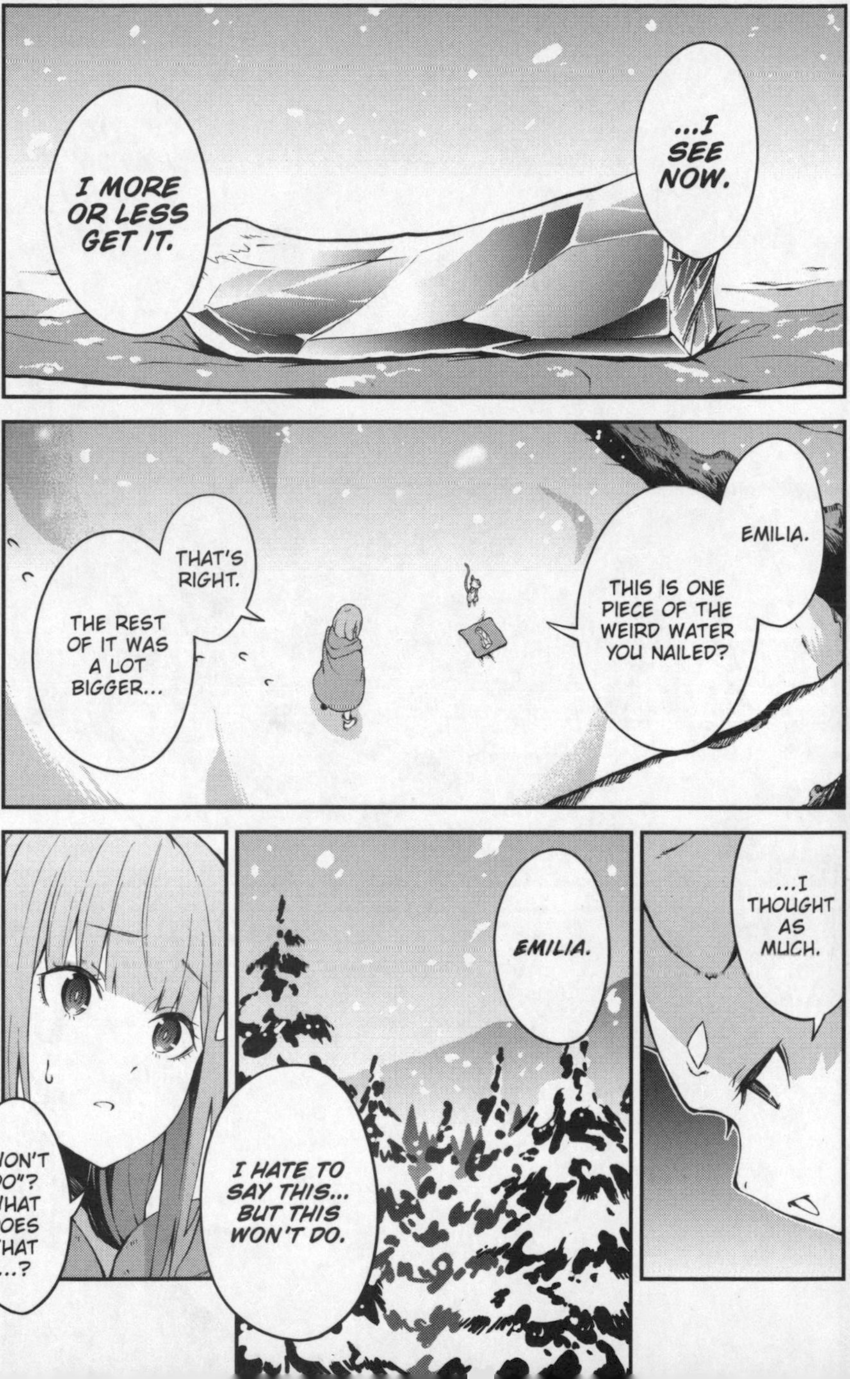
...I SEE NOW.
I MORE OR LESS GET IT.
EMILIA.
THIS IS ONE PIECE OF THE WEIRD WATER YOU NAILED?
THAT'S RIGHT.
THE REST OF IT WAS A LOT BIGGER...
...I THOUGHT AS MUCH.
EMILIA.
I HATE TO SAY THIS... BUT THIS WON'T DO.
"WON'T DO"? WHAT DOES THAT ...?

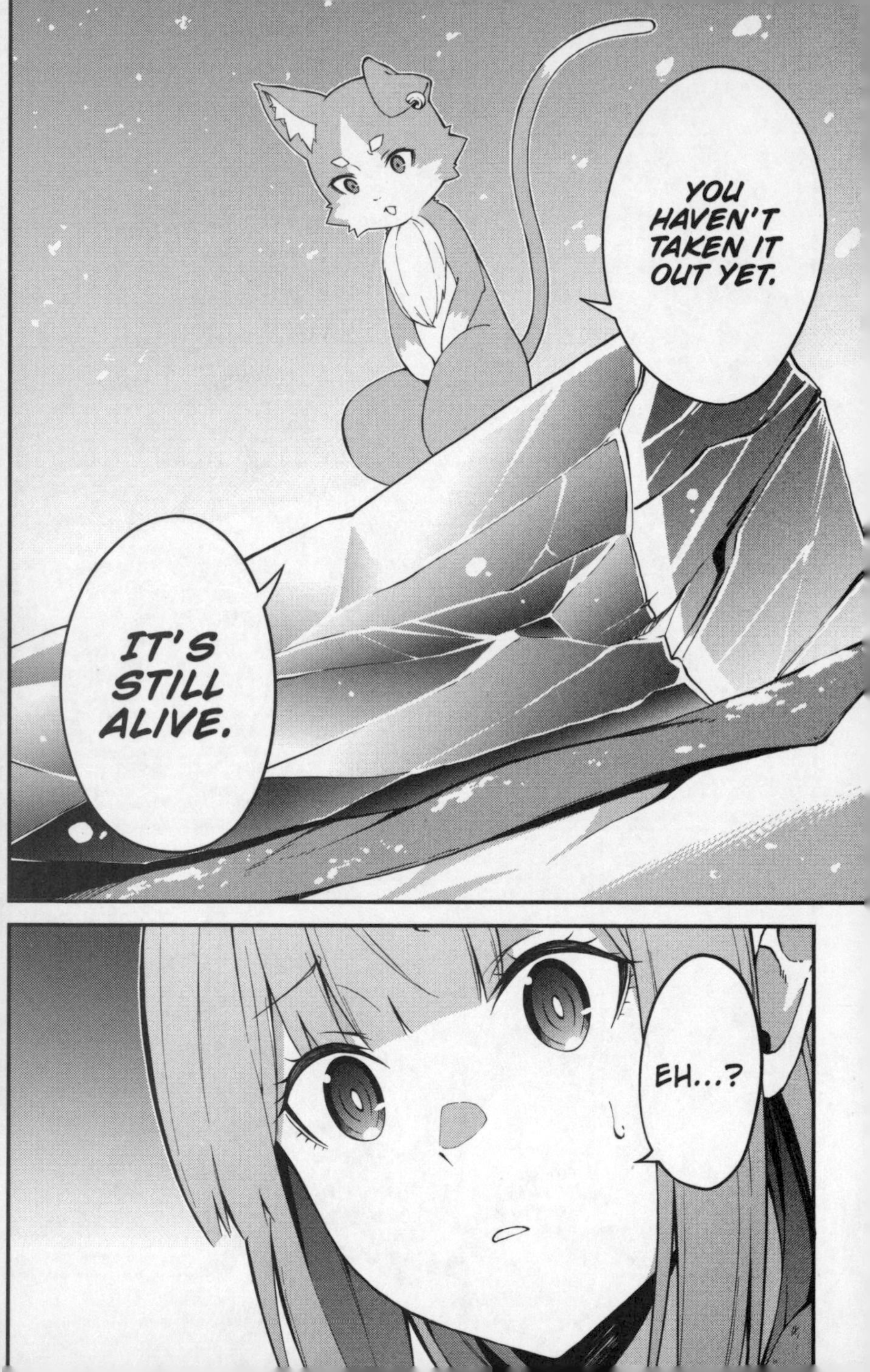
YOU HAVEN'T TAKEN IT OUT YET.
IT'S STILL ALIVE.
EH...?

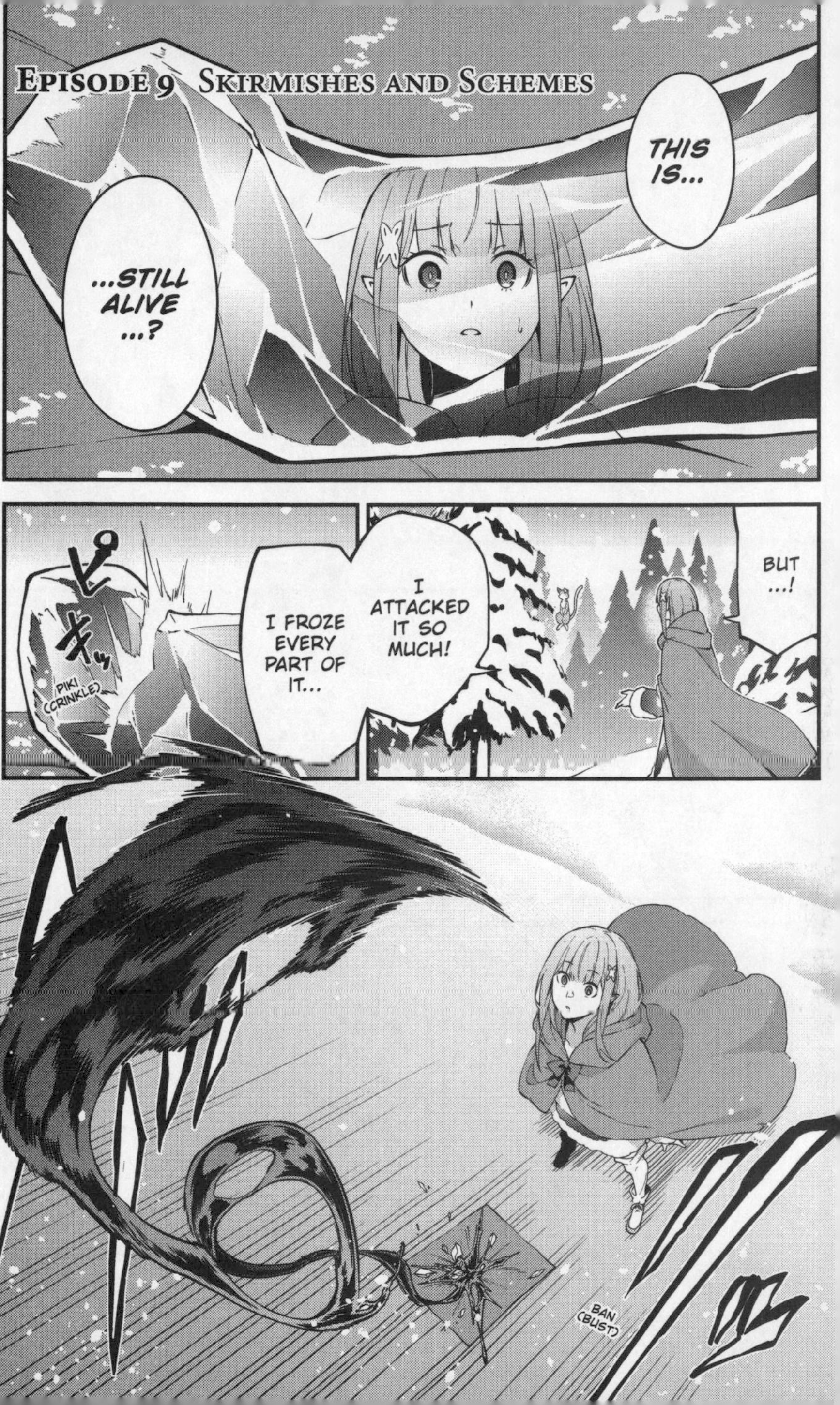
Episode 9 Skirmishes and Schemes
THIS IS...
...STILL ALIVE ...?
BUT ...!
I ATTACKED IT SO MUCH!
I FROZE EVERY PART OF IT...
PIKI (CRINKLE)
BAN (BUST)

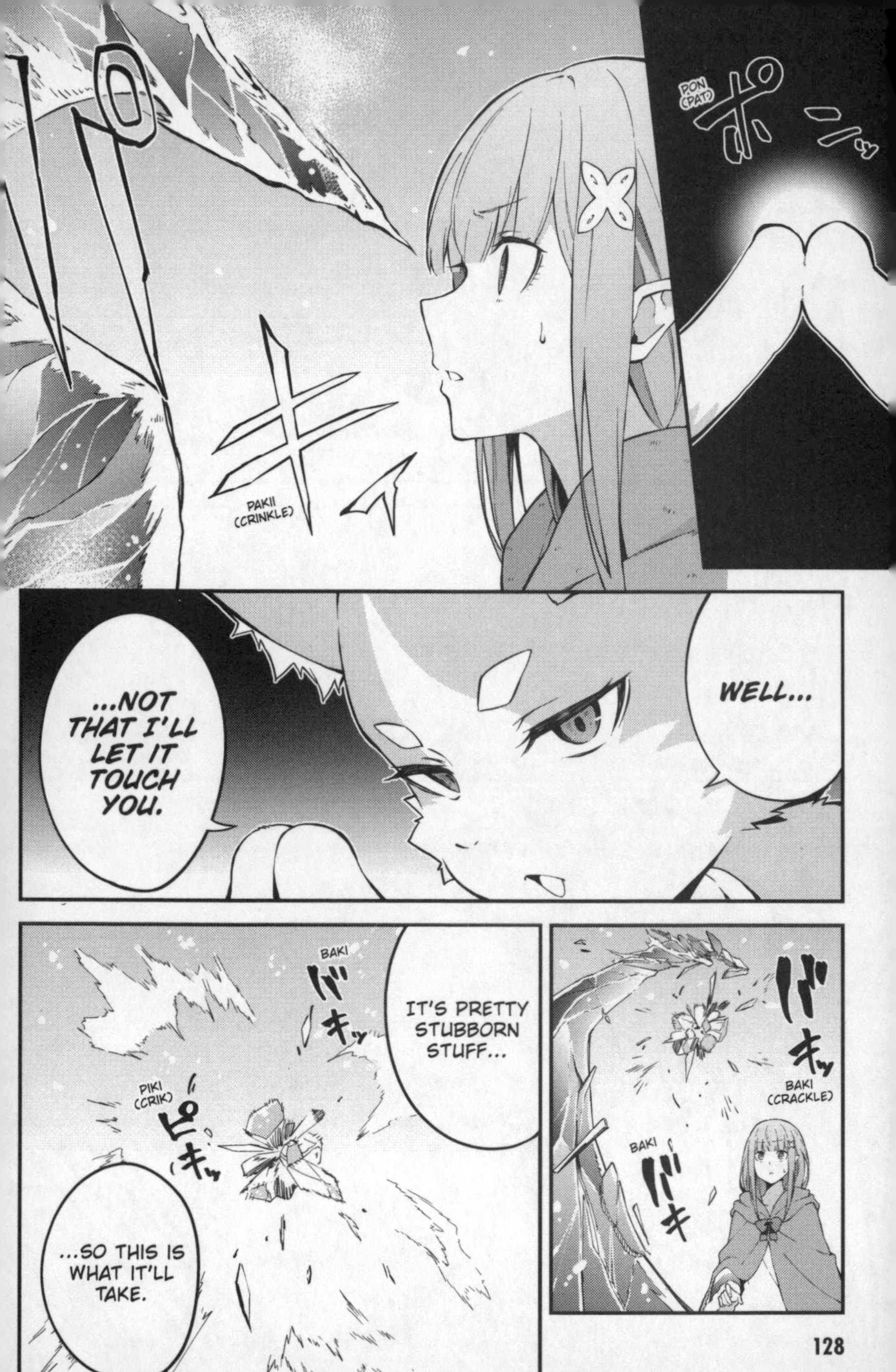
PON (PAT)
PAKII (CRINKLE)
WELL...
...NOT THAT I'LL LET IT TOUCH YOU.
BAKI (CRACKLE)
BAKI
BAKI
IT'S PRETTY STUBBORN STUFF...
PIKI (CRIK)
...SO THIS IS WHAT IT'LL TAKE.

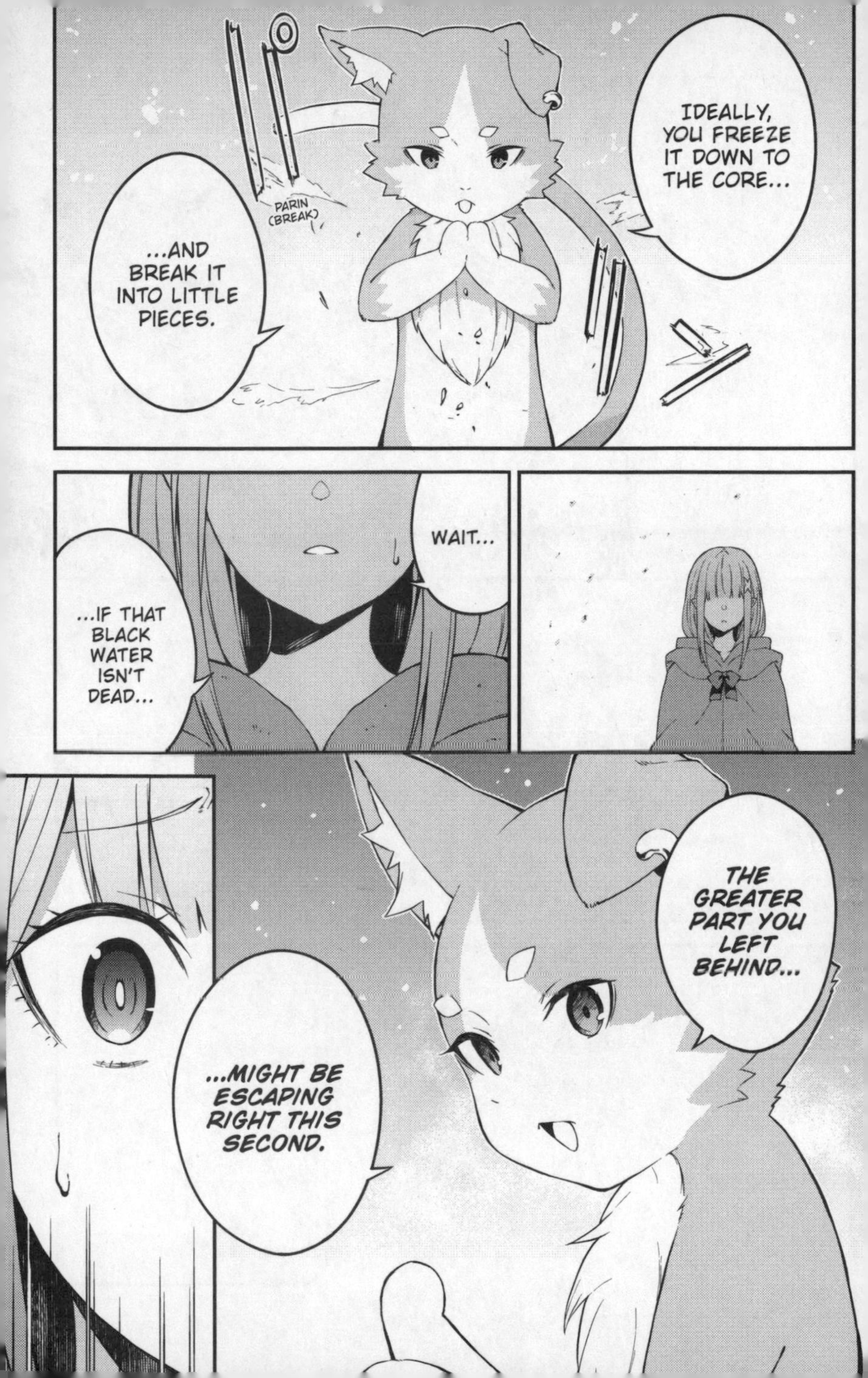
IDEALLY, YOU FREEZE IT DOWN TO THE CORE...
PARIN (BREAK)
...AND BREAK IT INTO LITTLE PIECES.
WAIT...
...IF THAT BLACK WATER ISN'T DEAD...
THE GREATER PART YOU LEFT BEHIND...
...MIGHT BE ESCAPING RIGHT THIS SECOND.

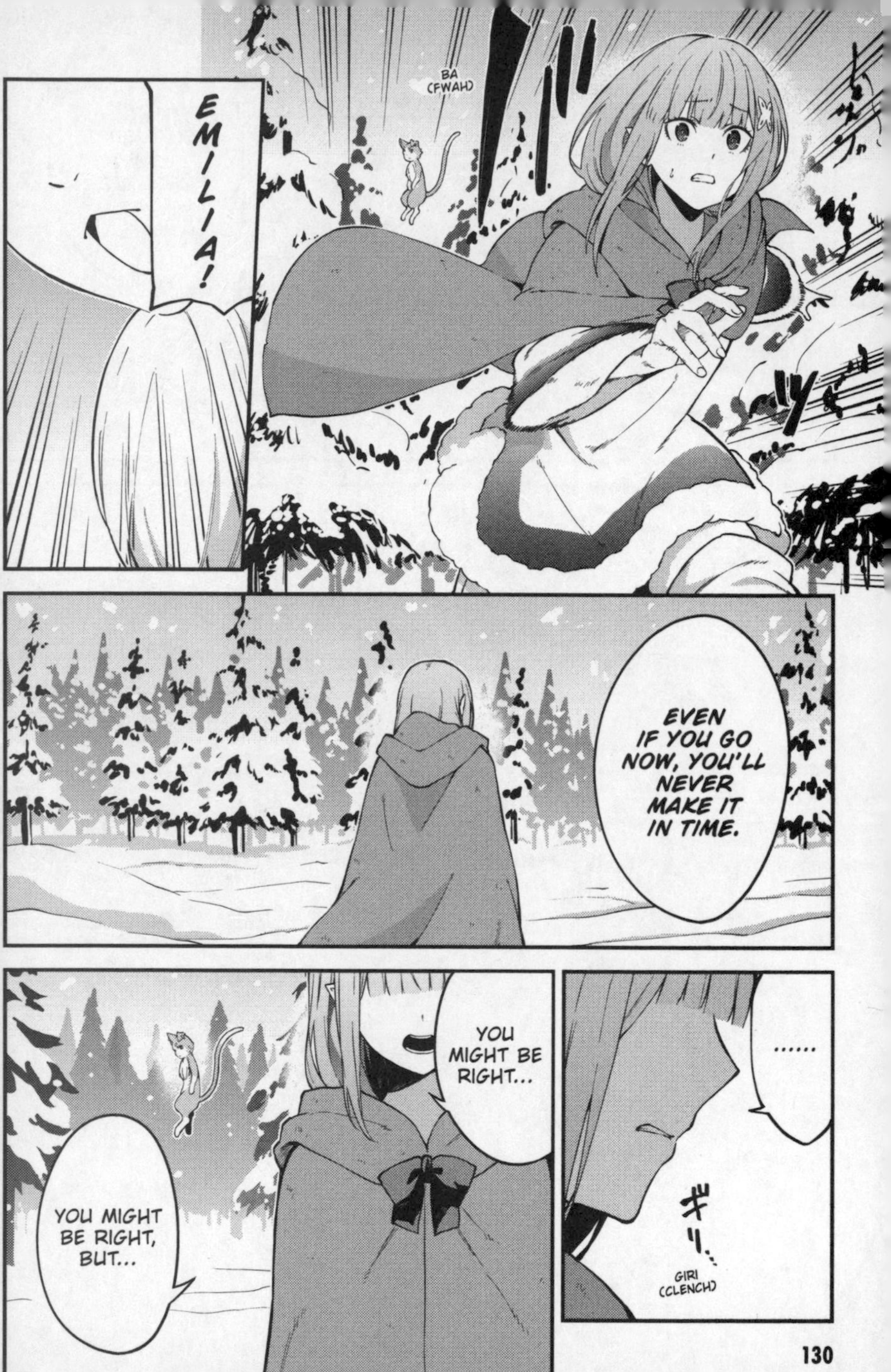
BA
(FWAH)
EMILIA!
EVEN IF YOU GO NOW, YOU'LL NEVER MAKE IT IN TIME.
......
ギリ…
GIRI
(CLENCH)
YOU MIGHT BE RIGHT...
YOU MIGHT BE RIGHT, BUT...

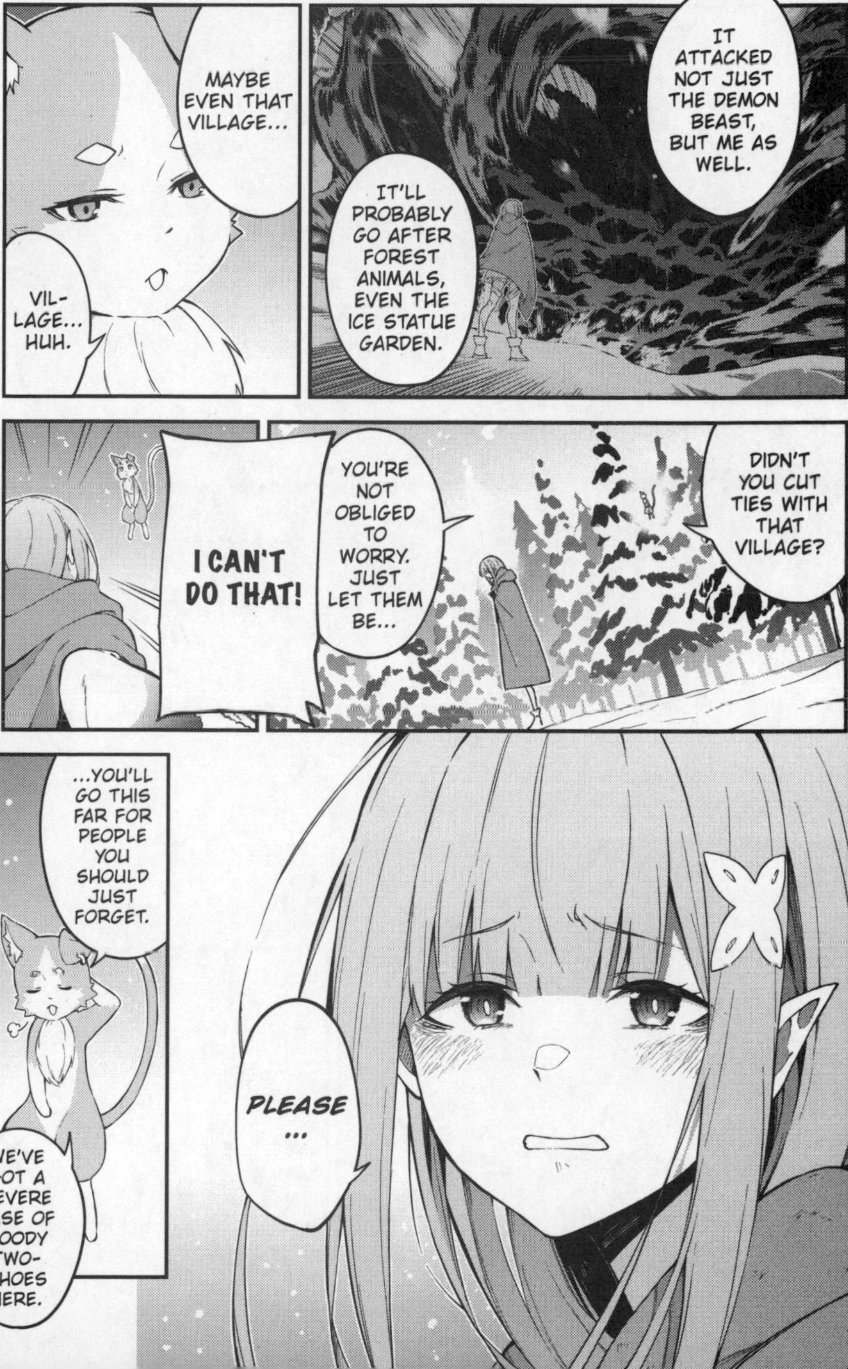
IT ATTACKED NOT JUST THE DEMON BEAST, BUT ME AS WELL.
IT'LL PROBABLY GO AFTER FOREST ANIMALS, EVEN THE ICE STATUE GARDEN.
MAYBE EVEN THAT VILLAGE...
VIL-LAGE... HUH.
DIDN'T YOU CUT TIES WITH THAT VILLAGE?
YOU'RE NOT OBLIGED TO WORRY. JUST LET THEM BE...
I CAN'T DO THAT!
PLEASE...
...YOU'LL GO THIS FAR FOR PEOPLE YOU SHOULD JUST FORGET.
WE'VE GOT A SEVERE CASE OF GOODY TWO-SHOES HERE.

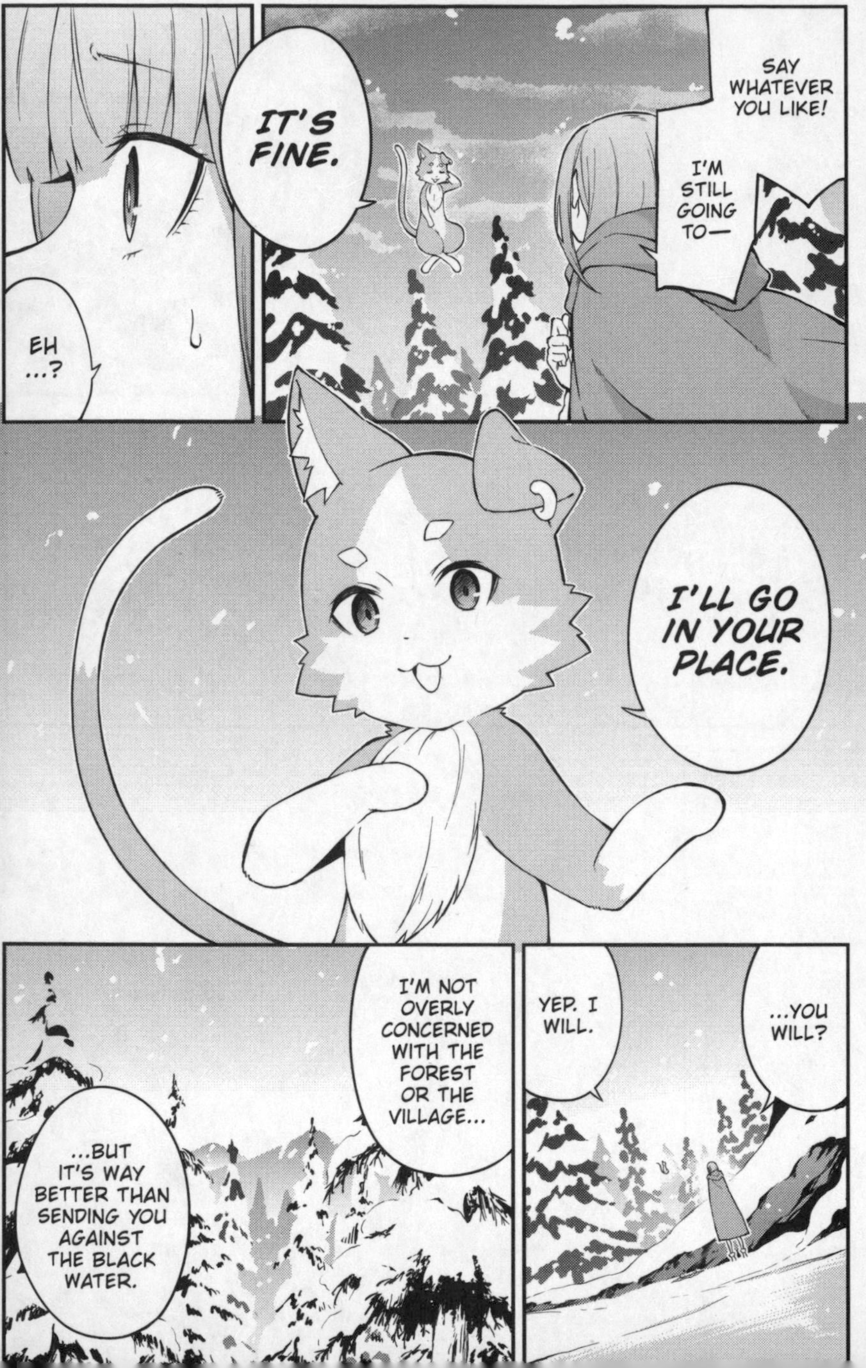
SAY WHATEVER YOU LIKE!
I'M STILL GOING TO—
IT'S FINE.
EH ...?
I'LL GO IN YOUR PLACE.
...YOU WILL?
YEP. I WILL.
I'M NOT OVERLY CONCERNED WITH THE FOREST OR THE VILLAGE...
...BUT IT'S WAY BETTER THAN SENDING YOU AGAINST THE BLACK WATER.

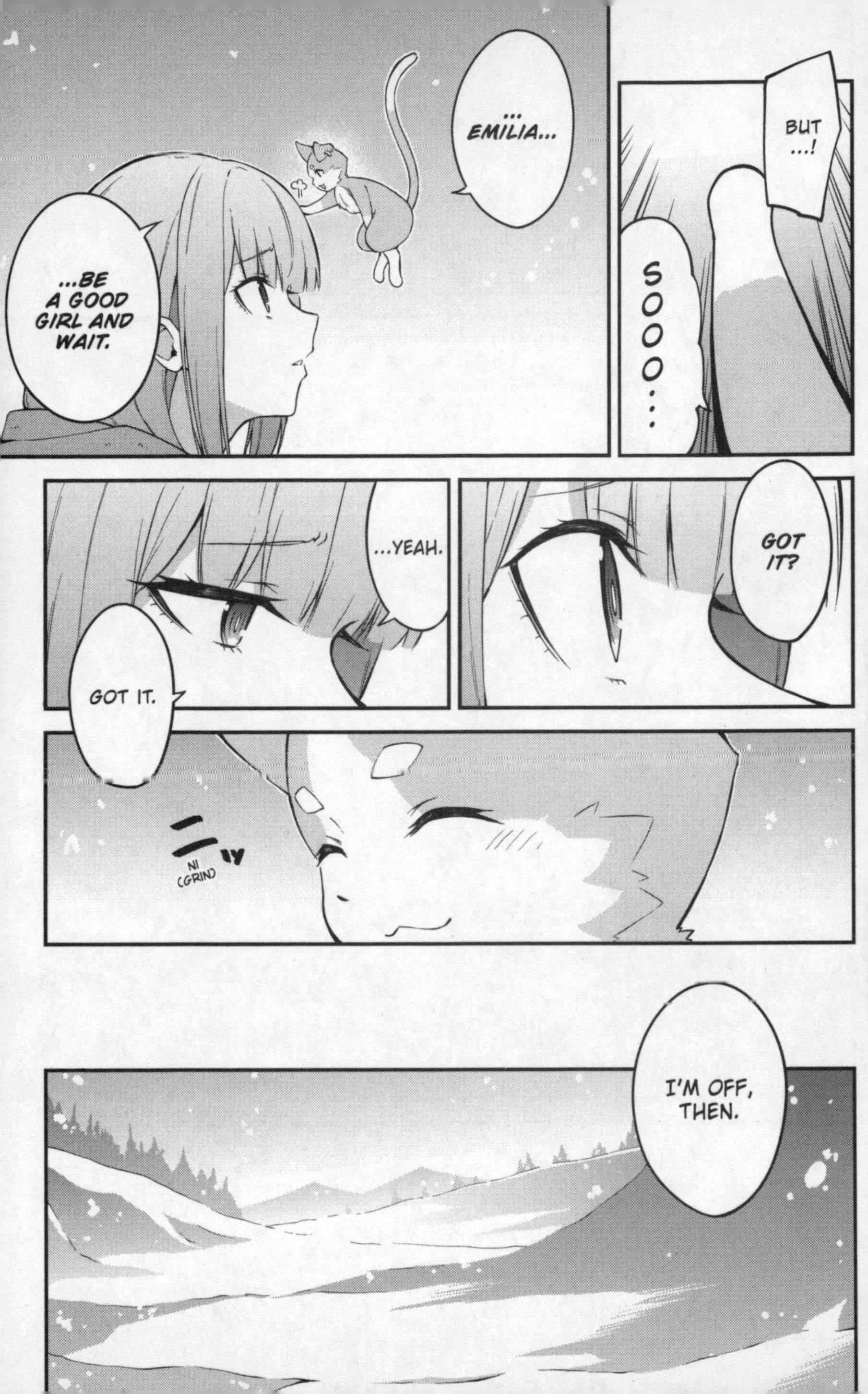
BUT ...!
SOOO...
...EMILIA...
...BE A GOOD GIRL AND WAIT.
GOT IT?
...YEAH.
GOT IT.
NI (GRIN)
I'M OFF, THEN.

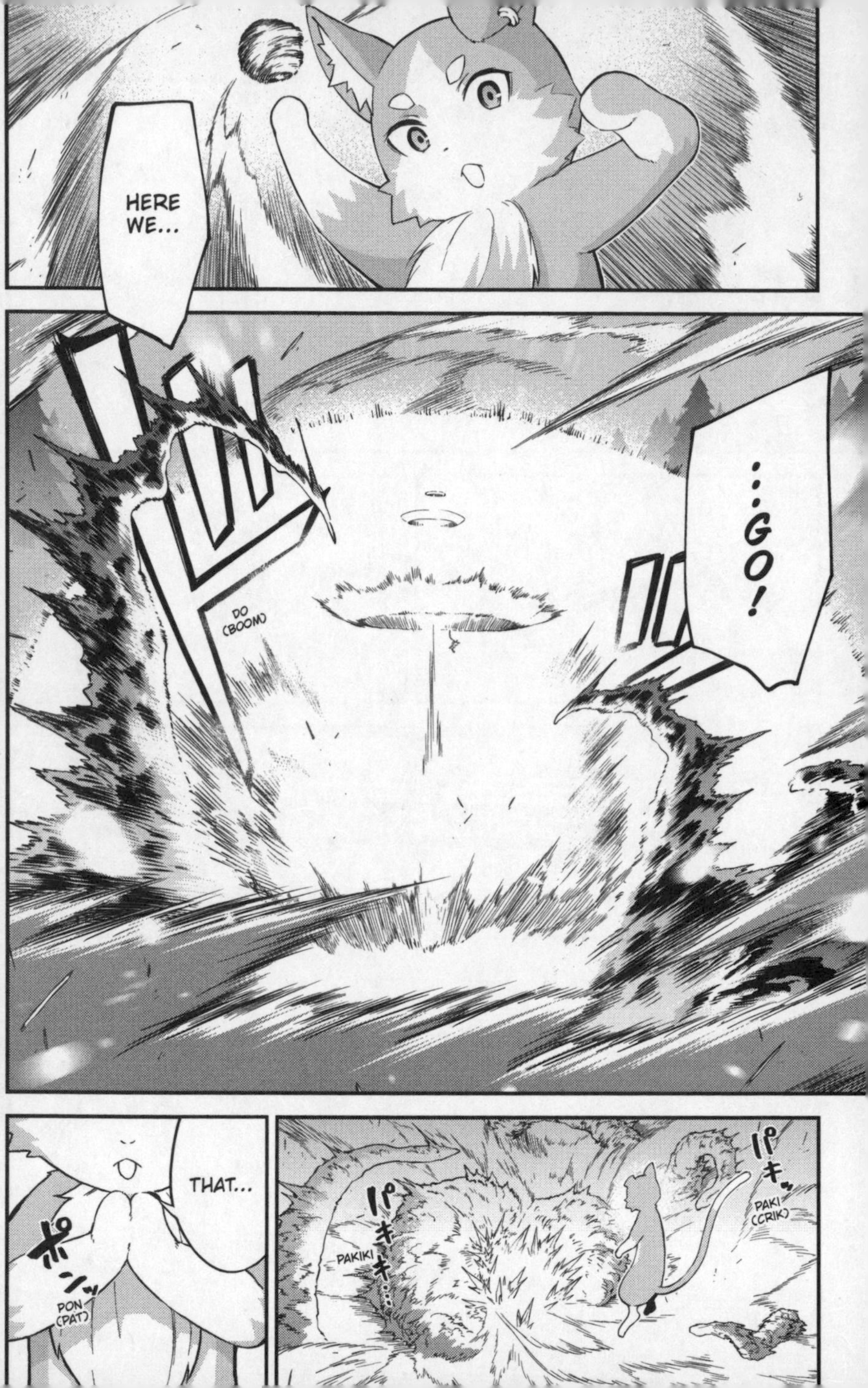
HERE WE...
...GO!
DO (BOOM)
パキッ
PAKI (CRIK)
パキキキ…
PAKIKI
THAT...
ポンッ
PON (PAT)

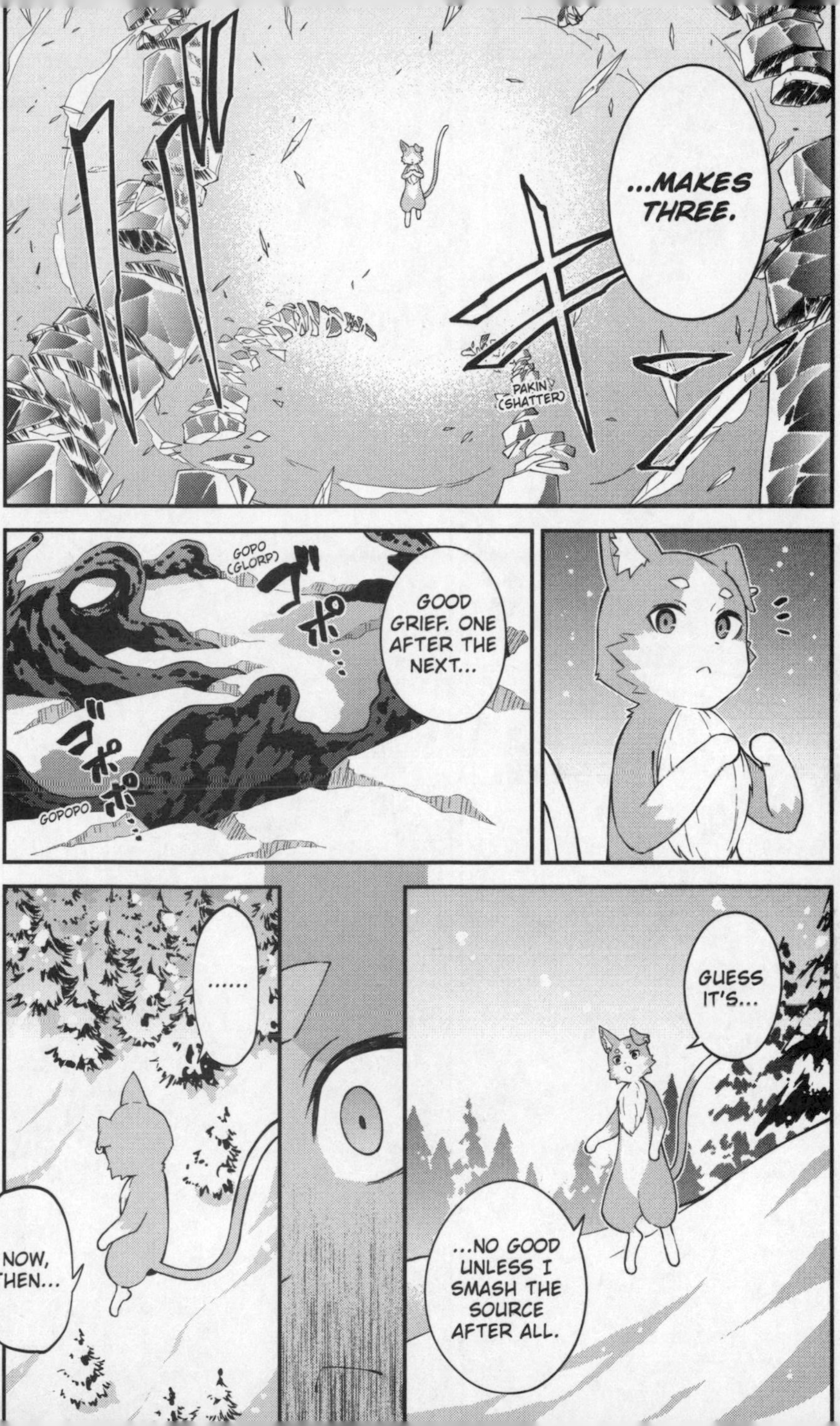
...MAKES THREE.
PAKIN (SHATTER)
GOOD GRIEF. ONE AFTER THE NEXT...
GOPO (GLORP)
GOPOPO
GUESS IT'S...
...NO GOOD UNLESS I SMASH THE SOURCE AFTER ALL.
......
NOW, THEN...

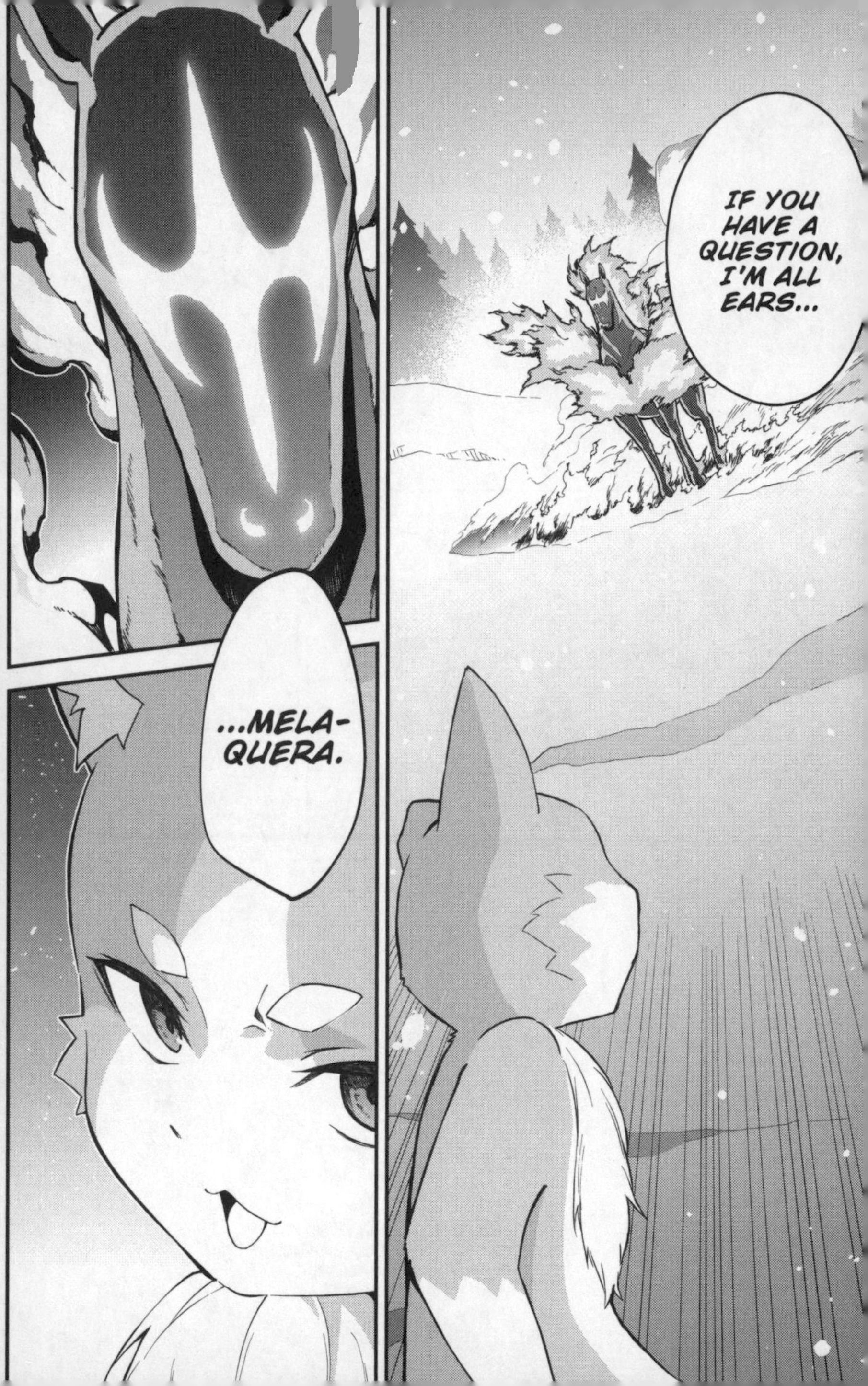
IF YOU HAVE A QUESTION, I'M ALL EARS...
...MELA-QUERA.

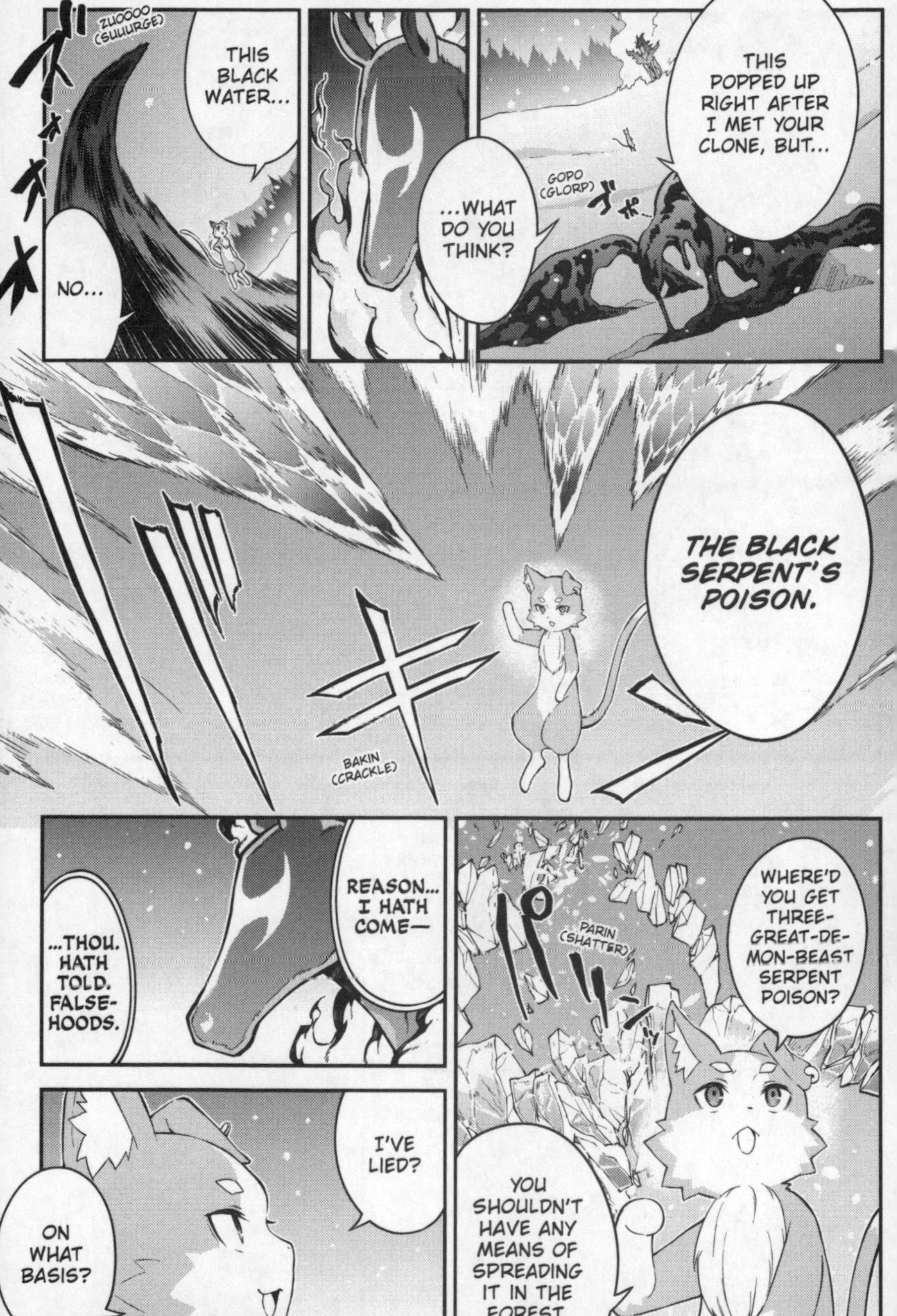
THIS POPPED UP RIGHT AFTER I MET YOUR CLONE, BUT...
GOPO (GLORP)
...WHAT DO YOU THINK?
ZUOOOO (SUUURGE)
THIS BLACK WATER...
NO...
THE BLACK SERPENT'S POISON.
BAKIN (CRACKLE)
WHERE'D YOU GET THREE-GREAT-DEMON-BEAST SERPENT POISON?
PARIN (SHATTER)
YOU SHOULDN'T HAVE ANY MEANS OF SPREADING IT IN THE FOREST.
REASON... I HATH COME—
...THOU. HATH TOLD. FALSEHOODS.
I'VE LIED?
ON WHAT BASIS?

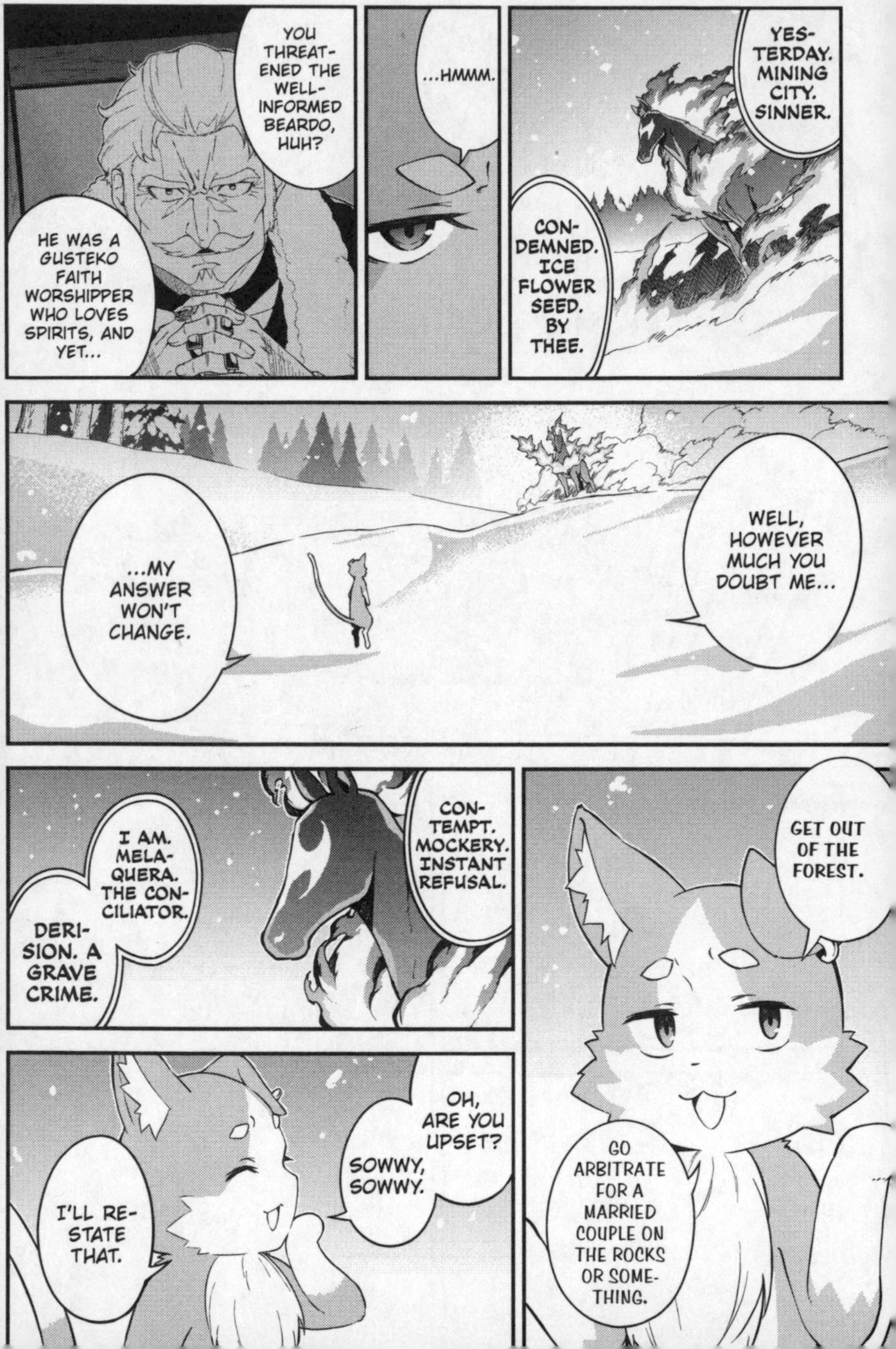
YESTERDAY. MINING CITY. SINNER.
CONDEMNED. ICE FLOWER SEED. BY THEE.
...HMMM.
YOU THREATENED THE WELL-INFORMED BEARDO, HUH?
HE WAS A GUSTEKO FAITH WORSHIPPER WHO LOVES SPIRITS, AND YET...
WELL, HOWEVER MUCH YOU DOUBT ME...
...MY ANSWER WON'T CHANGE.
GET OUT OF THE FOREST.
GO ARBITRATE FOR A MARRIED COUPLE ON THE ROCKS OR SOMETHING.
CONTEMPT. MOCKERY. INSTANT REFUSAL.
I AM. MELAQUERA. THE CONCILIATOR.
DERISION. A GRAVE CRIME.
OH, ARE YOU UPSET?
SOWWY, SOWWY.
I'LL RESTATE THAT.

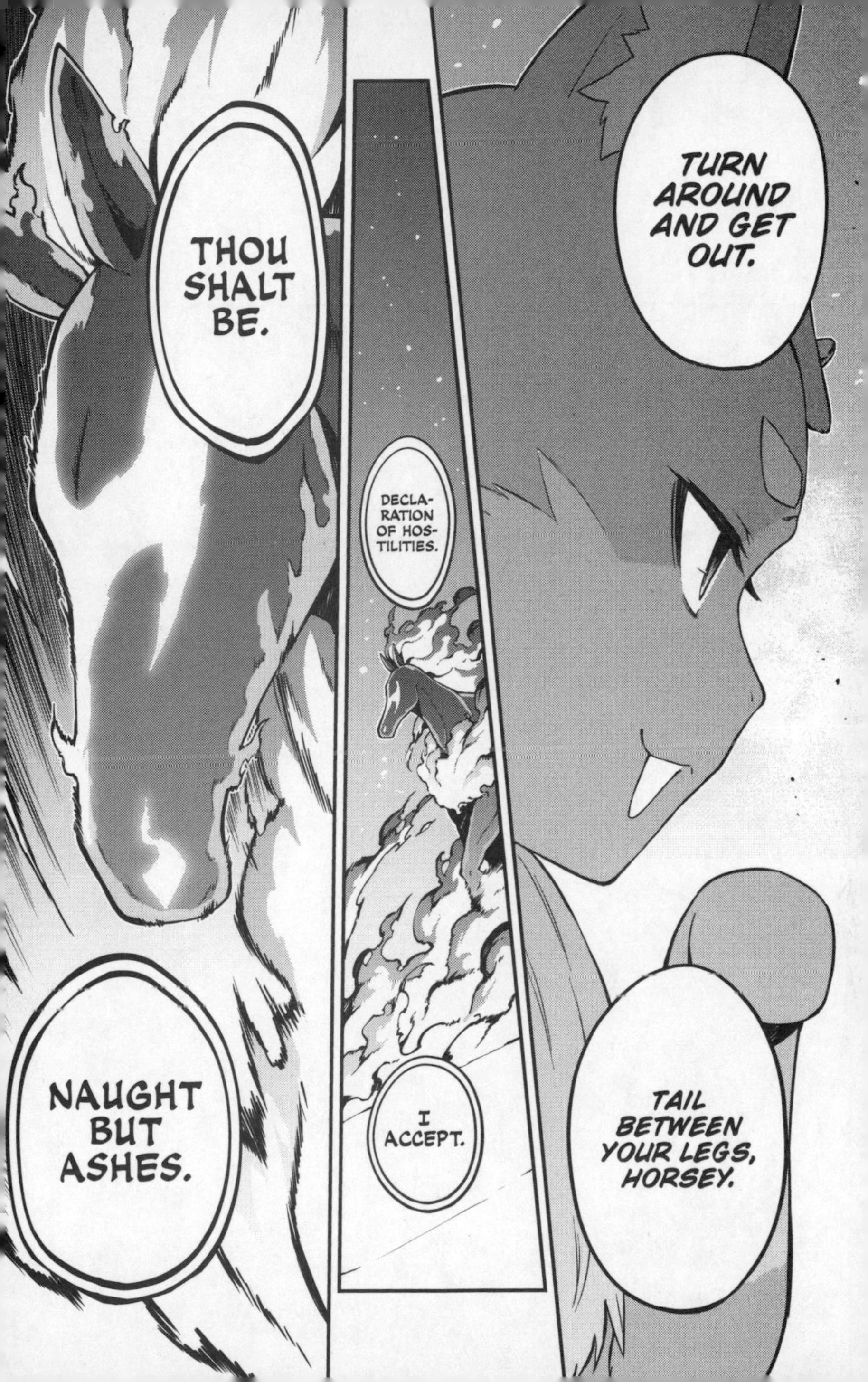
TURN AROUND AND GET OUT.
TAIL BETWEEN YOUR LEGS, HORSEY.
DECLARATION OF HOSTILITIES.
I ACCEPT.
THOU SHALT BE.
NAUGHT BUT ASHES.

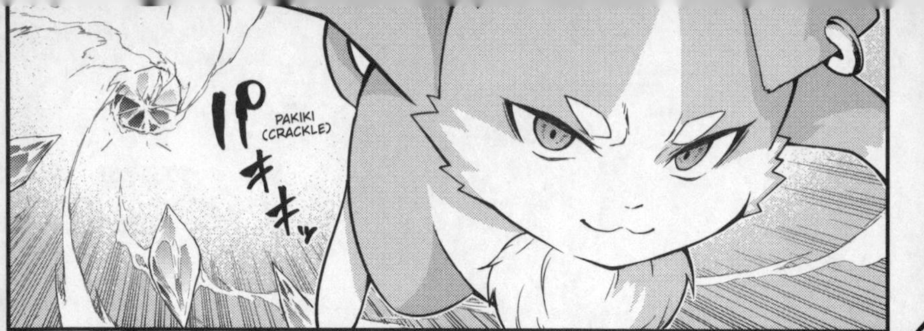
PAKIKI (CRACKLE)
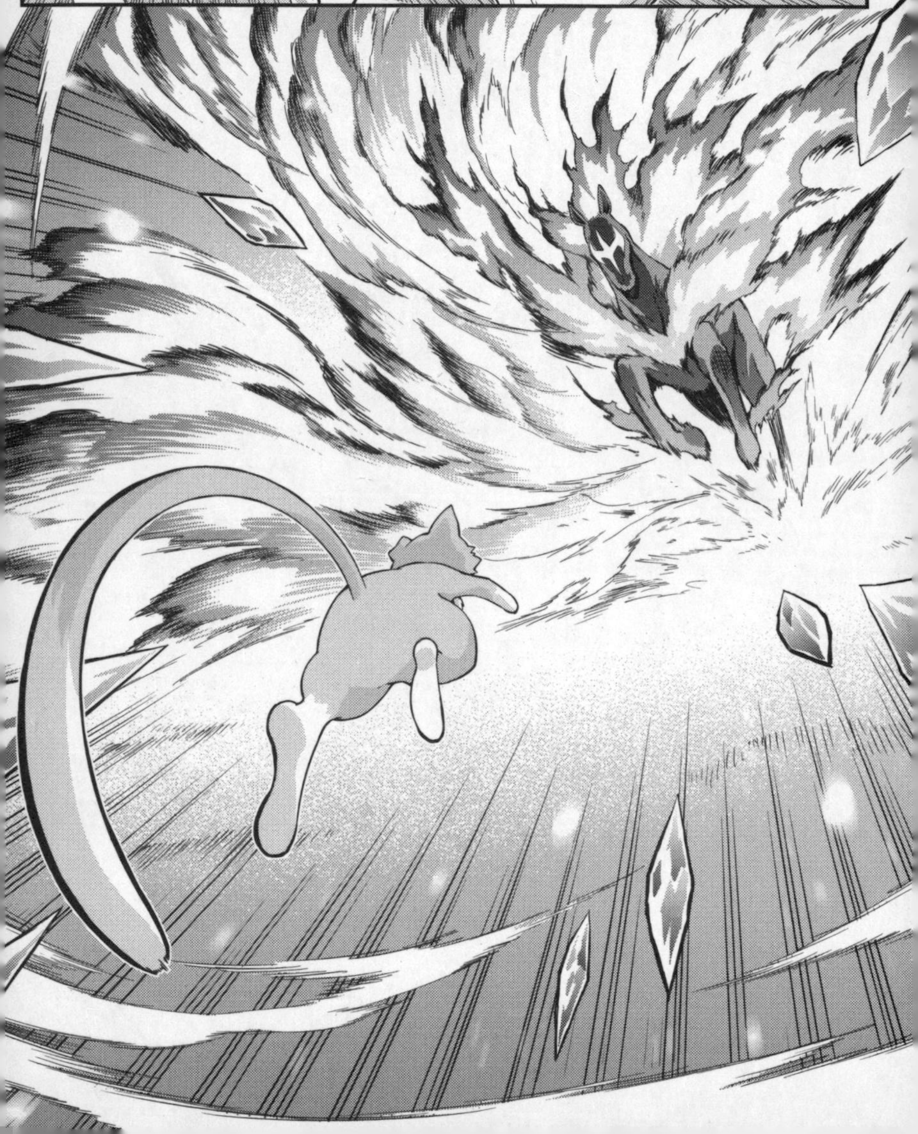

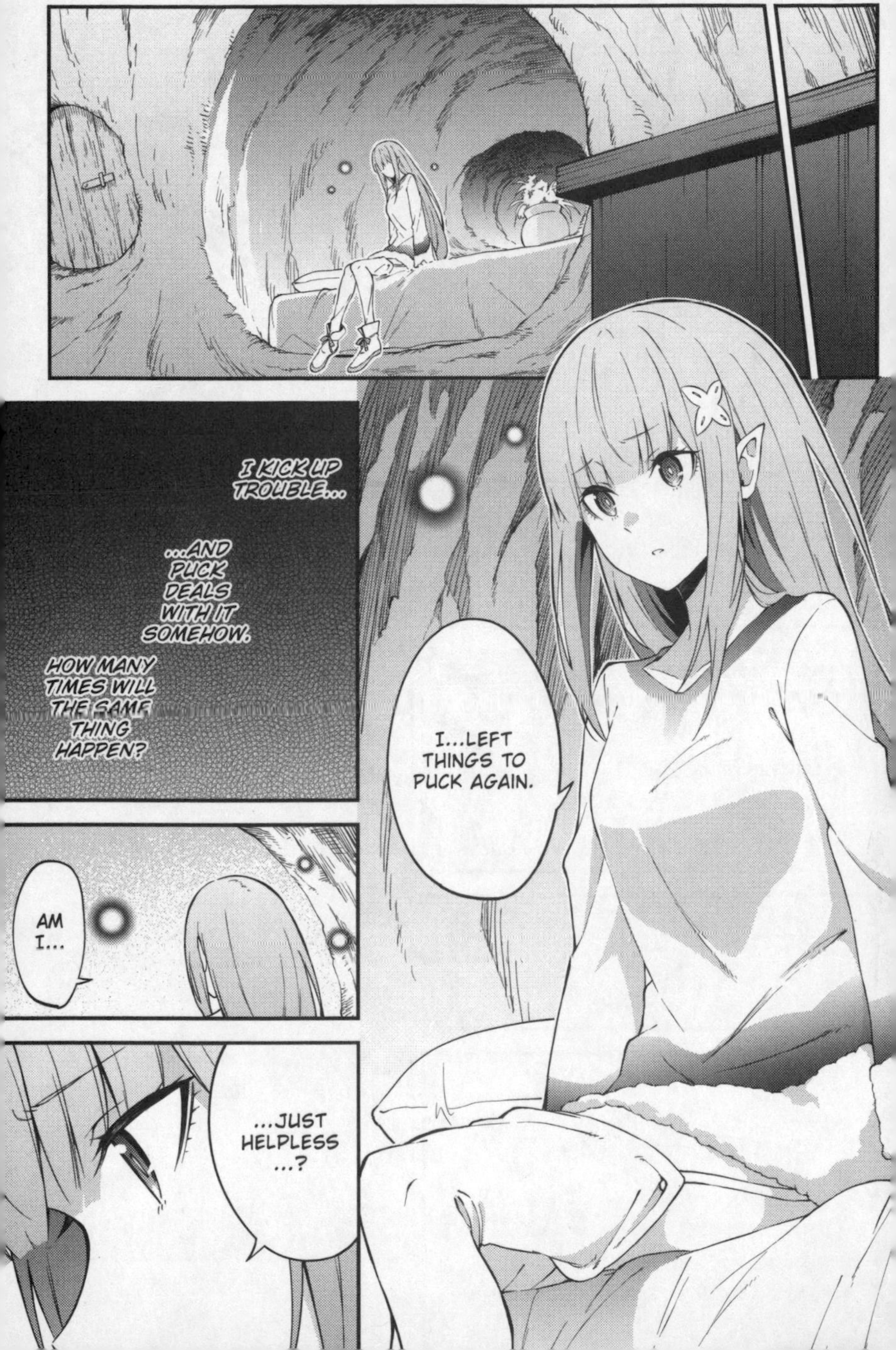
I...LEFT THINGS TO PUCK AGAIN.
I KICK UP TROUBLE...
...AND PUCK DEALS WITH IT SOMEHOW.
HOW MANY TIMES WILL THE SAME THING HAPPEN?
AM I...
...JUST HELPLESS ...?

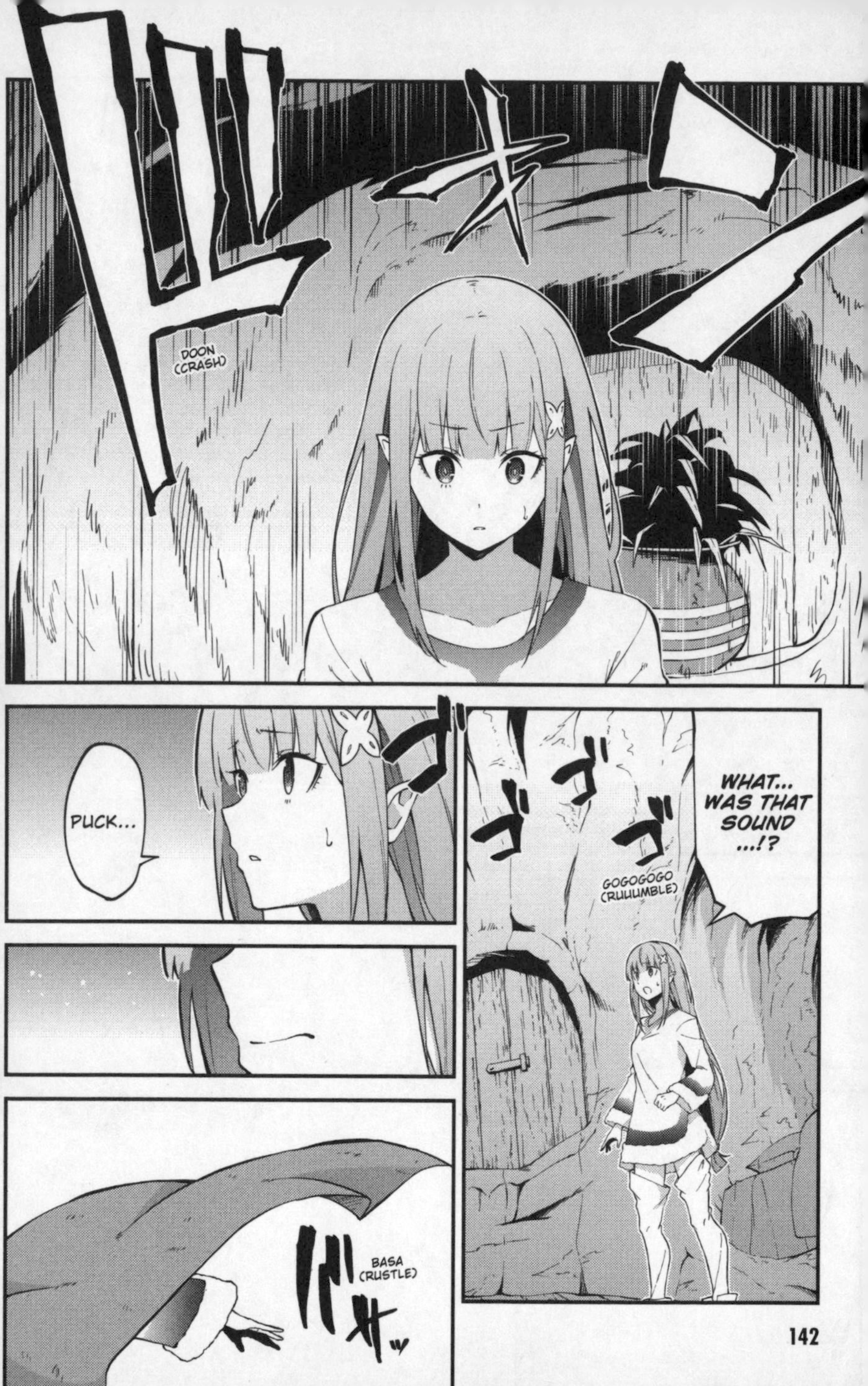
DOON (CRASH)
WHAT... WAS THAT SOUND ...!?
GOGOGOGO (RUUUMBLE)
PUCK...
BASA (RUSTLE)

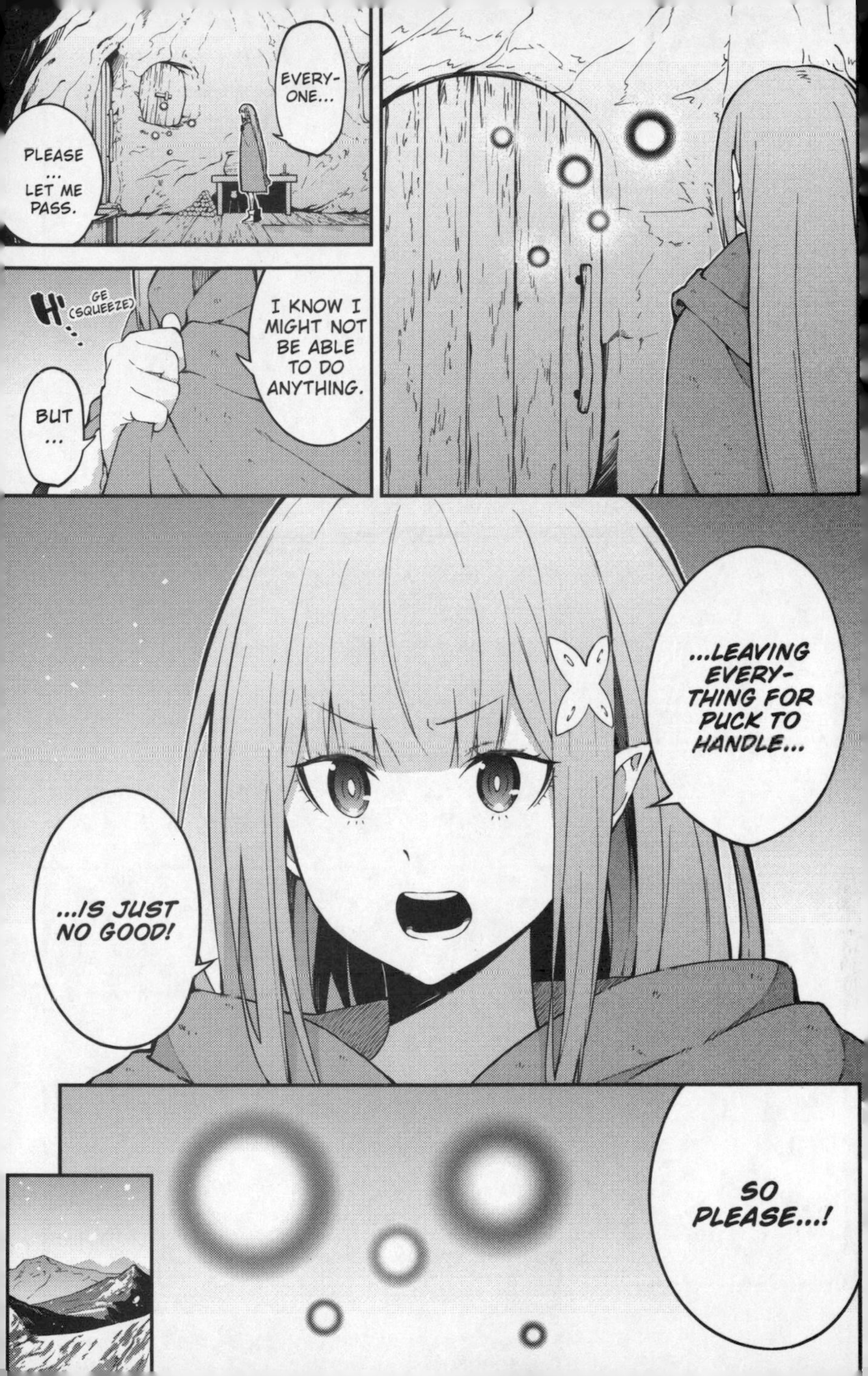
EVERY-ONE...
PLEASE ... LET ME PASS.
GE (SQUEEZE)
I KNOW I MIGHT NOT BE ABLE TO DO ANYTHING.
BUT ...
...LEAVING EVERY-THING FOR PUCK TO HANDLE...
...IS JUST NO GOOD!
SO PLEASE...!

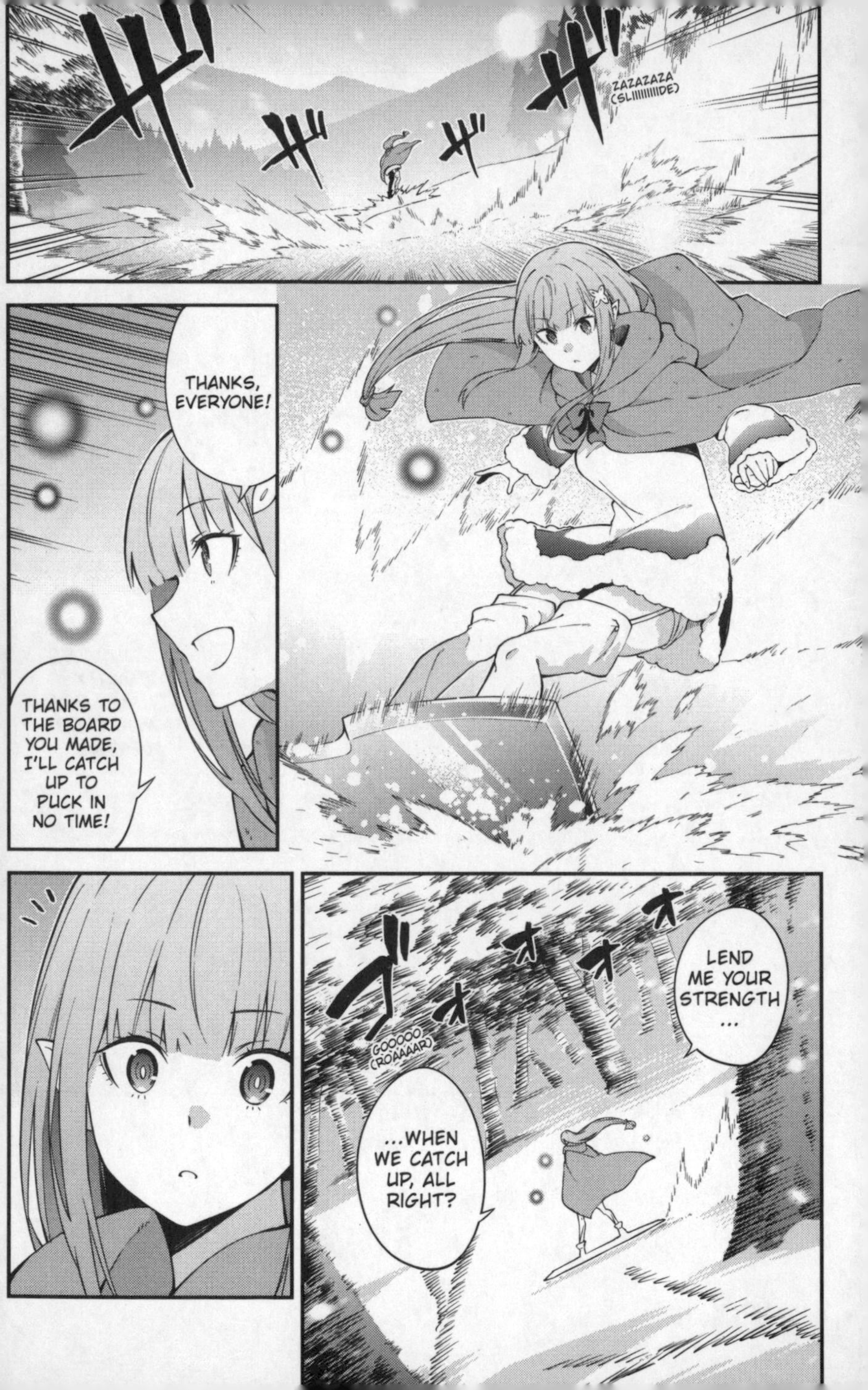
ZAZAZAZA (SLIIIIIIIIIIDE)
THANKS, EVERYONE!
THANKS TO THE BOARD YOU MADE, I'LL CATCH UP TO PUCK IN NO TIME!
LEND ME YOUR STRENGTH...
GOOOOO (ROAAAAR)
...WHEN WE CATCH UP, ALL RIGHT?

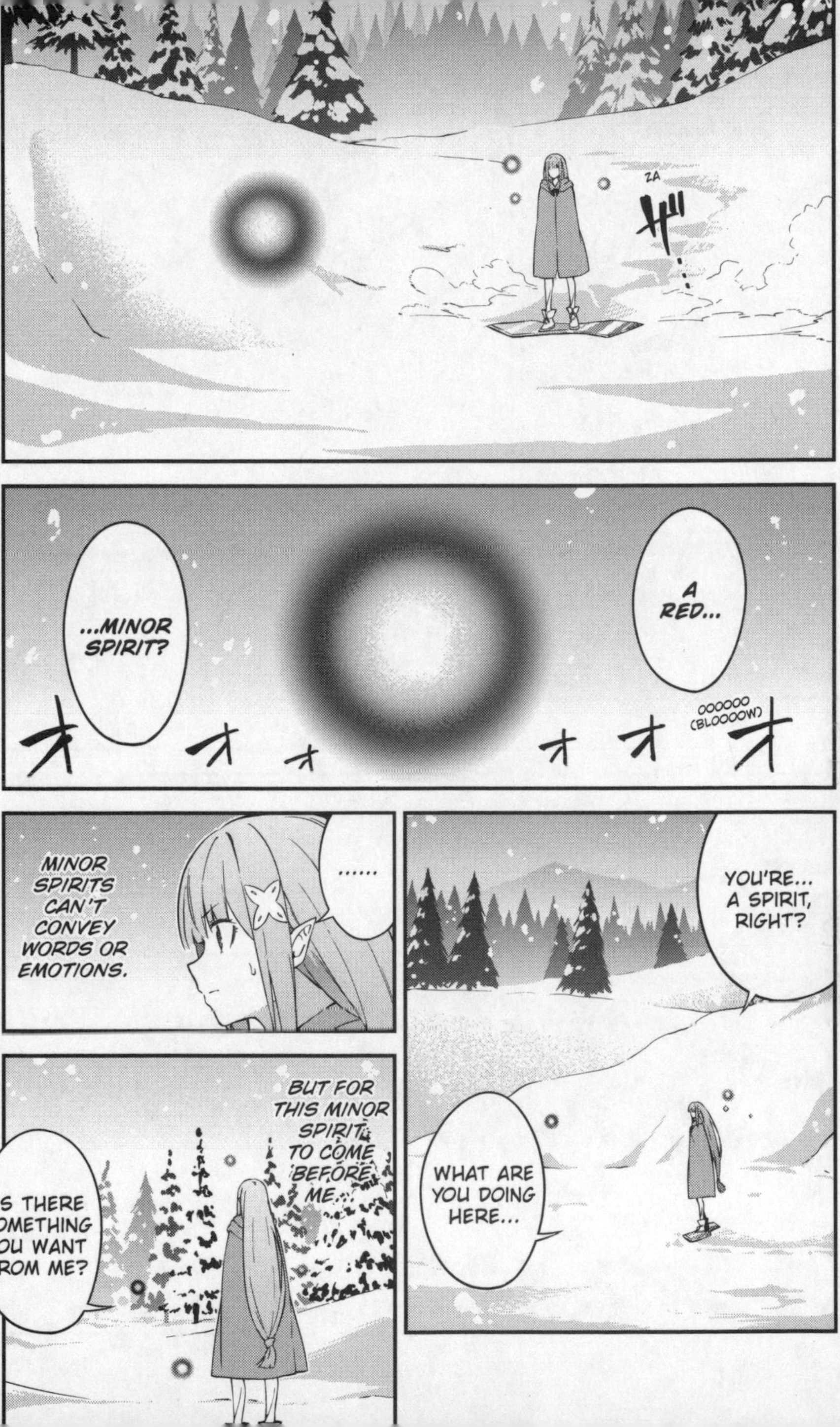
ZA
A RED...
OOOOOO (BLOOOOW)
...MINOR SPIRIT?
YOU'RE... A SPIRIT, RIGHT?
WHAT ARE YOU DOING HERE...
......
MINOR SPIRITS CAN'T CONVEY WORDS OR EMOTIONS.
BUT FOR THIS MINOR SPIRIT TO COME BEFORE ME...
IS THERE SOMETHING YOU WANT FROM ME?

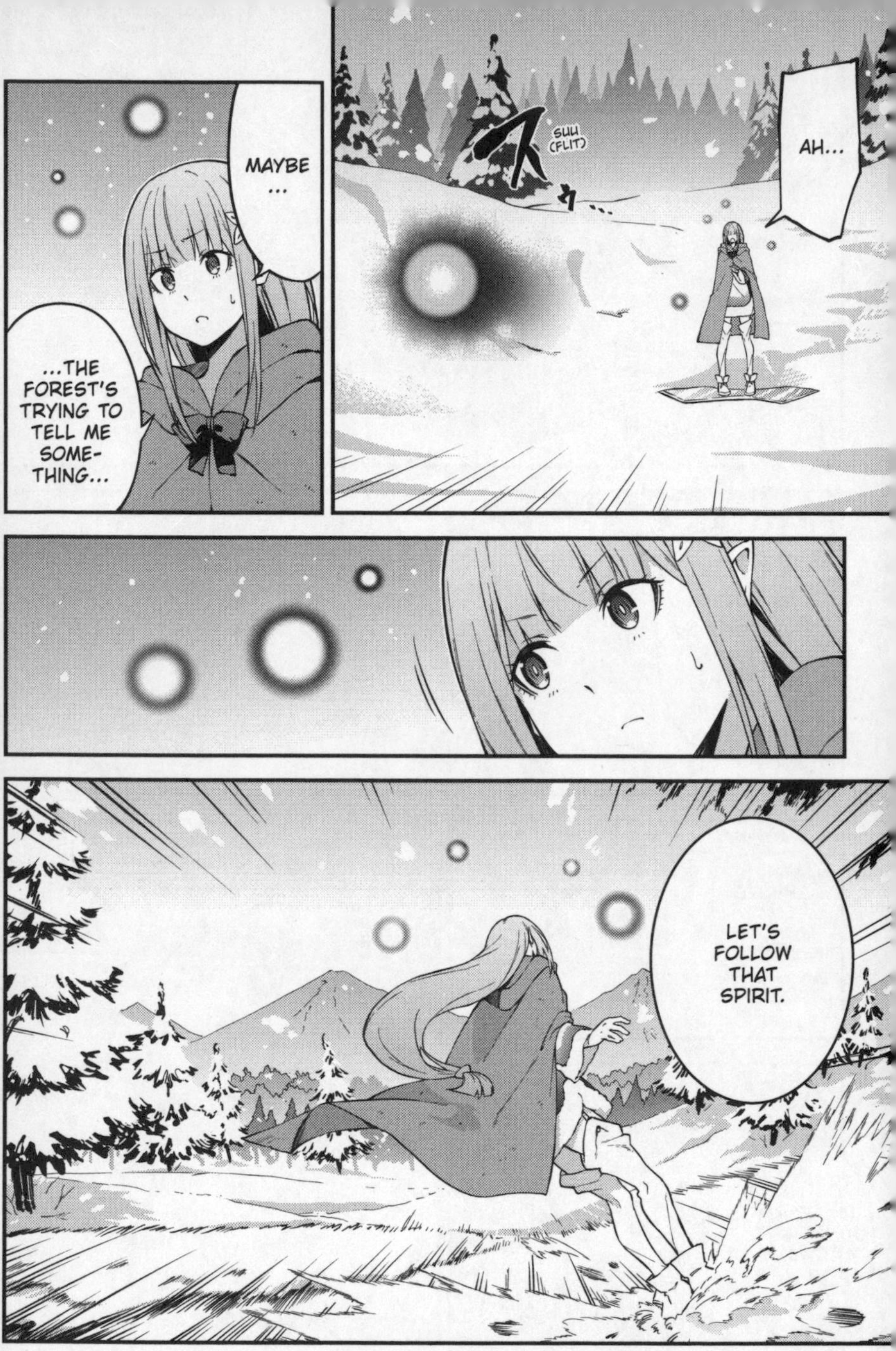
AH...
SUU (FLIT)
MAYBE ...
...THE FOREST'S TRYING TO TELL ME SOMETHING...
LET'S FOLLOW THAT SPIRIT.

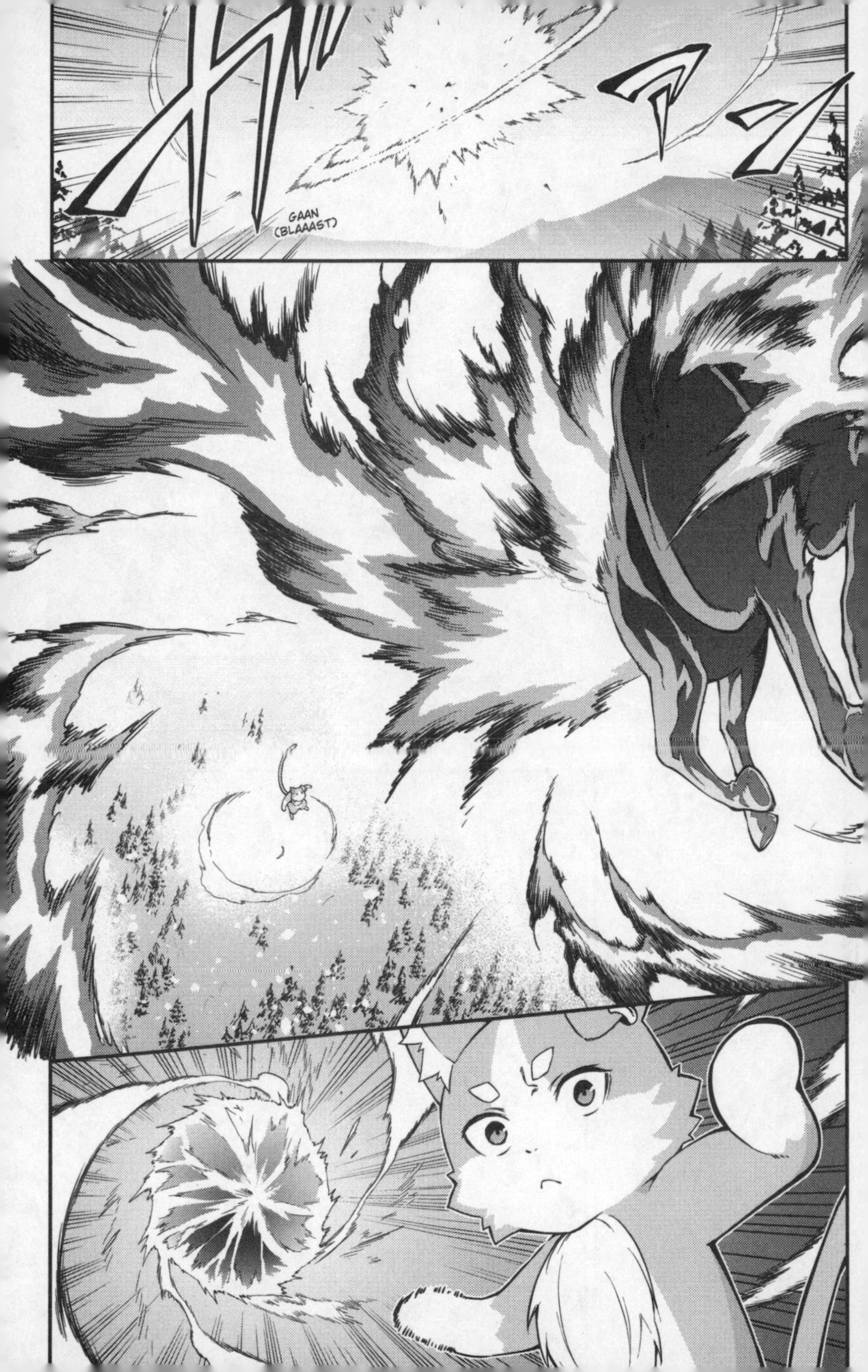
GAAN
(BLAAAST)

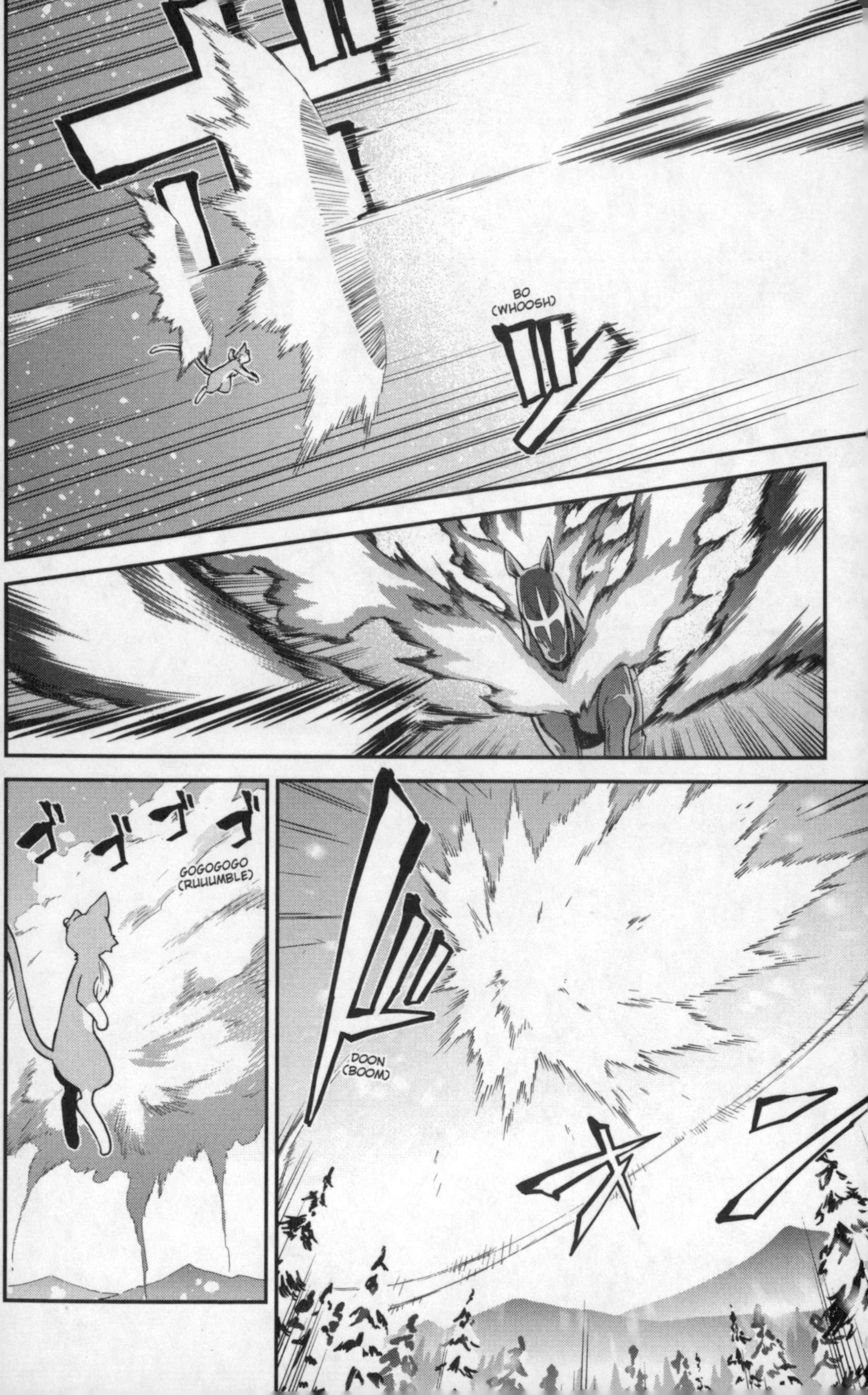
BO
(WHOOSH)
DOON
(BOOM)
ゴゴゴゴ
GOGOGOGO
(RUUUMBLE)

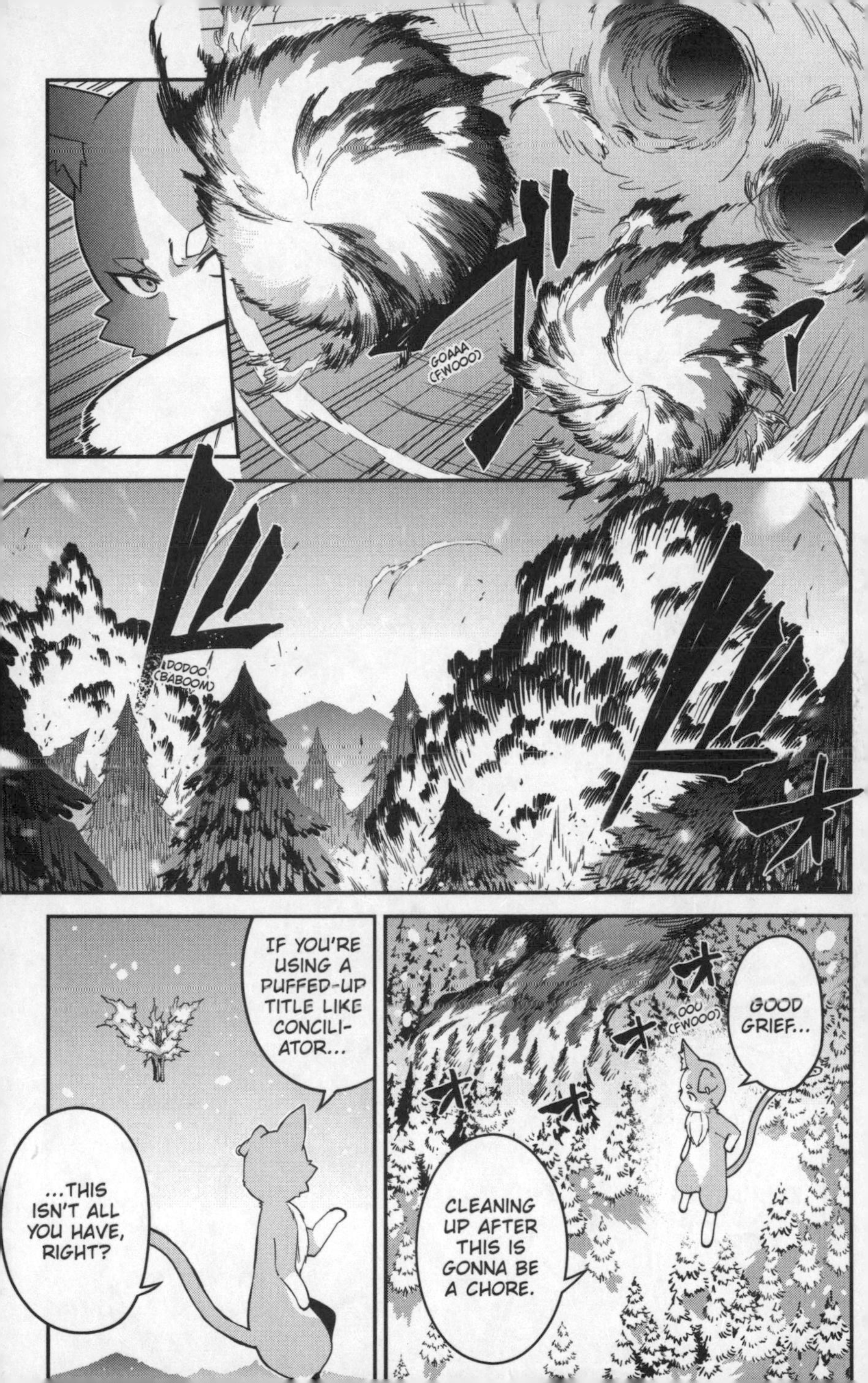
GOAAA (FWOOO)
DODOO (BABOOM)
OOU (FWOOO)
GOOD GRIEF...
CLEANING UP AFTER THIS IS GONNA BE A CHORE.
IF YOU'RE USING A PUFFED-UP TITLE LIKE CONCILI-ATOR...
...THIS ISN'T ALL YOU HAVE, RIGHT?

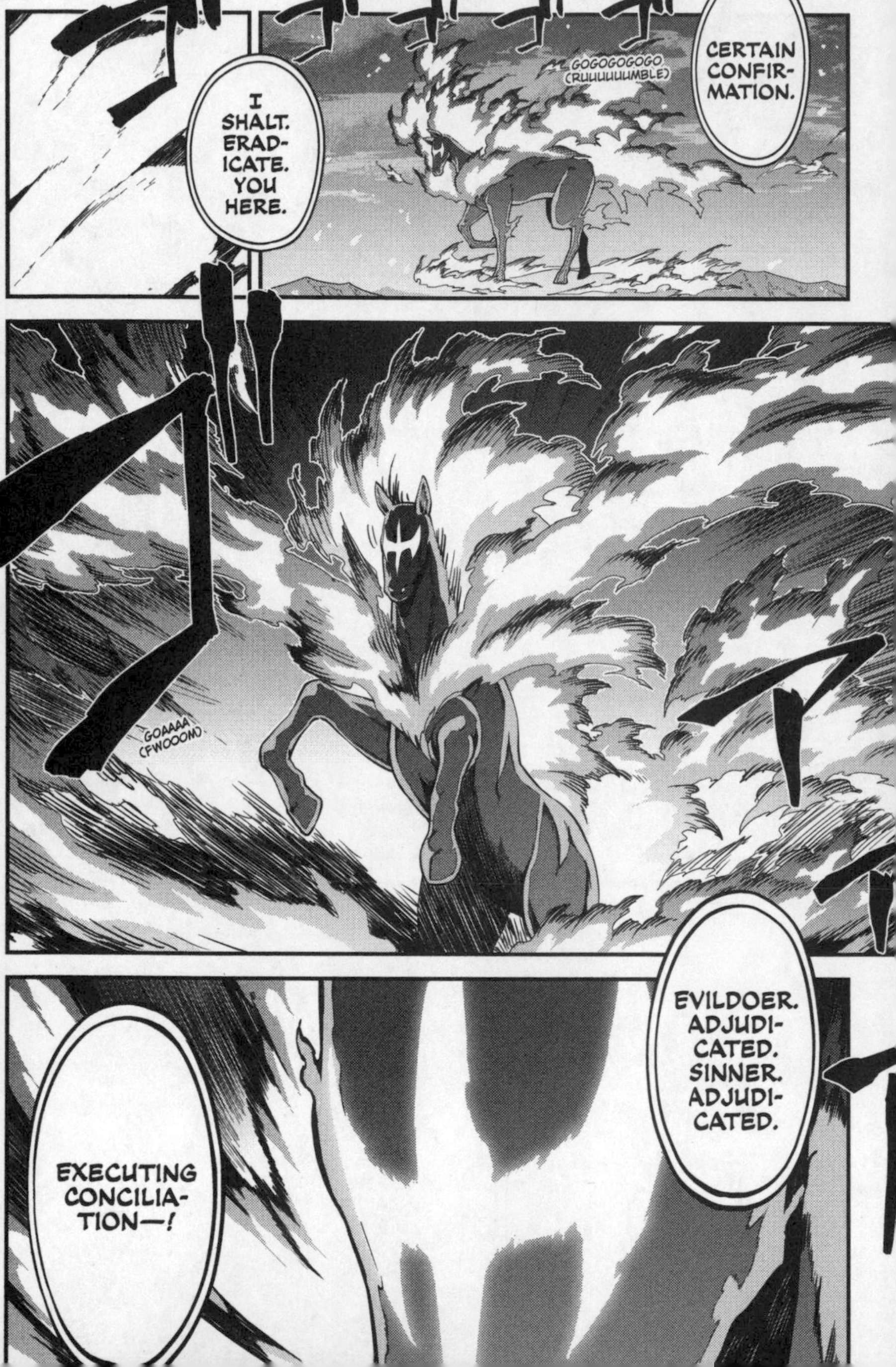
CERTAIN CONFIRMATION.
GOGOGOGOGO (RUUUUUUUMBLE)
I SHALT. ERADICATE. YOU HERE.
GOAAAA (FWOOOM)
EVILDOER. ADJUDICATED. SINNER. ADJUDICATED.
EXECUTING CONCILIATION—!

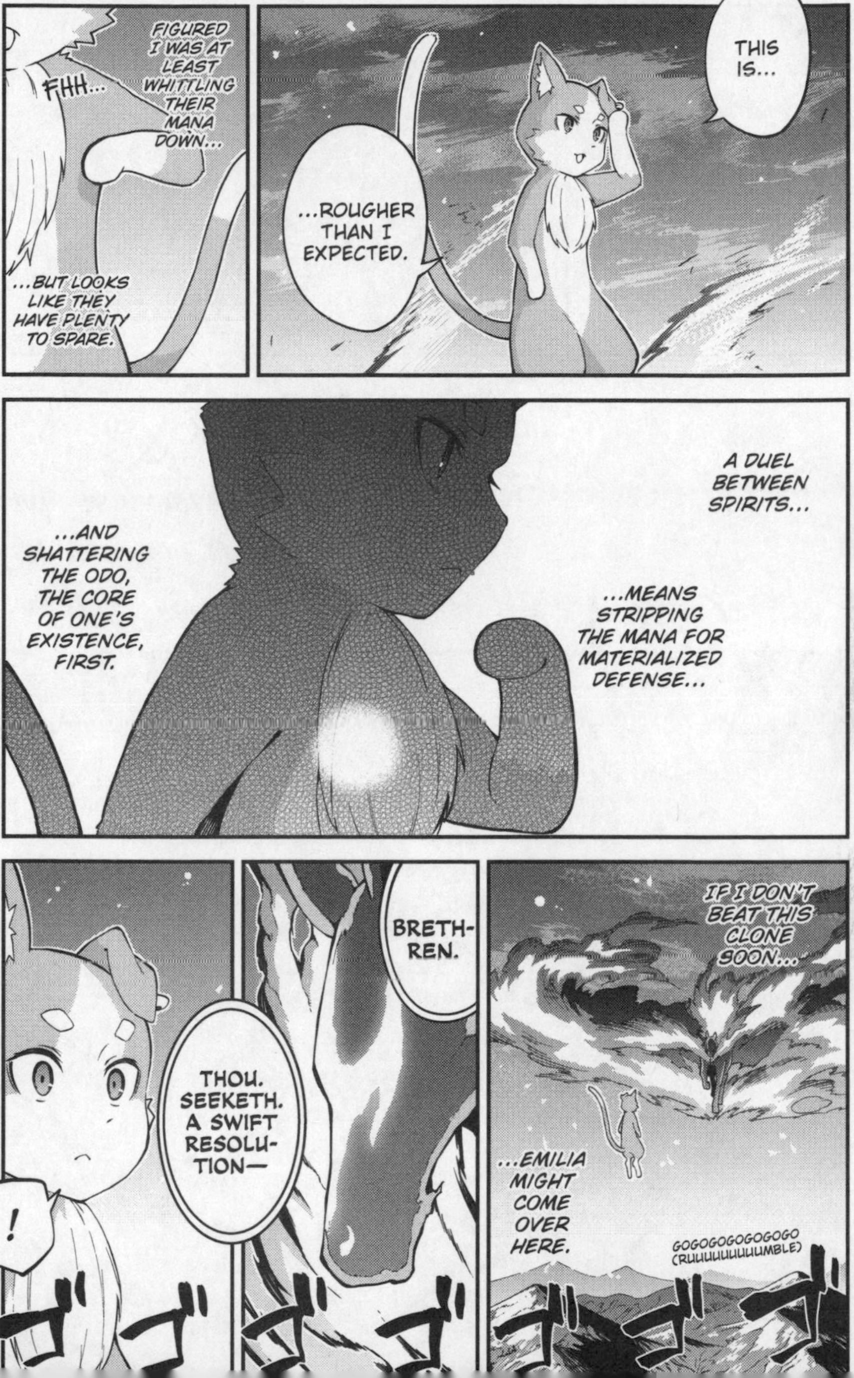
THIS IS...
...ROUGHER THAN I EXPECTED.
FIGURED I WAS AT LEAST WHITTLING THEIR MANA DOWN...
FHH...
...BUT LOOKS LIKE THEY HAVE PLENTY TO SPARE.
A DUEL BETWEEN SPIRITS...
...MEANS STRIPPING THE MANA FOR MATERIALIZED DEFENSE...
...AND SHATTERING THE ODO, THE CORE OF ONE'S EXISTENCE, FIRST.
IF I DON'T BEAT THIS CLONE SOON...
...EMILIA MIGHT COME OVER HERE.
GOGOGOGOGOGOGO (RUUUUUUUUUUMBLE)
BRETH-REN.
THOU. SEEKETH. A SWIFT RESOLU-TION—
!

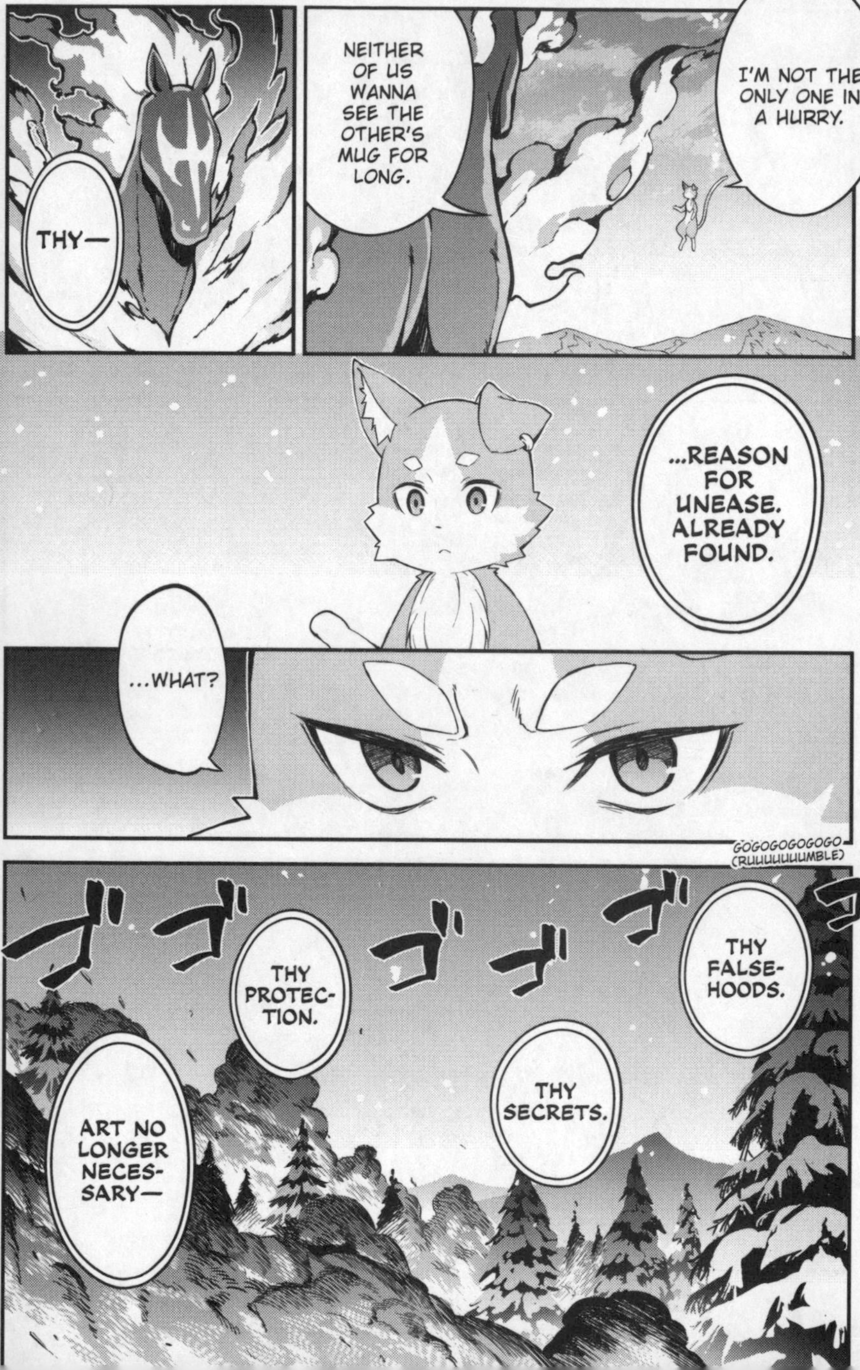
I'M NOT THE ONLY ONE IN A HURRY.
NEITHER OF US WANNA SEE THE OTHER'S MUG FOR LONG.
THY—
...REASON FOR UNEASE. ALREADY FOUND.
...WHAT?
GOGOGOGOGOGO (RUUUUUUUUMBLE)
THY FALSE-HOODS.
THY PROTEC-TION.
THY SECRETS.
ART NO LONGER NECES-SARY—

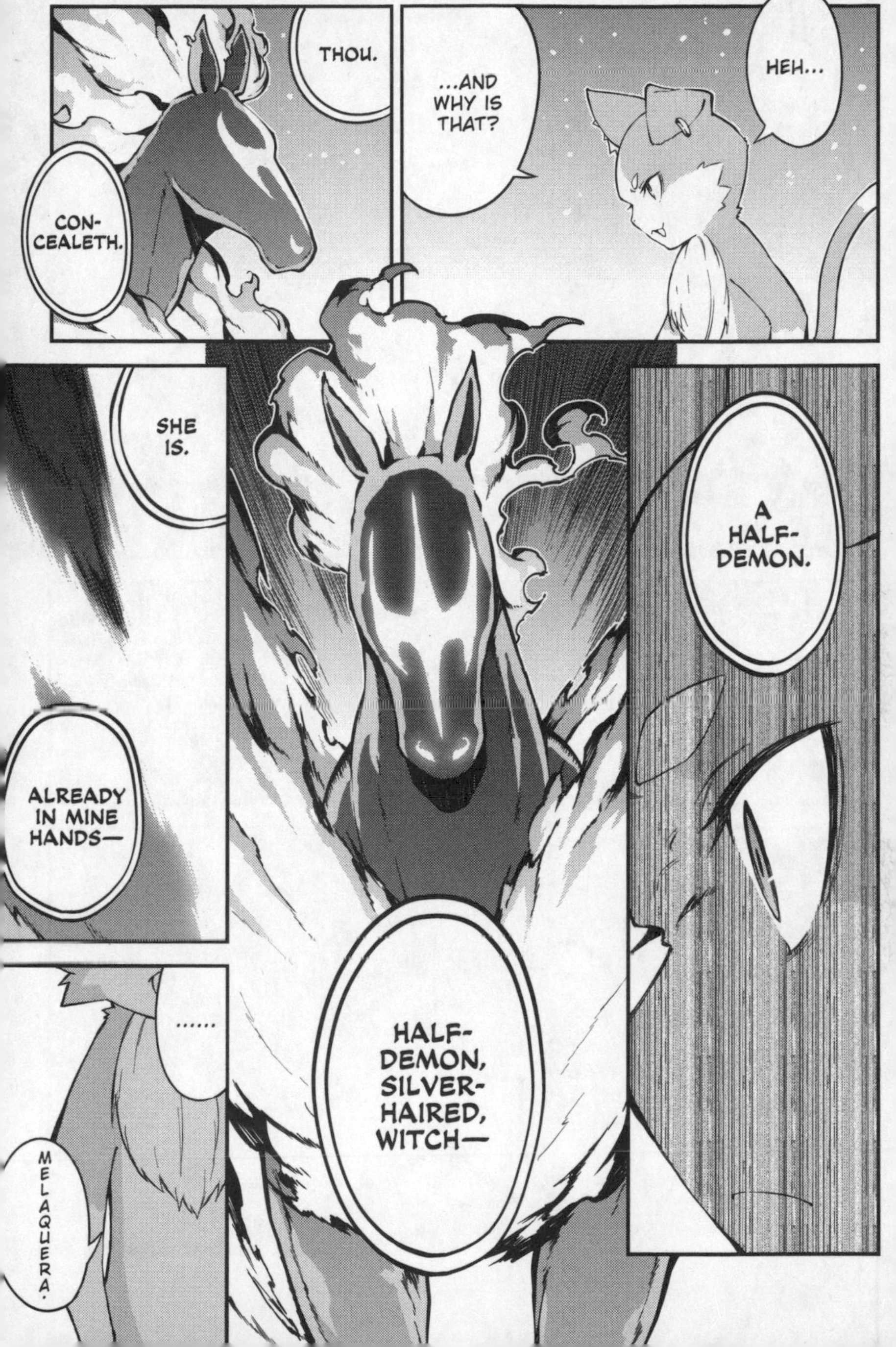
HEH...
...AND WHY IS THAT?
THOU.
CON-CEALETH.
A HALF-DEMON.
HALF-DEMON, SILVER-HAIRED, WITCH—
SHE IS.
ALREADY IN MINE HANDS—
......
MELAQUERA.

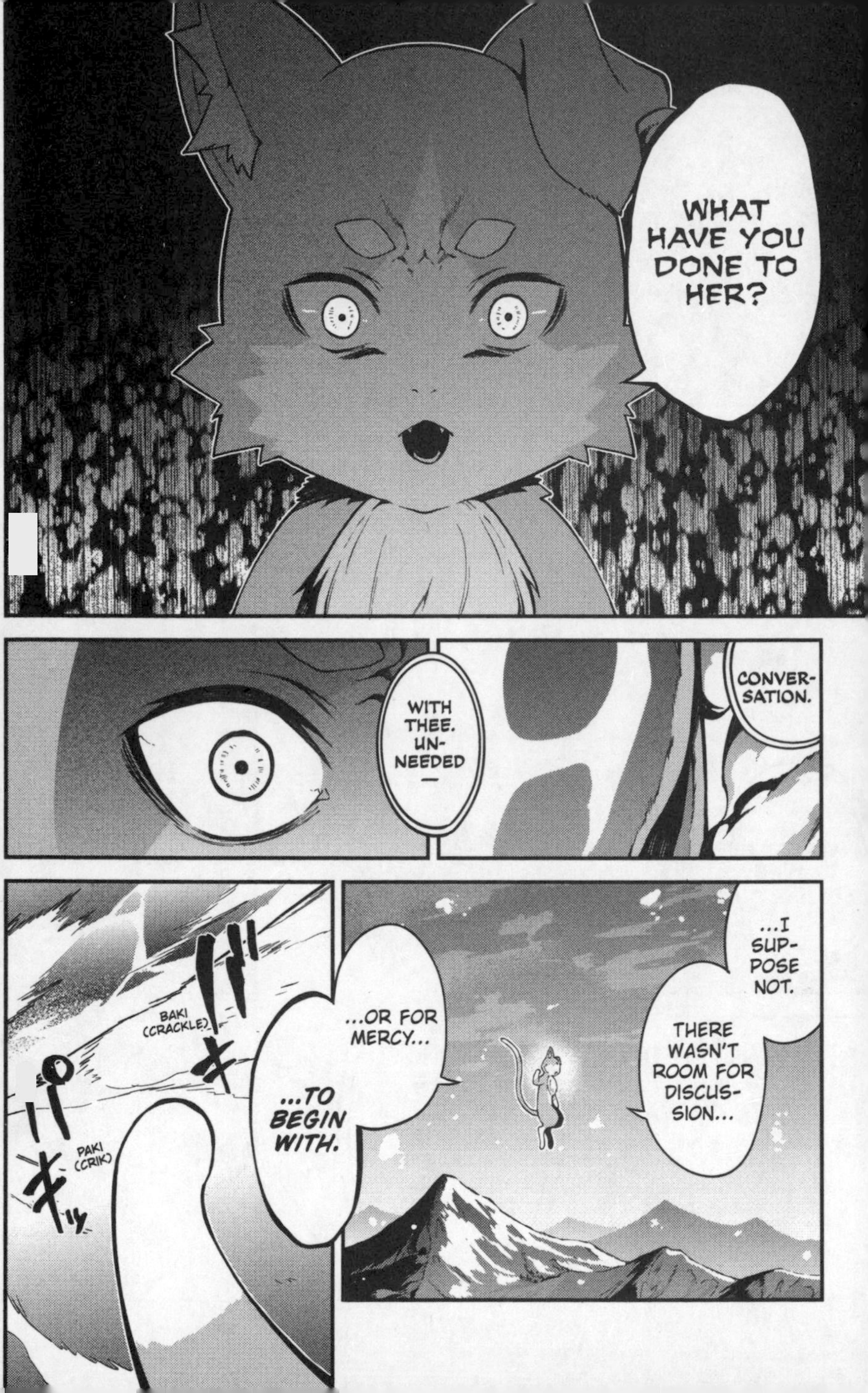
WHAT HAVE YOU DONE TO HER?
CONVERSATION.
WITH THEE. UNNEEDED —
...I SUPPOSE NOT.
THERE WASN'T ROOM FOR DISCUSSION...
...OR FOR MERCY...
...TO BEGIN WITH.
BAKI (CRACKLE)
PAKI (CRIK)

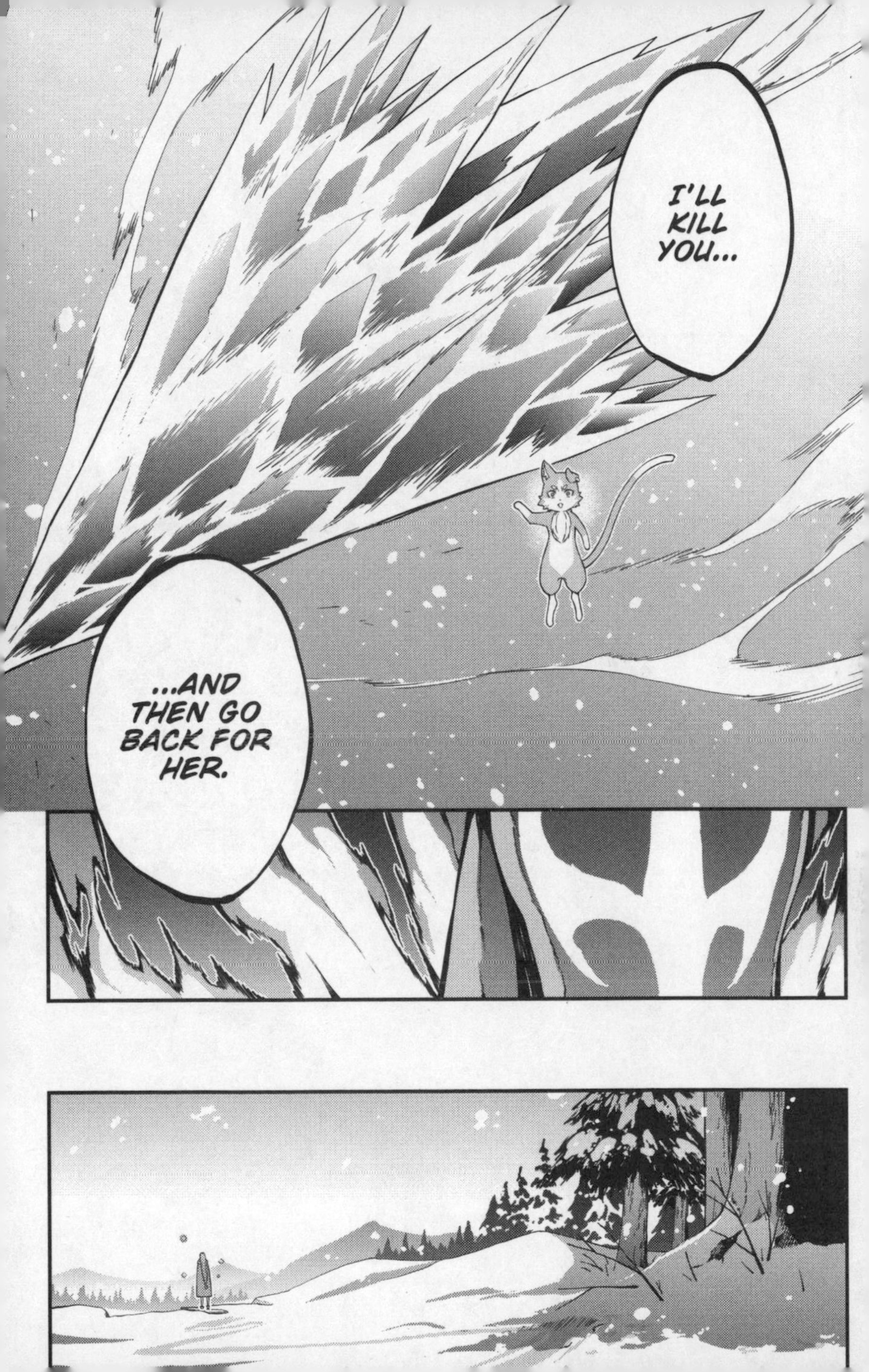
I'LL KILL YOU...
...AND THEN GO BACK FOR HER.

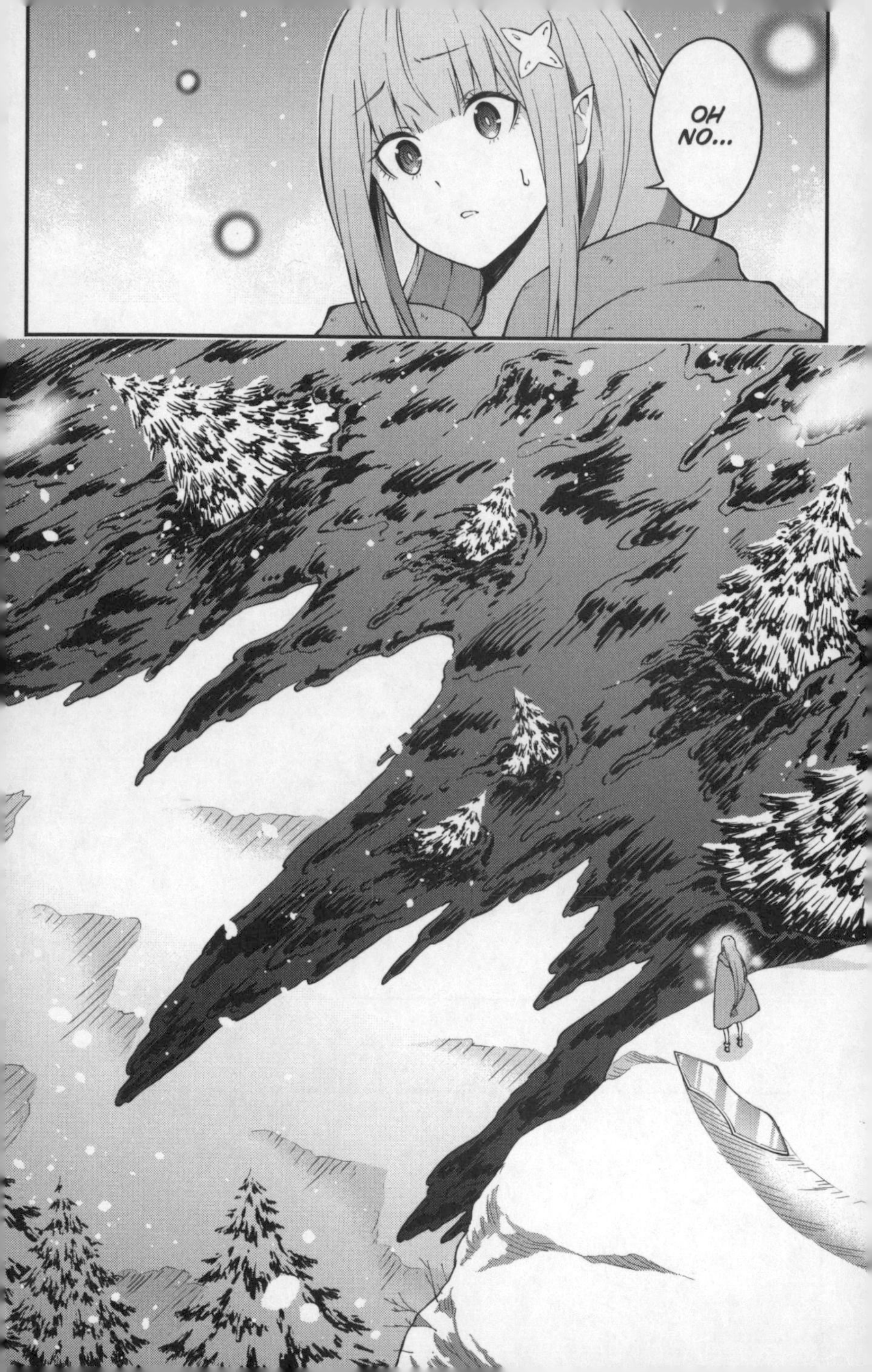
OH NO...

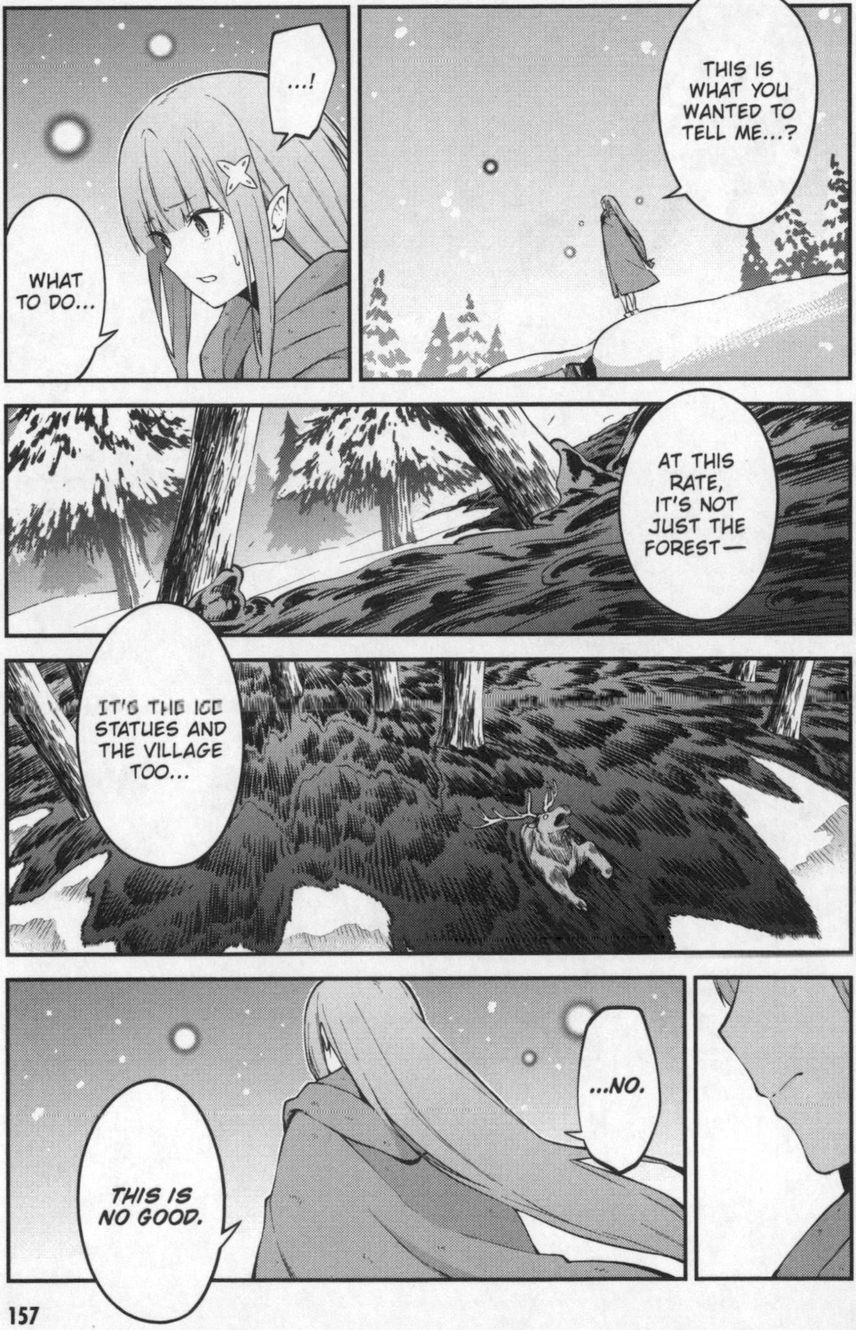
THIS IS WHAT YOU WANTED TO TELL ME...?
...!
WHAT TO DO...
AT THIS RATE, IT'S NOT JUST THE FOREST—
IT'S THE ICE STATUES AND THE VILLAGE TOO...
...NO.
THIS IS NO GOOD.

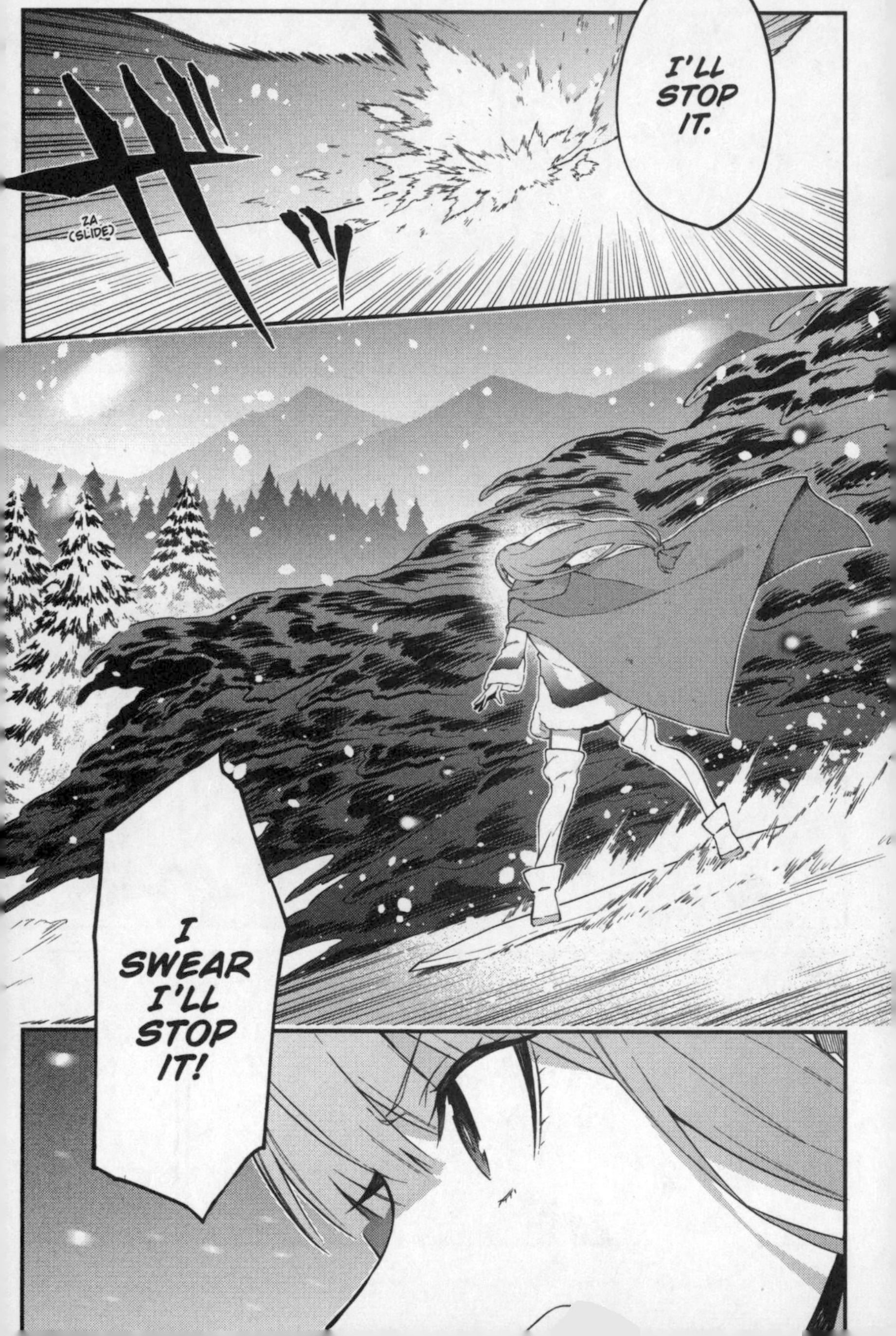
I'LL STOP IT.
ZA (SLIDE)
I SWEAR I'LL STOP IT!

Re:ZERO

-Starting Life in Another World-

The Frozen Bond

The only ability Subaru Natsuki gets when he's
summoned to another world is time travel via his own death.
But to save her, he'll die as many times as it takes.

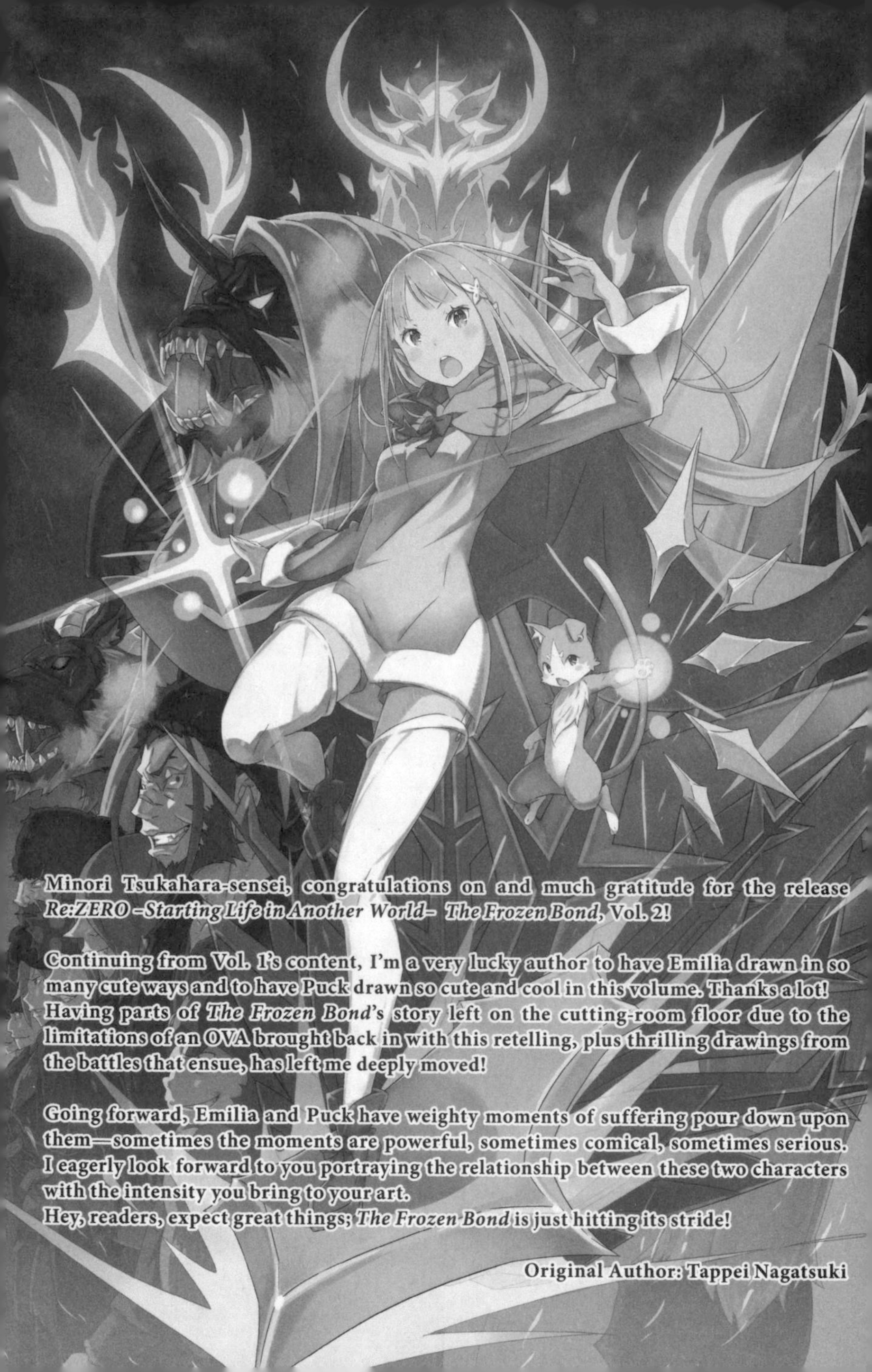

Minori Tsukahara-sensei, congratulations on and much gratitude for the release *Re:ZERO -Starting Life in Another World- The Frozen Bond*, Vol. 2!

Continuing from Vol. 1's content, I'm a very lucky author to have Emilia drawn in so many cute ways and to have Puck drawn so cute and cool in this volume. Thanks a lot! Having parts of *The Frozen Bond*'s story left on the cutting-room floor due to the limitations of an OVA brought back in with this retelling, plus thrilling drawings from the battles that ensue, has left me deeply moved!

Going forward, Emilia and Puck have weighty moments of suffering pour down upon them—sometimes the moments are powerful, sometimes comical, sometimes serious. I eagerly look forward to you portraying the relationship between these two characters with the intensity you bring to your art.
Hey, readers, expect great things; *The Frozen Bond* is just hitting its stride!

Original Author: Tappei Nagatsuki

STAFF

KAZUKI SATOU
SAKANO NOBORI

Special Thanks

NAGATSUKI-SAN
IKEMOTO-SAN
MANO-SAN
RIE
TAKAHASHI-SAN
Noshi-SAN
THE EDITOR

and you

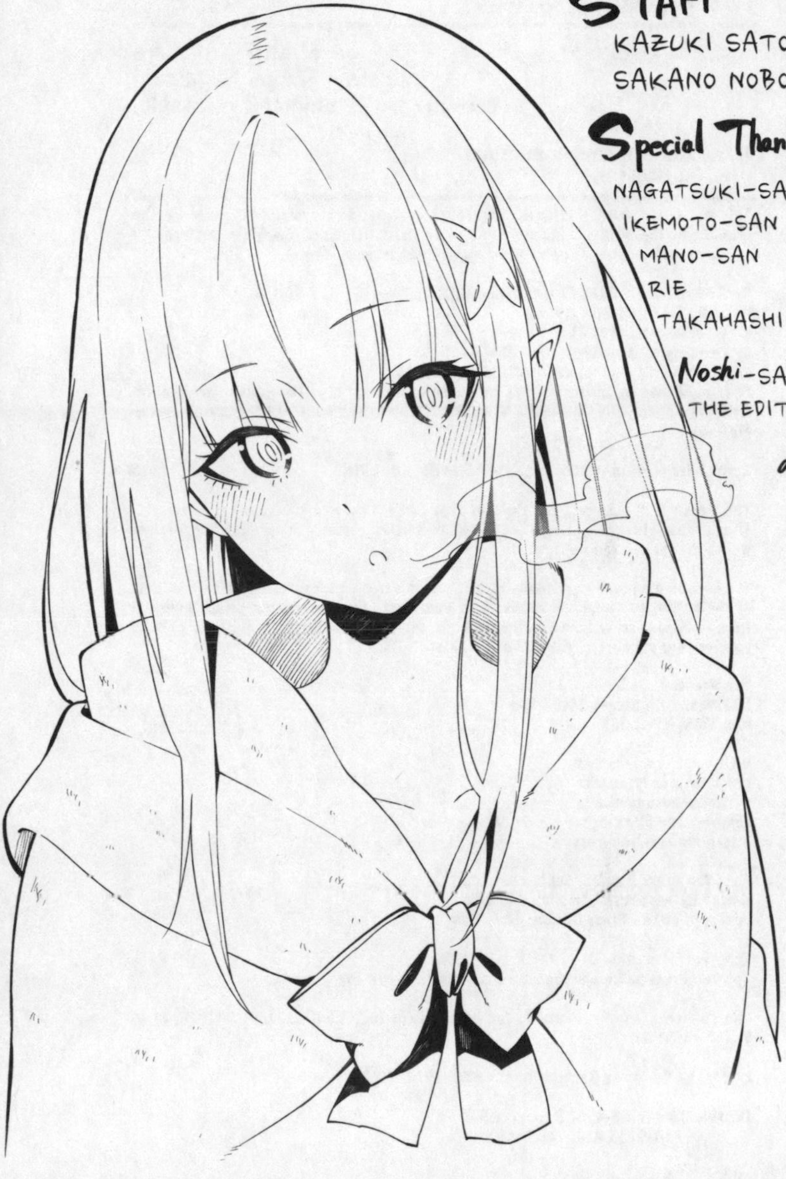

RE:ZERO -STARTING LIFE IN ANOTHER WORLD- ②
The Frozen Bond

Art: **Minori Tsukahara**
Original Story: **Tappei Nagatsuki**
Character Design: **Shinichirou Otsuka**

Translation: Jeremiah Bourque
Lettering: Viet Vu

Re:ZERO KARA HAJIMERU ISEKAI SEIKATSU
HYOKETSU NO KIZUNA vol. 2
©Tappei Nagatsuki 2021
Licensed by KADOKAWA CORPORATION
©2021 Minori Tsukahara/SQUARE ENIX CO., LTD.
First published in Japan in 2021 by SQUARE ENIX CO., LTD. English translation rights arranged with SQUARE ENIX CO., LTD. and Yen Press, LLC through Tuttle-Mori Agency, Inc.

English translation ©2022 by SQUARE ENIX CO., LTD.

Yen Press
150 West 30th Street, 19th Floor
New York, NY 10001

Visit us at yenpress.com
facebook.com/yenpress
twitter.com/yenpress
yenpress.tumblr.com
instagram.com/yenpress

First Yen Press Edition: September 2022
Edited by Yen Press Editorial: Carl Li
Designed by Yen Press Design: Eddy Mingki

Yen Press is an imprint of Yen Press, LLC.
The Yen Press name and logo are trademarks of Yen Press, LLC.

Library of Congress Control Number: 2022931579

ISBNs: 978-1-9753-4387-3 (paperback)
       978-1-9753-4388-0 (ebook)

10 9 8 7 6 5 4 3 2 1

WOR

Printed in the United States of America